THE MONEY MACHINE

HOW KKR MANUFACTURED POWER AND PROFITS

SARAH BARTLETT

WARNER BOOKS 39401-7 $12.99 U.S.A. ($16.25 CAN.)

KKR doesn't think you should read this book.
THE CRITICS DISAGREE

"Sure to generate concern.... Goes far beyond past critiques and presents a distinctly unflattering view of a firm more than willing to cut corners in pursuit of gain."
—Business Week

☛

"[A] considerable achievement in exposing KKR's means of ascent."
—Washington Post Book World

☛

"One of the first deeply critical looks at a firm that controls a host of companies, from RJR Nabisco to Safeway and Duracell."
—Newsweek

☛

"A well-researched and clearly written story about the rise and alleged abuse of power of the USA's biggest leveraged buyout firm.... Bartlett makes a credible case."
—USA Today

☛

"The talk of Wall Street.... Amid her immensely readable, and often scathing history of the men behind the KKR name, Bartlett makes some serious allegations....
Entertaining and iconoclastic."
—Financial Times

☛

"Fascinating ... authoritative.... Delves into the whos, hows and whys of KKR's growth and success.... This book will interest anyone who is interested in learning more about what happened in the 'go-go' 80s."
—Pittsburgh Press

☛

more ...

SARAH BARTLETT is a writer at the *New York Times* and has covered Wall Street and banking issues for more than ten years. Before joining the *Times* in 1988, she worked at both *Business Week* and *Fortune*.

THE MONEY MACHINE

HOW KKR MANUFACTURED POWER & PROFITS

Sarah Bartlett

WARNER BOOKS

A Time Warner Company

Copyright © 1991, 1992 by Sarah Bartlett
All rights reserved.

Warner Books, Inc., 1271 Avenue of the Americas, New York, NY 10020
Ⓦ A Time Warner Company

Printed in the United States of America
First trade printing: July 1992
10 9 8 7 6 5 4 3 2 1

Library of Congress Cataloging-in-Publication Number 91-65482

ISBN: 0-446-39401-7

Book design by Giorgetta Bell McRee
Cover design by Robert Anthony

CONTENTS

"Men, in the main, are strangely made. They can never strike the happy mean: the bounds of reason seem too narrow for them. They must needs overreact whichever part they play and often ruin the noblest things . . ."

—from *Tartuffe*, or *The Imposter*, by MOLIÈRE, 1664

———————

"I allowed myself to get too caught up in what I was doing to consider the consequences or to stop myself from doing what I knew was wrong. . . . I now recognize that by accomplishing less, I might even accomplish more.

—MICHAEL MILKEN, 1990

PREFACE

For the last ten years I have had a front-row seat on one of the biggest financial booms in U.S. history. As a reporter at *Fortune, Business Week,* and, finally, the *New York Times,* I was one of a cluster of financial journalists in Manhattan struggling to keep up with the changes wrought on society by the financial engineering that so dominated the last decade.

Sometimes the individuals I covered seemed truly exceptional in their insights about the inner workings of the financial markets, while others were just as striking for the narrowness of their focus and their seeming obliviousness to the larger impact of their activities. Some were charming and witty, and a few were, yes, arrogant and vicious—though not as many as one would guess from the exaggerated portrait of the decade that now seems to be emerging.

In attempting to chronicle this extraordinary period, I

became fascinated with the concept of power: how it was amassed by certain individuals, the use to which they put it, and the deference that was then accorded them by others. Of all the individuals I encountered, none seemed better examples of this phenomenon than the founders of Kohlberg Kravis Roberts & Company, the firm that has come closest to making *leveraged buyout* a household term.

Here were three men who started a firm in 1976 with a few million dollars and just ten years later had control over what is believed to be the largest corporate empire in the world. How did they do it? What was it about these individuals, their personalities, their motivation, that catapulted them to the top in such a way? Was it their inventiveness, their brilliant strategy, or was it a matter of being in the right place at the right time? And why did their names arouse such intense emotions, ranging from envy, to awe, to fear?

In early 1989, when I was writing about Wall Street for the *New York Times,* I began to look into KKR, as it is commonly known, to see if there was anything new to say about the firm. In making the rounds of investment bankers I had come to trust over the years, I heard that some of KKR's deals were not doing well. The reports surprised me because the firm had an impeccable reputation, and if it was running into problems, that would certainly be newsworthy.

The more I learned about the firm and its history, the more fascinated I became. It seemed to me that though the three partners had founded their business on a great insight, and it had made them wealthy beyond their wildest dreams, they had gradually allowed themselves to veer off track, to the point where the activities they were then engaging in were a perversion of the principles that had been responsible for their original success. It struck me that what was happening to KKR was, in some ways, emblematic of what was happening to Wall Street in general: a rush for money and power that carried within it the seeds of its own undoing.

I tried to convey some of these ideas in a lengthy article about KKR that ran in the business section of the *New York*

Times in August of 1989. Although the article was generally well-received, though not by KKR, I was frustrated by how much of the story I still felt I did not know or understand, and therefore that I had not yet told.

In the course of writing that article, I had an occasion to meet Jerry Kohlberg, one of the three founders of KKR, who left the firm in 1987 and had since made himself unavailable to the press. The meeting was strictly an "off-the-record, get acquainted" session that I knew would be of no use for that particular story but that I hoped might lead to something more fruitful further down the road. True to my expectations, Kohlberg said nothing about his former firm during that meeting, but agreed to serve as a future resource for Wall Street stories in general, provided his comments were for my use only and would not appear in print. Since many of my most useful sources on Wall Street had also insisted on this frustrating form of communication, I agreed, figuring it would be better to hear his perspective than not to.

A few weeks after my KKR article was published, I began to consider the possibility of writing a book that would develop some of the themes the article had touched on, since I felt this subject was rich enough to warrant the year or more such an effort would almost certainly require.

After several months of reflection, I approached Kohlberg and asked him if he would agree to be interviewed on the record about his experiences concerning KKR. Since our initial meeting, we had exchanged several phone calls and he had provided some general insights on several stories unrelated to KKR, but he was not what I would call one of my "better" sources. When I asked for his cooperation on a book, I didn't really know where such a dialogue would take me, but I thought that simply having his views exposed in a public forum would be interesting, since they had never before been aired in any depth.

To my surprise, after giving the idea some consideration, he agreed. He also placed no conditions upon his cooperation. Although he said he approached such a project with trepidation, he said he felt it was time to "set the record straight."

I later approached Henry Kravis and George Roberts, the other two founders, who are still at KKR, and asked them for their cooperation. I explained that the book would explore the theme of power and how and why certain individuals were able to amass it, and that they would be key figures in it. They agreed to cooperate, though their response was slightly less surprising because they had generally made themselves available to reporters in the mainstream business press.

Once I took a leave of absence from the *Times* and began working full time on the book, I asked each of the three men to give me names of people who they felt had been influential in their lives, in defining who they became as individuals. Over the next nine months I interviewed their relatives, their former classmates, their best friends, and their teachers. I also interviewed dozens of people in the business community who had either worked for them in some capacity, sold them companies, or invested with them. Almost all of the interviews were taped—with the subject's permission, of course. The few instances where I quote from secondary sources are marked with footnotes.

In the course of my reporting, I encountered some damaging material concerning the business practices of KKR and certain individuals who are closely aligned with the firm. In some cases, it comes down to one person's word against another's. In a few instances, the main source of information is Jerry Kohlberg. In others, it is Hedi Kravis, Henry's ex-wife.

Many readers may wonder why a journalist would take seriously the words of an ex-partner or an ex-wife, since either of them could be embittered and have an ax to grind. I was acutely aware of this danger while I was researching and writing this book. But just as one cannot accept blindly the words of those who are in a position to be biased, so it seemed to me one could not dismiss their observations out of hand, either.

In the end, I relied on standard journalistic techniques for trying to ascertain the truth. First and foremost, was there any independent evidence that either corroborated or undermined their allegations? How truthful was Kohlberg on other issues, especially where the answers to certain questions required him to reveal unflattering information about himself? Was there anything in any of the principal characters' personal backgrounds that might indicate a penchant for telling the truth or, alternatively, for obfuscating? How did each of the individuals in the book respond when confronted with negative information about themselves: were they evasive, did they try to twist words in their favor, or did they acknowledge certain faults and accept responsibility? Did any patterns emerge? Did some people consistently try to offer misleading information or obstruct my research? Or did they invite further probing and place no limits on where my questions led? How would each of the individuals be hurt or helped by certain information becoming public, and what might their motivation be in airing or suppressing it?

At the end of a year of sifting and sorting, a bias clearly emerges in the book in favor of Kohlberg. From the standpoint of dramatic storytelling, this is rather unfortunate. For as Kohlberg's character unfolds in the book, many readers will probably find him irritatingly correct. I share their frustration. This is a man who comes to a full stop and then puts his turn signal on when he goes around the corner in a parking lot! As one of his cousins told me after I had confessed my frustration with what seemed to be the meager results of my reporting, "When he says it's ten after two, it's ten after two. It's not fifteen after two, or twenty after two, it's ten after two." I finally came to accept that concern for precision as the real thing.

Having said that, Kohlberg is certainly no hero. He has an ego just like everybody else, and he bears responsibility for questionable activities that occurred while he was at the firm, whether he knew about them or not. In the end, however, I concluded that Kohlberg really was as obsessively straitlaced as he appeared and that the perspective he shared, though tinged with some bitterness, also had a real basis for credibility.

Hedi Kravis's allegations against her ex-husband and his lawyer, Dick Beattie, most of which emerge from a recent court case, are also controversial. In discussing the possible motives for her comments, Hedi's friends point out that she is hardly the stereotypical embittered ex-wife and, if anything, has been one of Henry's great defenders. As my own reporting independently confirmed, it was she who had misgivings about her marriage from the start and who initiated the separation and divorce. And she has seemed to be genuinely happy about Henry's 1985 marriage to Carolyne Roehm and the fact that he had finally found someone better suited to his needs. The two did not socialize together much after their divorce; however, until Hedi's recent lawsuit against him, they were on friendly terms and would frequently talk by phone regarding their three teenage children.

It is also hard to see what Hedi would gain from telling false tales about her ex-husband and his lawyer. If she *were* to have done so in her court papers, that would only leave her open to charges of perjury. And her allegations against Dick Beattie are only likely to inflame still further her dispute with Henry, making it even less likely that he will voluntarily agree to pay more in child support, as she is seeking.

In the end, I decided that individuals like Kohlberg and Hedi Kravis had a lot to lose by stating what they believed, and that both were credible sources. Unfortunately, that conclusion, and its corollaries, puts me at odds with some of my colleagues at competing publications—a position few reporters, including myself, like to find themselves in. It seemed to me, however, that if I was going to remain true to the theme of the book, and to probe the many and varied dimensions of power, I could not leave the business press out of the equation just to avoid being accused of competitive sniping or sour grapes.

I make no claim to having any monopoly on the truth, for that remains as elusive as ever. What I do hope is that I have fairly presented another "take" on a confusing decade that will probably require many more years and many more books to fully comprehend.

RAY

One by one, the cars pulled up to the white gatehouse, the windows silently glided down, and the occupants' names were given to the guard on duty, who carefully checked to make sure that they were on the guest list before slowly raising the white arm that had been blocking the half-mile drive to the exclusive Southern Hills Country Club. Off to the right, as the cars followed the winding road up the hill, was a popular skeet-shooting spot, while several lonely golf tees lay off to the left.

The steady stream of cars eventually came to rest in front of a pale gray, two-story clubhouse, more distinct for its daytime views than its external appearance. From its commanding position on top one of the area's higher knolls, club members have a breathtaking view of all of Tulsa and the grassy surrounds that form Oklahoma's Osage Hills.

On that particular evening, January 10, 1990, there hap-

1

pened to be a strong wind blowing from the southwest. So, although the night air was mild, the passengers made a mad dash from their cars into the relative calm of the club's entry hall. The drivers were only too happy to hand over their car keys to the club's valet parking staff. Inside, the women peeled off their coats and fixed their hairdos before making their way with their escorts to the ballroom where other women, similarly encased in long, shimmery evening gowns and flanked by their tuxedo-clad menfolk, stood in clusters drinking and chatting as the Tulsa Youth Symphony Quartet played quietly off in the background.

Although most of the 275 guests that night were from Tulsa, a few had flown in for the occasion from as far away as Colorado, Texas, and California. They were gathering to watch the governor of Oklahoma, Henry Bellmon, bestow an award upon Henry Kravis, local boy made good. Many of those present that night were old school chums of Henry's, some amazed at how well their former classmate had fared. Others were close friends of the family and relatives eager to clap and cheer the night's guest of honor. All had paid $125 for the privilege of paying tribute.

To many in the ballroom that night, Henry Kravis's life was indeed deserving of celebration. Though he sprang from sleepy Tulsa, where he earned an undistinguished record at the local public school, by the time he was in his early forties he had become one of the richest men in the country and one of Wall Street's most illustrious tycoons. The latest list published by *Forbes* magazine of the four hundred richest Americans pegged him at the $550-million mark, not bad for a man barely graying. As one of three founding members of a firm called Kohlberg Kravis Roberts—the two others being Jerome Kohlberg, Jr., and Henry's cousin, George Roberts—Henry had made his money by taking over companies using mountains of debt and selling them several years later at vastly higher prices. But while many other takeover artists had ended up in jail or flamed out after a few successes, Henry's upward climb had been long and sure.

In 1976, he and his two partners had started their firm with just $120,000. Fourteen years later, they had convinced enough banks, pension funds, and insurance companies to lend them over $58 billion to buy thirty-six companies. At last count, their sprawling enterprise employed 350,000 people. Not even the venerable banker J. P. Morgan, at the height of his career, had amassed such an empire. At one point in the late 1980s, KKR companies, whose products are as timeless as Winston cigarettes, Oreo cookies, and Duracell batteries, were generating more money from sales than all the exports of Australia and New Zealand put together.

So it was not entirely surprising that Henry Kravis was being singled out for an honorary award. But his eminence went well beyond facts and figures; it had a personal side to it as well. With his expensive suits, his cocksure ways, his constant tan, his jet-setting lifestyle, Henry had become a convenient symbol for the glamorous life on Wall Street. When the actor Michael Douglas was trying to conjure up the character of Gordon Gekko for the movie *Wall Street,* he turned for inspiration to his former prep-school classmate Henry Kravis, even naming Gekko's chauffeur after Henry's driver, Mohammed.

Without a doubt, Henry's life had a certain storybook quality to it. He had barely become a well-known figure on Wall Street before he had been granted complete and unconditional access to some of the snootiest, most prestigious corners of Manhattan's ruling class. Not only was he invited onto the boards of some of Manhattan's most-sought-after charities, such as the Metropolitan Museum of Art and the Central Park Conservancy, but he had even been appointed the chairman of Channel 13, one of the most respected public television stations in the country. Every three months, this youthful Wall Street whiz would sit at the head of a large table surrounded by other New York luminaries and discuss issues like the financial impact of a series on the greenhouse effect or chimpanzees in Tanzania. It was all rather wonderful.

But Henry hadn't stopped there. From his base in Manhattan's financial and society circles, he had claimed a position in high-powered Washington circles. He became friendly with a number of senators and congressmen, was one of the most active fund-raisers in the Republican Party, and was known to be on a first-name basis with President Bush, who would seek his opinion on certain economic and financial issues.

There was no doubt about it. In choosing to honor Henry Kravis for the kickoff event of Oklahoma Homecoming '90, Governor Bellmon had clearly picked a winner. The evening was intended to instill pride in the state and inspire future generations of Oklahomans. Seated among the guests that night were Henry's parents, Ray and Bessie, both in their eighties, Henry's somewhat eccentric older brother, George, Henry's current wife, the fashion designer Carolyne Roehm, and his daughter from a previous marriage, fourteen-year-old Kimberly. Henry had jetted in on his private plane, a Falcon 900, which was parked at Tulsa's airport, ready for his crack-of-dawn departure the next day.

After the guests had waded through their elaborate four-course dinner—drinking an '82 cabernet sauvignon with their choice of lobster, roast beef, or quail breast, and nibbling on a sumptuous poached-pear and chocolate-rum-ball dessert—the round of speeches began. First there was the mayor, offering his warmest greetings to the crowd. Then Governor Bellmon talked about the symbolic importance of the evening. And finally, the man they had all come to honor, Henry Kravis, approached the podium to share his thoughts with the crowd.

"What a great place Tulsa is to grow up in!" Henry exclaimed to the group, who cheered his acknowledgment of the land that bore him. Though his reputation had grown larger than life, the Kravis who stood before them that night seemed unchanged from his earlier years. His small stature was still startling—he was just five feet six by some people's reckoning. And he had not lost that unfailing politeness that his parents had drummed into him. His hair was as wavy as ever, though now it was graying at the temples. And just as when he was a child, Henry was immaculately groomed, his kerchief pointing just so out of the left-hand pocket of his tuxedo.

Henry spoke warmly that night of his early days in Tulsa and how important they had been to his later success. He joked about his early introduction to inventory management, when he collected old newspapers from the neighborhood and earned $3.50 for each load that he and his mother delivered to the newspaper recycling plant. And he attributed his sales and marketing abilities to the days when he sold magazine subscriptions door-to-door on behalf of his high school. He was, he acknowledged, "always striving to be the top salesman of the day. Some of you are probably still getting magazines I sold you thirty-two years ago!" The crowd roared with laughter at the notion.

Gradually, though, Henry got serious. He talked of the "moral compass" that growing up in Tulsa had afforded him. "In the Tulsa of my youth, people had time for each other, for friendships. They weren't caught up in the moment," he said. When he left Tulsa and ended up in New York, his hometown experience left him "better able to withstand the lure of the 'siren of instant gratification,' the temptations of the 'big time.' If I am better able to keep on an even keel, to steady myself in the choppiest waters of the East, and to navigate the most difficult Wall Street terrain *without* losing my way, perhaps it is because of my early life in Tulsa, where I built my own foundation for life."

His wife, Carolyne, he added, shared his same hometown values, growing up as she did in Kirksville, Missouri. That might have come as a surprise to some in the audience, who had seen pictures of Carolyne in women's magazines draped across Louis XV furniture in her $5,000-plus sequined evening gowns. But they applauded politely when the governor presented the strikingly tall and thin Carolyne, dressed in a low-cut sleeveless gown, with a basket of Oklahoma products:

salsa, a jar of *picante* sauce, "Oklahoma Crude"—a calorie-rich fudge sauce—and chocolate "cow patties," a local delicacy consisting of round chocolate wafers dotted with peanuts.

Guests who attended say the performance Henry and Carolyne gave that night was flawless: they were success incarnate, yet still humble enough to acknowledge their beginnings. They never seemed to lose their charm as they received endless congratulations and shook innumerable hands.

Who in that room that night could possibly have guessed some of the questionable business practices that Henry had employed on his upward climb? There was no reason to think anything other than the obvious: that he had gotten where he was because he was smarter than others, harder working, quicker to seize a promising investment opportunity that made his investors fabulously rich. No one knew, or could even imagine, the extent to which Henry and George Roberts—having successfully edged their other partner, Kohlberg, out—had made their way to the top by plying money and favors on those in a position to help and intimidating the few who tried to oppose them. Nor was anyone in the crowd that night likely to have guessed the extent to which Henry and George's financial success might have come at the expense of their own investment partners.

Their image remained intact in part because they relied upon a finely tuned system of seduction. They secured people's loyalty by doling out liberal amounts of whatever worked. In most cases it was money; but in some instances, it was merely prestige and status. The end result was the same: KKR enjoyed a high degree of cooperation that its less-generous competitors did not. As Henry and George went about applying this approach, and the individuals they encountered willingly went along, some of the nation's leading institutions and individuals were compromised: public officials, law firms, corporate chieftains—even the press, which came to have a large stake in Kohlberg Kravis Roberts's continued success.

Unfortunately, the money that Henry and his partner were using to lubricate this system was for the most part not their own. It had been given to them to invest on behalf of 3 million working people, mainly public-school teachers, firemen, policemen, and some private-sector employees whose retirement money was managed by about twenty different pension funds. A host of commercial banks had also invested some of their money with KKR in the hopes of earning high returns. Few of the people representing these groups seemed to have any idea what was really going on, or if they did, they preferred not to roil the waters.

Of course there was not a hint of any of this that night. Who would think of questioning the motives of a man who takes phone calls from President Bush, who endows a college chair in "leadership," who preaches about the importance of business ethics? No, the evening was quite sublime, especially as far as Ray and Bessie, Henry's parents, were concerned. After the speeches were over, the guests were entertained by the lovely voices of the Tulsa Youth Opera. The choice seemed particularly fitting, for Carolyne Roehm was known to adore the opera. Every year she insisted on dragging Henry off to Salzburg to listen to some of the world's great divas.

No, the evening could hardly have gone more smoothly. The Kravises' friends had all been in attendance, the food was superb, the speeches had all been warm and uplifting. Ray and Bessie were thrilled by the honor being paid to their son. To be sure, their joy was dampened later that night when Ray's appendix burst and he had to be hospitalized, forcing them to cancel their long-planned departure the next day for the Virgin Islands, where they had intended to celebrate their sixtieth wedding anniversary. But even that unfortunate development did little to tarnish the warm memories of that night, or to diminish the other sweet irony that probably few in the room that night appreciated: Henry had been honored in a club that for decades would not have Ray Kravis as a member.

* * *

Growing up Jewish in Tulsa was very different from growing up in Tulsa. On one level, it would be hard to imagine a more tranquil place to live. Like a welcome splash of green in the middle of America's great bare plains, Tulsa is filled with shady, tree-lined streets where comfortable middle-class houses sit amply apart from their neighbors, and children ride furiously around street corners on bikes, glaring at passing cars. Men saunter around in blue jeans that hang low on their hips; women, meatier than their bicoastal counterparts, wear their loose-fitting polyester outfits with pride. It's the kind of place where everyone knows everyone else; where pedestrians observe the DON'T WALK signs when there isn't even a car in sight; where lunchtime often means eleven-thirty.

Underneath that placid Norman Rockwell veneer, however, is a long history of intolerance toward anything foreign, and that word is loosely defined. Although Indians mingled freely with white settlers who arrived in the Indian territory in the mid-1800s, and several of the town's earliest leaders were of mixed blood, it was a much different story when blacks began to arrive in Tulsa after the turn of the century, when oil was first discovered. Black families were immediately relegated to a slum area, later dubbed Little Africa, where living conditions were horribly squalid. Interracial tensions grew so great in the early 1920s that the town became the site of some of the country's earliest race riots. In one particularly violent episode, fears of a mob lynching triggered street riots that left more than thirty dead, hundreds seriously injured, and Little Africa a heap of smoldering cinders. The Ku Klux Klan chapter that opened after that episode became so active that the governor ultimately had to declare martial law in Tulsa and send in the National Guard.[1]

As whites, of course, Tulsa's Jews were spared such horrible atrocities. But they were discriminated against nonetheless. Jews, after all, were even more of a minority than blacks. In the 1940s and 1950s, when Henry Kravis was growing up, there were only about eight hundred Jewish families in Tulsa, out of a total population of about one hundred and seventy-five thousand. In a town that considers itself very much a part of the Bible Belt, and is home to 183 Baptist churches and Oral Roberts University, there are three lonely synagogues.

Tulsa's Christians were perfectly happy to do business with Jews—indeed, Jews comprised some of the most prominent businesspeople in the community. It's just that no one wanted to socialize with them. On weekends, the WASPs retired to Southern Hills to play golf, drink Bloody Marys, and go swimming, while the Jews gathered at the smaller and more modest Meadowbrook Club.

It might not have been so galling had Ray Kravis, Henry's father, not been the success story that he was. The son of a British tailor who emigrated to America when Ray was just five, Ray had set goals for himself that went well beyond his father's haberdashery in Atlantic City. After gaining an engineering degree from Lehigh University in Bethlehem, Pennsylvania, this tiny man—just five feet four inches by some people's estimates—accepted a job offer from a family friend and moved to Tulsa to seek his fame and fortune. It was 1925, and Tulsa, then in the midst of an oil boom, was very much a magnet for ambitious young men.

Despite his engineering background, Ray showed an early aptitude for finance and number-crunching, a skill he took one step further by taking evening courses in tax accounting. Indeed, it was in the course of poring over tax court decisions late one night some years later that Ray made a discovery that would change his life: a loophole that would enable oil properties to be packaged and sold in such a way that any profits would only be taxed at the rate of 15 percent, instead of the 81-percent rate that was then being applied to oil properties. Ray had discovered one of the earliest forms of a tax shelter, an art form that tax lawyers and accountants have since developed into an enormous business. Armed with his knowledge of both accounting and oil, Ray quickly found himself at the epicenter of a burgeoning market in oil and gas properties.

Although Ray is frequently referred to by family members as a petroleum engineer, that does not begin to capture his talent. "I laugh when I read stories about Henry Kravis that say his father was a well-known geologist or valuation engineer. His father is a financial mogul, a tremendously successful businessman," says Bill Elson, the president of Elson Oil Company, who has known Ray Kravis for four decades. Ray did not analyze rocks or go trudging around in the muck in search of good drilling spots; he was a dealmaker, just as his son is now. The only difference is that in Ray's day the objects of desire were oil properties, not corporate assets.

Ray became so well known for his tax-sheltering skills that Joe Kennedy, the irascible father of the former president and no slouch himself when it came to business skills, sought out Ray as his personal scout in the oil market. Kennedy viewed oil properties as an ideal way to shelter the millions he had made in real estate. For years, Ray invested Kennedy's money, along with some of his own, and made both a small fortune. Although Kennedy is widely understood to have detested Jews, he and Ray were friends. The two would sometimes play golf together in Palm Beach, where they both spent their winters, Ray having bought a 3,800-square-foot penthouse apartment some years earlier. Ray and Bessie were invited to attend Eunice Kennedy's wedding to Sargent Shriver in 1954. And many years later, when Edward Kennedy decided to put together a collection of written tributes to his father, Ray Kravis was one of his father's friends to whom he turned for a contribution.

Ray was not shy about enjoying the fruits of his labor. He bought land in one of Tulsa's most exclusive neighborhoods and erected an enormous house on the wooded, 180'-by-320' lot. Built of a soft-beige native stone, the sprawling, 10,000-square-foot home where Ray and Bessie still live has four bedrooms on the second floor and two servant's quarters over the three-car garage.

Visitors to the plush home arrive at a two-story-high entrance hall whose most prominent feature is an intricate, wrought-iron handrail that gracefully winds its way up the thickly carpeted stairs to the second floor. The craftsman who forged the handrail had previously worked on the palace of Haile Selassie, the late emperor of Ethiopia.

Like many American families, the Kravises live not in their showpiece living room, which has the feeling of a shrine, but in a less formal, wood-paneled family room where the floor-to-ceiling picture windows look out over an English-style garden. It is in that room that the Kravises have their built-in bar, their built-in television, and Bessie's reclining sofa. Adjoining the family room is a greenhouse, which opens out in the summer onto a large stone patio.

Besides being fancy, Ray wanted his house to be *modern*. He installed one of the area's first radio-controlled garage door-openers. The kitchen was outfitted in pale-green steel cabinets and contained all the mechanical labor-saving devices that had then been developed. There was an elevator to the second floor for those evenings when Ray and Bessie were too weary to climb the stairs. So elaborate and eye-popping was the Kravis home that the *Tulsa Tribune*, writing about it in a feature story in April of 1950, called it "one of the largest and most modern homes to be constructed in Tulsa in 10 years."[2]

Ray splurged on more than his house. He liked cars— the bigger and fancier the better. In the days when Henry was growing up, there was a gold Imperial Cadillac with a vanilla-colored convertible roof for Bessie, and a Lincoln Continental for Ray—the only one in town. To make his cars even more distinctive, Ray liked to use those personalized "vanity" license plates. Sometimes he would use numbers, such as 1 and 2, or more recently, simply RFK.

Ray always loved his cars. Even now, when he gives a

tour of his house, the last stop is the garage, where, with a flourish of his arm, he says, "And this is my Lexus!" The expensive new Toyota sits next to his Mercedes 560, "the largest of their tour cars," Ray explains.

By the mid-1960s, Ray's accomplishments had become well known in Tulsa and were creating more than a little stir. For a man of such modest beginnings to have made and kept so many millions of dollars earned him the respect and admiration of the entire community. He also began to play a more active role in cultural groups and charities, and Ray and Bessie's exploits gradually became fodder for the local society pages. The Tulsa paper chronicled their exotic trips, their attendance at black-tie affairs, their invitation to a White House dinner—even the news that Bessie's jewels had been stolen from a safe at New York's swanky Pierre Hotel.

But if Ray and Bessie's star was rising, it counted for little within the town's WASP establishment. It took years before Ray was invited to join the prestigious Southern Hills—he was the first Jew to be accepted—and two other premier establishments, the City Club and the Tulsa Club. And it was even longer before he was asked to become a board member of a local bank, another first. "There was a lot of prejudice when I first came," says Ray. "It was hard to get in, they didn't want you."

Of course, not everyone cared about getting into places like the Southern Hills Country Club. Many of the Kravises' friends said they felt more comfortable at Meadowbrook; that was where all their friends were. But for the Kravises it seemed to be a point of pride. Ray wanted the acceptance. "Most others are not concerned with getting into Southern Hills," observes oilman Elson. "All they aspire to is making a living. It's the ones who achieve financial success who want to conquer something else."

So Henry grew up a little prince in a big castle, but that castle lay in hostile territory. Henry's two closest friends, Donald Renberg and Bernard Robinowitz, were friends not through school, where they often were not even in the same class, but through their ties in the Jewish community. Don and Henry comprised two of the five in their Sunday school class. The boys belonged to a Jewish youth group, and all three played golf together at Meadowbrook.

Despite their relative isolation, the Three Musketeers, as they liked to call themselves, led a fairly charmed existence. They would get together after school and do the things that boys did in those days: ride bikes, hang out at the town's first mall, eat pizza, or go bowling. Sometimes they would simply hang out at Henry's. "I used to love going over to the Kravises' house. My God, I mean, my mother made me do everything! But I'd go over there, and he's got two maids and a butler and a chauffeur and an elevator. I didn't even have to walk down the steps!" recalls Renberg, still reveling at the thought of all that luxury.

Though the three were popular in school, they were never fully accepted. There were only one or two other Jews in their class of several hundred, and they were regarded as different from the rest. It took them years before they were invited to join the school's social club, for instance. And after they were finally allowed in, Renberg remembers walking down the hall with Bernie and Henry to attend one of the first meetings and hearing one of his classmates stand in front of them and say loudly, "Oh, oh. Here come the Jews."

"I think that being Jewish in Tulsa, Oklahoma, puts a whole different perspective on things. You feel persecuted, you almost feel like you are black. This was a very prejudiced little community," says Renberg, who remained close to Henry for years and was an usher at his first wedding. Renberg recalls one time when a girl Henry was dating got a little drunk and started calling Henry a kike. He was taken aback by her behavior and turned in confusion to his father, who comforted his son over the ugly incident.

But if Ray was troubled by the community's lack of acceptance of his accomplishments and his family, he showed no sign of letting it get in his way. He forged ahead with local charities, showering large amounts on the Tulsa Ballet Theatre, the Tulsa Philharmonic, the Tulsa Opera, and ultimately securing seats on many boards. And he took his position in Tulsa and parlayed it into one in New York's financial circles, where Jews were more readily accepted. Ray had an infectious way about him that made it easy for him to win friends. Although such a small physique might make some men shy, or alternatively, overly aggressive, Ray was simply charming. He had a kind, jovial face and eyes that frequently twinkled with delight as he gently teased his companions or told a witty joke. He loved to surround himself with pretty women, and even today, in his late eighties, he flirts readily with pretty waitresses and tries to impress young women with his vitality by making a muscle and suggesting they give it a good squeeze.

Ray's playful personality was a hit on Wall Street, but his timing was also impeccable. For in the 1950s and 1960s, everyone was eager to get in on the oil and gas bonanza. "No one investing in oil and gas in those days made a move without first consulting Ray Kravis," said Alan Greenberg, a native of Oklahoma City who is now the chief executive of Bear Stearns and who began his career in the firm's oil and gas department. Although Ray had contacts with all the leading firms, WASP preserves included, his closest ties were to Goldman Sachs & Company and Bear, Stearns & Company—the vast majority of whose partners were Jewish. Ray Kravis became their window into the oil and gas world, and they were Ray Kravis's key to breaking into New York.

Ray became particularly friendly with Gustave Levy, one of Wall Street's most highly respected traders, who became the senior partner of Goldman Sachs & Company, and Salim, or Cy, Lewis, who was then Bear Stearns's senior partner. Levy and Lewis could be snarly and cantankerous to their business associates, but when they got together on the golf course with Ray, who regaled them with stories, or when they made a tour of some of New York's more prestigious drinking holes, flanked by pretty young women, they were a boister-ous, fun-loving group.

For a number of years, Cy, Gus, Ray, and another Wall Street executive would go off to some faraway spot—once it was Scotland—and do nothing but play golf and go out on the town. (Upon his return, Ray would reward Bessie for her tolerance with baubles: rubies, diamonds, sapphires, which she would later bitterly refer to as her "stripes.") In 1954, Ray and Cy Lewis attempted an even more ambitious trip: an eight-week odyssey around the world where the object was to play golf at every stop.

"We played in England, in France, in Italy, not in Turkey because the course was terrible," recalls Ray, and India and Pakistan. Everywhere they went, they were wined and dined by local dignitaries who had been alerted to their arrival by Ray's good friend Joe Kennedy, who had developed a wide circle of international contacts during his tenure as the U.S. ambassador to Great Britain in the late 1930s.

Years later, when the American Jewish Committee launched its prestigious Herbert H. Lehman award, the clique was still intact. Gus Levy won it in 1968; the year after, the honor belonged to Cy Lewis; and in 1970, the award went to none other than Raymond Kravis. The night the award was presented, sixty of Ray's friends, including the mayor of Tulsa, made the trip to New York to be present at the awards ceremony at the Plaza Hotel. (Seventeen years later, Ray had the honor of presenting the same award to his son Henry.)

Today, Ray looks back on his life with a great deal of pride in his accomplishments. His office, where he can still be found most days, is littered with plaques, certificates, and photographs that attest to the success he attained. They cover his walls, they sit on his desk, they line the long cupboard that runs behind his leather chair. Even the one object that stands out from the clutter—a large oil painting of his two sons, dressed identically in white-sleeved shirts and navy-blue shorts—has the sense of being a trophy.

Ray lives, it would seem, in a three-dimensional scrapbook. Ask him questions about his famous son, Henry, and he will quickly revert back to his own accomplishments. He'll ask if you know that he, Ray, has just been inducted into the Tulsa Hall of Fame, or that he, Ray, is on the board of numerous Tulsa charities, or that he knows George Bush well, or that a wing of a local museum and a performing arts center in West Palm Beach are both being named after him.

Friends and colleagues say Ray has never been particularly shy about his achievements. Many can recite in surprising detail Ray's exploits with famous people, how many clubs he belongs to, the boards on which he is a director. "You always knew," said Elson. "He told stories, like about the Kennedys. He didn't make it a secret."

THE BOYS

Ray's ambition did not stop with himself. It extended to his children, and he intended to see to it that they continued what he had started. While other Tulsans looked on in amazement, this immigrant who had started with next to nothing and by the seventies was worth an estimated $50 million began launching the next generation, working his network of New York cronies to position his son for great things to come.

Henry was Ray's brightest hope. The couple's first child had been named George Roberts Kravis—after Bessie's father. But Ray says that, tragically, the little boy smothered to death in his crib when he was just four and a half months old while they were away on a trip. It took Bessie years before she wanted to have any more children, and some family friends think the terrible incident may have contributed to her heavy drinking in later years.

Finally, however, nine years after they were married, Bessie gave birth to a second child. They named the boy George Roberts Kravis II. And five years later, in 1944, she delivered Henry Roberts Kravis. He was six weeks premature—always in a hurry, his father later took to saying.

The two boys could not have been more dissimilar. George was quiet, withdrawn, off in his own world. He spent his free time playing with any and all electrical gadgets. Bessie used to say that George was born with a screwdriver in one hand and an electric cord in the other. She constantly feared that he would electrocute himself.[1]

Henry was more the kind of boy to whom Ray could relate. Quicker than George and more outgoing, Henry knew how to flash that endearing smile that mothers and teachers seemed to fall for. He was never particularly studious, but that didn't bother Ray. "Read books? Not Henry. He was well liked, he was popular with everybody. The instructors liked him, everybody liked him. He was an easy fellow to get along with. Even now, everybody really likes him," says Ray, burbling with delight over his son's success.

At an early age, Ray had Henry out on the golf course learning to swing clubs and putt like a grown-up. When it came time to interview at various boarding schools, the first question on Henry's list, which he wrote down and carried around with him on a clipboard, was, did the school have a golf team? A chip off the old block.

"Dad spent more time with Henry," said Henry's brother, George. "They both liked golf." Henry even seemed to have Ray's financial acumen. In the eighth grade he was elected class treasurer and, according to the school yearbook, racked up such "a nice, fat bank account" that other grades wanted to know the class's secret.

Of course there's nothing unusual about a son's trying to be like his father. It's just that in Henry's case, Ray had set a particularly high standard. "I was not afraid of him. No, it never was that. But I became in awe of him and I just didn't want to be rejected," says Henry. "My father was demanding. For example, he'd say, 'All right, you want to play golf. Fine. You're going to get up early and play golf. I don't care how late you stay out as a teenager, but you're going to get up and play in the morning.' "

Renberg, Henry's childhood friend, says that Henry followed his father around as if he were a saint, hanging on to every word he uttered. Today, Henry attributes much of where he is to a drive, a determination to excel, that was instilled at an early age. "I was always competing with myself, trying to do better than I had before," he said. "I had this desire to do well at whatever I did. I've often thought about it. Does one do well because of fear? The fear of failure."

Despite having an older brother, Henry grew up almost as if he were an only child. Not only was there a five-year age gap between him and George, but their difference in temperaments also kept them apart. George was often away in the summer at camp when Henry was growing up. And from the time that Henry was nine, his older brother was away at boarding school, the name of which Ray cannot recall.

"George was never there. I don't know where he was, but I never saw George," says Renberg, who used to prowl around George's room with Henry, exploring George's stash of electronic equipment. George can't remember much about growing up with his little brother either.

No, it was another George who ended up being more like a brother to Henry, namely George Roberts, Henry's first cousin, who lived in Houston. George was the son of Carolyn and Louis Roberts. Lou was Bessie's brother, a loud, backslapping oil broker whose gregarious ways had attracted Carolyn, a beautiful blond Houston belle. Like George Kravis, George Roberts was named in honor of Bessie and Lou's father, who emigrated from Russia to the United States in the 1890s.

George Roberts was born in 1943, just four months before Henry, and the two boys developed a close friendship from a very early age. The families frequently took their vacations together in the summer, and Carolyn Roberts and Ray Kravis both remember their sons playing at the beach at Marblehead, a fashionable summer resort in Massachusetts, building sand castles that might today seem like early symbols of the corporate empire they were to assemble.

"I think that's when the children really began to know each other," says Carolyn Roberts, now a widow, seated on a pale green couch in her overstuffed Houston apartment. "But with Henry and George, from that point on, even as small kids, they always had a certain rapport. Henry would come here when school was out—they were five or six years old at the time—and stay at my house as much as at his own. And he and George would always pick up where they left off. Their personalities just jelled."

When they were in Houston, the two would spend the days swimming in the huge pool at the glamorous new Shamrock Hotel, or playing cowboys and Indians around the log cabin that the Robertses had built in their backyard. Except for the fact that George's face was more angular, the two boys almost looked as if they were twins. In Tulsa, George would tag along with the Three Musketeers, although Donnie and Bernie didn't share their friend Henry's enthusiasm for his cousin. "I remember George Roberts as being combative, tough, a pretty aggressive guy, more aggressive than Henry," says Bernie. Donnie says he was just "real weird." In all the times that he came to visit, he recalls, "George would never say a word. I don't think I've ever seen him talk for more than twenty seconds."

But if George Roberts was considered hopelessly quiet by the other members of the Tulsa gang, to Henry he was a blood brother. Ray and Carolyn remember that from the time the boys were six or eight years old, the two would sit around and talk, and one of their favorite daydreams was about going into business together.

George attributes his interest in business to his relationship with his father. "From the time I'd been old enough to start to understand things, I'd sit in my dad's den and listen to him talk on the phone and ask him questions about things. And he would take me on business trips with him when I was fifteen or sixteen, meetings where they'd be discussing a merger of something, or talking about drilling a well. . . . I used to know how to read a set of [oil] logs pretty well. And he taught me about finance."

Carolyn remembers her son's early inquisitiveness. After her husband had finished a business call, "George would say, 'Dad, what does it mean when you say you work out a formula this way or that way, what do you mean by that?' And my husband was one, regardless of what he had to do or what he had on his mind, the kids came first. And he'd sit down and explain it to him the best he could."

Lou presented an altogether different image of business to George than Ray did to Henry. He was much more of a wheeler-dealer than his brother-in-law. With no technical skills to speak of, and only several semesters at college, Lou was the consummate happy-go-lucky dealmaker. He was constantly on the lookout for a new prospect, a get-rich-quick scheme.

"He was pretty flashy, George's dad," recalls Renberg. "He was always trying to be a big shot." When he went to New York on business trips, for instance, Lou would often reserve a big suite at the Stanhope, a fashionable hotel across the street from the Metropolitan Museum, in order to entertain potential business partners, on whom he would bestow lavish gifts.

Sometimes Lou's gambits would work, and for a brief moment, the family would feel fabulously rich. And then before long, one of his deals would crater, and they would go back to not knowing how they would make ends meet. "I grew up, I guess, in a family that financially had a lot of ups and downs," recalls George today, sitting almost motionless as he stares out at the San Francisco Bay from his forty-fifth-story office. The instability, he said, reflected both the vagaries of the oil business and his father's personality. "My father was a wildcatter, in the classic sense. He was a real gambler, an optimist. So, we didn't know whether we were rich or poor, and many times we were both."

Though the Robertses were plagued with financial uncertainty, they never let it get in the way of being a close family. Evenings would find them all gathered around the dinner table, often including Carolyn's parents, poking and teasing and challenging each other on everything from foreign policy to a neighbor's latest mishap. During these raucous evening affairs, George was always the quiet observer. His older sister, Linda, a rebel by nature and full of mischief, was forever chatting and making jokes. With Linda, his swashbuckling father, and his talkative mother to contest with, George had a hard time getting a word in edgewise. He came to play the role of the quiet, steady one who, in the midst of chaos, could always be counted on to remain unflappable.

From the time that he was a child, George was told again and again that he would have to fend for himself. "My father was very clear about what was expected of me," said George. "He said, 'Look, I don't have a business to give you, so you're going to have to go out and earn your own living in the world.' " Lou promised George that he would give him a good education, but that once he left school or decided to get married, that would be the end of Lou's financial support. From then on, Lou told his son, he would have to be on his own. "He kept drumming that into me from the time I was little, and I've tried to drum that into my own kids. So, as much as he was up and down, it was a pretty consistent level of signals and messages of what was expected of me," George recalls.

If George and his cousin Henry had fantasies of going into business together, they both had a long way to go before getting there. First there was the small matter of an education. Despite Henry's mediocre performance in school, Ray aimed high. After Henry finished the eighth grade at Tulsa's Edison Junior High, he was sent off to Eaglebrook School, a strictly run boarding school in the historic New England village of Deerfield, Massachusetts, in the fall of 1958. Ray had heard about Eaglebrook from friends who had sent their own sons there.

Both Ray and Henry say that the reason he went away to boarding school was that Edison High School was undergoing extensive construction and Henry's classes were being disrupted. In fact, as Henry's classmates will tell you, and as the school's yearbook shows, the construction at Edison had been completed a full year before Henry left Tulsa. "It was that Eastern education would make him more competitive," says schoolfriend Renberg, clearly amused by the Kravises' version. "Very few families sent their kids away. It was expensive then. But Ray Kravis had the foresight to realize it would make Henry more competitive."

Not that there was anything wrong with Edison High or its brand-new facilities. It's just that the life it prepared its students for was not necessarily the one that the Kravises had in mind for Henry. In those days, Edison was the kind of place where girls took classes in homemaking, where they learned about formal table-setting and how to use household equipment. Boys, meanwhile, spent their afternoons in "shop," learning about auto mechanics, drafting, or doing metalwork.

It was this foresight, this understanding of where they might fit in life, that seemed to distinguish the Kravises from other wealthy Tulsa families. Although the oil boom showered fortunes on many local businessmen, few seemed to have the vision, the know-how, or the gumption to parlay that into an entirely new social status for themselves and their offspring. Ray, on the other hand, through his contacts in the business community and on Wall Street, had developed a keen sense of what schools Henry should attend, what clothes he should wear, what sports he should master, what foods and wines he should learn to appreciate, and what traveling experiences would make his son "well rounded."

It wasn't that Henry was particularly brilliant or gifted,

says his friend Renberg. "Henry is a person who did his homework, who followed direction." But without Ray, says Renberg, he would have been nothing. "You can't talk about Henry Kravis and George Roberts without knowing the background of how they were developed and nurtured and matured by the process set up by Ray Kravis. Ray Kravis knew where to send them, how to educate them, who to expose them to, who they needed to know. I was always impressed by it. Henry would say, 'I'm meeting this person, I'm going to New York, I'm going to be interviewed by this person, Dad wanted me to do this.' Ray orchestrated everything."

In general, Henry was a willing subject. He didn't, however, enjoy his stay at Eaglebrook very much. "It was a shock," he recalls, "it was real regimentation. In those days, you had to go to Lord and Taylor and they'd outfit you in the Eaglebrook uniform: a little blue blazer or a gray corduroy jacket. In the summer you could wear a madras jacket. And that was it. You couldn't wear loafers, you had to wear tie shoes, and you went out and saluted the flag every morning whether it was snowing or whatever."

To make matters worse, Henry had to spend two years there before going on to his next destination. Since he came from a public school in Tulsa, Oklahoma, it was decided that he should repeat the eighth grade. That is something else you will not hear from the Kravis family. They uniformly explain that Henry graduated one year behind his friends Donnie and Bernie and his cousin George, all of whom are the same age, because his birthday falls in January. In fact, Henry only fell one year behind his friends after the eighth grade.

After Eaglebrook, Henry's next stop was Loomis Chaffee, an even more elite prep school in a sleepy Connecticut town six miles north of Hartford. Less well known than schools such as Andover or Exeter, with somewhat looser academic standards, Loomis Chaffee was nonetheless considered a perfectly acceptable boarding school for prominent

New England families. Once again, Ray heard about it from friends who were sending their sons there. At Loomis, Henry could mingle with the children of upper-class Establishment families and absorb and adopt their culture. Among the school's better known graduates are Arthur O. Sulzberger, whose family has long owned and run the *New York Times,* and George P. Shultz, who became the secretary of state under President Reagan.

Henry loved his three years at Loomis and still considers it his happiest time in any educational establishment. (He now sponsors three disadvantaged students a year there.) The setting could hardly have been more uplifting, or more likely to instill self-confidence in a young man being groomed for success. The campus is like a miniature of the University of Virginia, whose very formal school grounds were designed by Thomas Jefferson. Loomis's main school building, topped by a copper cupola, sits grandly overlooking a long, rectangular green lawn that is lined on either side by stately, three-story dormitories. The boys enter and leave their red-brick dorms every day through an impressive colonnade of white columns—a heady environment for fourteen-year-olds.

Henry, or Hank, as he was known then, spent three idyllic years there in the early 1960s, playing football, wrestling—he was cocaptain of the school's varsity team in his senior year—and developing close friendships, many of which he retained for years.

A popular student, Henry was elected to the Student Council twice, once as vice president and the second time as a member of the executive committee. When he graduated, the school commended him with a book prize for his "unselfish leadership qualities."

Hank also developed a reputation as something of a ladies' man. Described in his class yearbook as an "ardent" member of the Dance Committee, Hank could always be counted on to do some serious swirling with girls from nearby schools at the occasional mixers. "Thanks to his Oklahoma drawl, his panhandle sincerity and his lovely black hair [another nickname was 'Kink'] Hank managed to win himself the reputation of Class Lover," according to his yearbook.

Loomis Chaffee was also where Henry took his first serious step into the life his father had mapped out for him. In his senior year he took an economics course and found it absolutely fascinating. Jim Wilson, who taught the course and has stayed in touch with Henry ever since, remembers Hank as an extremely attentive student who, like the proverbial apple-polisher, sat as close as he could to the teacher and was constantly volunteering answers while other students hung back. Henry was very intense about learning the material, very focused. "He was a very competitive person; he was going to do well," says Wilson.

Wilson was surprised by how much Henry already seemed to know. "He came with a greater awareness of the world of business than other students—that was clearly from his family. It's fairly unusual for kids to have a sense of what business is," Wilson reflects. Henry not only knew more than the others, he even looked the part. Wilson remembers Hank being far and away the best-dressed boy in the school. His pants were always pressed, his shoes shined, he had matching socks, and he always wore a tie pin, which most boys his age regarded as an object of derision, if not a tool of torture.

Loomis had one flaw. It did not have a golf team. But Henry managed to find a course nearby where he could practice on weekends. His friends teased him about being the only boy in school rich enough to own a leather golf bag.

During the summers, Henry would go back to Tulsa and pick up where he had left off with his old sidekicks, Donnie and Bernie. They would always be waiting eagerly for him, determined not to let their friend's time in an upscale boarding school turn him into one of those stuffy preppies.

Indeed, Donnie considered it his personal mission to organize Henry's social life so that upon his return he didn't miss a beat. More of a partygoer than Henry and less serious about getting ahead or making money, Donnie considered himself an expert in the dating category, and tried to pass along certain tips to his friend, whom he regarded as easily infatuated by girls, but clumsy in his approach. The boys would frequently double or triple date, taking advantage of Ray's big Lincoln and his black chauffeur to enhance their image.

Finding the right girls for Henry often took some doing. "Henry always had a thing about beautiful women," says Renberg. Yet his friend's size and his religion were clear drawbacks to some of Tulsa's fair maidens. Renberg would try to overcome those obstacles by reminding girls of Henry's wealth and status. "We used to work on the girls' psyches," he recalls with obvious relish. "We'd tell them, 'Not only is this guy handsome and well liked and well respected in his peer group, in academia, in Eastern prep schools, but his parents are worth twenty-five million dollars.' We'd have these girls so psyched up, and Henry would love it, he'd pick them up at the door and . . ." Donnie gave a snap of his fingers to show how easy it all was.

Often times, that was all it took. Once introduced, Henry's polite manner and congenial nature would win over many girls. And he was attentive—very attentive. He was always making sure they weren't too cold or uncomfortable or lacking for anything.

But sometimes all the attentiveness and gifts in the world weren't enough. He was often dismissed for being too serious, too straight. He never smoked, for instance, in an era when that was considered a rite of passage. Renberg says some people would complain to him, "What's so big about Henry? He's straight, he's dull, he doesn't do this or that," a criticism that Renberg would then strive valiantly to counter. But Renberg knew what they meant. He had seen that single-minded side of Henry, too. It's just that he chose to ignore it and to undermine it as assuredly as he could.

One surefire way to loosen Henry up, to make him forget about his destiny in the business world, or his ambition to excel, was to get him drunk, which, when Henry was a teenager, was evidently not very hard to do. The boys would raid

Ray's liquor cabinet or go out carousing in the local bars. It was only then that a wild underside of Henry's personality would show itself.

One night, for instance, Donnie, Henry, and another boy went to the local diner around midnight to dry off a little after dropping off their dates. As the boys paid their checks one by one and began walking out, Henry, the last in line, got into a fight with a local drunk who was propped up near the cash register. The next thing Donnie knew, Henry was running down the street screaming, "Run! Run! The police are after us!" At first, Donnie thought Henry was pulling his leg. Those doubts were quickly overcome, however, when a policeman came tearing around the corner, dropped to one knee, and took aim at Henry with his gun. At this point, Donnie's older brother, Bob, who had followed the boys out of the diner, came up behind the policeman and knocked the pistol out of the cop's hand. Donnie, who was by then a few blocks away, panting in the bushes, thought he was safe until he felt the cold steel of a pistol pressing up against his temple. Apparently, in the ruckus that Henry had created at the diner, the police thought he was trying to rob the cash register. The boys explained who they were and no charges were brought.

GEORGE

George Roberts's high school years were not quite so exciting. After he had finished junior high school, his parents hoped to send him to one of Houston's private schools. But in the early sixties, as was not atypical, those schools had informal quotas for the number of Jewish students they would accept. George took the aptitude tests, but didn't score high enough to secure one of those precious places. So after a year at San Jacinto public high school, during which George drifted sideways, earning very average grades, Lou and Carolyn decided they had no choice but to pack their young son off to boarding school.

Unlike Henry, who landed in a cushy prep school, George's home for the next three years was a military school in Culver, Indiana. The Robertses had intended to take their son to visit five or six different schools, including several on the East Coast. But Culver was the school that Lou had attended when he was a boy, and so it was the natural first stop. Almost as soon as they arrived at the picturesque, lakeside campus, Lou dragged his son off to the gym to show him a picture that was still hanging there of his days as a boxing champion. For young George, who had traipsed after his father for years, that was about all it took. "Well, where did George want to go to school? Culver. I knew that was a foregone conclusion," says his mother, who is in her early seventies and still trim and attractive. The family never visited any other school.

When Carolyn and Lou dropped George off at Culver that fall, and she saw the barracklike conditions her only son would be living in, Carolyn had serious second thoughts. She cried the whole car-ride back to the Chicago airport. "Military schools are for bad boys," she sobbed to her husband, "but George is a good boy! Why does he have to go there?"

Indeed, George had always been an easy child for Carolyn to take care of, especially compared to her rambunctious daughter. While Linda's bedroom would always be littered with clothes, making it virtually impossible to clean, George was tidy beyond a mother's wildest dreams. He always hung his shirts an inch or more apart in the closet so they wouldn't get wrinkled and would put on a clean shirt and tie for any occasion without prompting from his parents. When friends came over to his house to play, George always insisted they clean up their mess before going home. "Well behaved and clean," says Carolyn, her head nodding with wholehearted approval. "George is still that way. He is immaculate."

Military school only served to enhance the orderly side of George's personality. It also gave him a good physical and mental workout, as this small boy suddenly found himself up against scores of big, beefy Midwesterners. When George arrived at Culver the fall of 1959, the school sized him up as a mediocre student. He had scored only middling grades on standardized tests, and since he came from a public school in Texas, with his diminutive stature and reserved personality, the school's administrators were not very optimistic. Based on the admissions' office's initial assessment, "I would have thought, if he can get C-pluses, we'll be doing all right," said Alexander D. Nagy, who was assigned to be George's counselor, or house parent.

But George seemed determined to beat the odds against him. Not blessed with intuitive intelligence or physical might, he used the only weapons he had at his disposal: boundless energy, self-discipline, and determination. He organized his day down to the last minute and worked and worked at every subject or sport he was engaged in until he finally beat it into submission. It was a technique George has used ever since to conquer new and foreign territory.

He didn't spend much time developing friends or horsing around. "He was someone who wouldn't waste a day. It was as if he had to account, at the end of the day, for how he had spent his time," recalls Nagy. "You would always have an impression that for him, life was serious, school was serious, competition was serious."

Each of the eight hundred or so boys in the school was assigned to a military unit that competed against the others, scholastically and athletically. George was in Battery C, an artillery unit that Nagy oversaw. He was housed in what was known as the Main Barracks, an old, ivy-covered building filled with double rooms.

Every morning George would rise at reveille—a cannon would go off at 6:25 and the boys were allowed three minutes tolerance. Like the others, he would pull on the gray pants and blue double-breasted jacket that made up the school uniform, make his bed, polish his shoes, and get ready to march to breakfast in military formation. There were daily calisthenics classes, and twice a week, there were elaborate military drills. As a member of Battery C, one of his jobs was to help keep clean the 105-howitzer cannons that were displayed and set off during the school's military parades.

In class, George was always referred to as Mr. Roberts; teachers were addressed only as "sir." The academic schedule was rigorous, and no excuse was considered acceptable for incomplete homework—students were expected to take care of that themselves. The school was run on the honor code. Lying, for instance, was considered an expellable offense, and anyone who knew of another who had lied or cheated was expected to turn in that errant student. Those who committed lesser violations faced a range of penalties—from heavier cleanup duty to walking around in a circle for hours at a time, holding a rifle perfectly upright.

After just a few months of Culver's discipline, the boy's transformation was evident. When George came home for Christmas, "I didn't know whether to kiss him or shake hands. He was a little maaan," said Carolyn with her long, languid Southern drawl. She immediately withdrew her objections to Culver.

"Did I like it?" George pauses to think. "I didn't dislike it."

George threw himself into sports. He played basketball and volleyball and became one of the school's best soccer players until he tore the cartilage in his knee one day and had to stop. And like his father before him, George made it onto the wrestling team. Nagy says that George's athletic abilities made him a valued member of Battery C. "He was very much of a boy's boy, very involved in those things that competitive teenage boys do for their activities," said Nagy.

In class, George did well in subjects such as history, English, and Spanish, the latter of which he had had an opportunity to practice in Texas. But he stumbled over math and science, a shortcoming that he eventually overcame in his business career. George was one of those students who never said much in class, but when he did contribute, he was listened to respectfully by his peers.

During the three years that George was at Culver, he gradually recast himself, largely through willpower, from a boy of middling abilities into one of the school's most highly regarded students. He graduated cum laude in 1962—one of the top ten students of his class of 193. His military rank—cadet lieutenant—was the highest for which he was eligible.

"He had a feistiness and determination that sometimes goes with that physical build," says Nagy, who has since become Culver's dean and remains in touch with George. "There has to be within the young man a driving, motivating force." How else, Nagy wondered, could George have made so much of himself from such modest beginnings? George, he concludes, "is clearly an overachiever."

The year that George graduated from Culver, he was faced with perhaps one of the most traumatic events that could ever befall a young man. His father, whose office he had sat in for hours as a young boy, dreaming of the day he would be a businessman, too, was arrested and sent to prison. Lou had failed to file income tax forms for several years, and when the Internal Revenue Service finally caught up with him, he decided, rather than go to trial, to plead guilty. According to records at Seagoville, a minimum security federal prison just outside Dallas, Lou was given a two-year sentence and was released on parole after ten months.

Friends of the family say the Robertses faced this turn of events stoically and turned inward for moral support. Carolyn, a strong, proud woman, stood by her husband despite the social ostracism caused by his jail sentence. Those who know George well say he was deeply traumatized by the event, but remained dutifully loyal to his father, too. When George got married five years later, he asked his father to be his best man. "George was very close to Lou," says Carolyn softly, "very close."

Unfortunately, that was not the end of Lou's problems. In the fall of 1972, two IRS agents went to the Robertses' home and informed the couple that they were the subject of a criminal investigation. The government believed that in offering to make restitution for his previous crimes, Lou had again attempted to hide large amounts of income. On a hot, muggy day the following May, Lou was arrested again, dragged off to jail and held overnight. The charge this time: eleven counts of tax fraud, including failure to disclose $220,000 in assets, and underreporting income by $503,000 over four years. Bail was initially set at $100,000, though later reduced to $50,000. "Oil and Gas Broker Indicted on Tax Charge," said the headline in the *Houston Chronicle* the next day.

Thanks to exhaustive efforts on the part of the family's lawyers, who made a series of motions to dismiss the case and requested separate trials for different counts, the date of Lou's trial was continuously delayed. But his health began to deteriorate. He was not in good shape to begin with, having suffered from diabetes and rheumatoid arthritis for over twenty years. His doctors had prescribed steroids to mitigate the arthritic pain, but they had only helped to make him, as one doctor described later, "moderately obese."

Lou's health problems were further compounded when he developed an ingrown toenail in the big toe of his right foot. It subsequently became infected, and though he treated it with antibiotics, it became gangrenous. He finally had to have the toe amputated in October of 1974, but it was too late. The gangrene had spread up his leg, and the next month, Lou had to have a second operation—this time his right leg was amputated above the knee.

While he was recovering from that operation, Lou suffered heart failure and remained in the hospital for about six weeks, heavily sedated. He was unable to sit up for long periods of time in bed, and having never learned how to use his artificial leg, he could not walk. "Mr. Roberts has deteriorated quite a bit during this time and has been a difficult surgical problem, as well as a difficult medical problem," Dr. Henry Glass wrote to Lou's lawyer, describing his condition. "His capacity for memory to me has decreased and his ability to withstand long periods of conversation or any physical or mental trauma has been impaired greatly since I first knew him in 1970."

When Lou got out of the hospital, he was bedridden and required constant attention. His daily diet consisted of three codeine pills and four tablets of the painkiller Darvon. After three years of legal maneuvering and faced with a defendant who was deemed too weak to undergo a trial, the government finally dropped its suit against Lou in November 1975. Still riddled with arthritis and diabetes, Lou drifted downhill and finally died in 1977.

George has rarely confided to anyone about his father's misfortunes. To cover over the incident, he tends to use the throwaway phrase that his family suffered financial "ups and downs." Since his friends knew his father was an oil wildcatter, that always seemed enough of an explanation. Still, many friends sensed that the relationship was pivotal.

"I think George's father was a very different person than George was," says Donald R. Stephens, who came to know George well later. "I know he was very cyclical in his finances. I think it may be one of the things that made George very conservative."

According to one person who did know the full story and became close to George later in his life, "it was clearly extremely influential—unquestionably. It was probably one of the central events of his life." The reason he knows that, he added, "is that he said one sentence to me when we were driving in a car. He said, 'My dad disappointed me a great deal.'" And for the painfully shy George, that simple statement amounted to a highly personal admission.

George went off to college in that fall of 1962, despite the family's troubles. The school he attended was Claremont Men's College, a loose-knit affiliation of five colleges on one campus located in a suburb of Los Angeles. Ray says George ended up there because he passed along the name of the school to his nephew after coming across it in an article in *Time* magazine, which described it as the Oxford University of the U.S. George's counselor, Nagy, had also recommended

Claremont because he thought the boy would do better in a smaller setting.

It was also the school that George liked the most of the ones at which he was offered a place. Despite his good record at Culver, both Yale University, which he had had his heart set on, and his other top choice, Stanford University, turned him down—a result once again, George believes, of his inability to score well on standardized tests.

Claremont proved a welcome respite for the quiet, serious-minded George. After three years in a Midwestern military school, sunny, girl-infested California offered him his first taste of unadulterated freedom. Life improved even more when George was joined there the next year by his cousin and close friend, Henry. Loomis had advised Henry that his grades were not good enough to get him into Stanford, where he really wanted to go. So the young Kravis had only applied to Claremont, Washington and Lee in Lexington, Virginia, and his father's alma mater, Lehigh. But the only one he had any real interest in was Claremont, where he thought he would have more fun being with his cousin George.

The two young men had a grand time exploring southern California. The sprawling campus, at the foot of the San Gabriel Mountains, was within easy driving distance of Los Angeles' bikini-laden beaches, the racetrack at Santa Anita, and the crap tables of Las Vegas. The two cousins experimented liberally in all three pursuits. Henry clearly set the pace in the dating category, but it was George who met his bride-to-be at Claremont, the strikingly beautiful Leanne Bovet, a debutante of Swiss Episcopalian heritage known best for her soft blond hair and shy manner.

Both men majored in economics, though George was the better student. He found the work fairly easy and applied the work habits he had honed at Culver to whatever subject happened to be at hand. "Let me put it this way: I was a very organized student. I always knew what I had to do to get done what I had to get done," says George matter-of-factly.

"So when everybody else was running around worrying about finals, I'd pretty much have studied for them." Though both men ultimately made the dean's list, George graduated cum laude, an honor he neglected to mention to his mother and Leanne, who learned of it only when they happened to glance down at their graduation programs.

It was the summer of 1964, after his sophomore year in college, when George's life finally took a turn for the better. He had returned home to Houston, to a summer job at Battelstein's, one of Houston's department stores. His assignment was to unpack dresses and other garments in the store's unairconditioned warehouse and load them onto racks, which would then be rolled into the store. It was hot, sweaty, monotonous work, and a far cry from what the serious-minded George wanted to be doing with his time.

Ray felt sorry for his nephew and decided that he'd better extend a hand. He was always having to come to the rescue of his wife's brother's family, and friends say he frequently groused about Lou's constant screwups. On this particular rescue mission, Ray called his nephew and asked him if he'd be interested in working on Wall Street. "George said, 'I'd love it,' so I made a few calls. I called Cy [Lewis] and said, 'George is bright,' and he said, 'Send him here,' " said Ray.

And that was all it took for George Roberts to end up working the next summer for one of the top ten firms on Wall Street when he was just twenty-one years old. "That's Ray's claim to fame, that he took him out of the ready-to-wear business and put him in New York," says Carolyn, clearly irked to hear that Ray was still taking credit for her son's launching.

Though a few friends thought it odd that Ray would be taking such an interest in the son of his wife's brother, Ray's actions were not entirely altruistic. Henry was already working summers at the firm that was run by his father's good friend Gus Levy, the senior partner of Goldman Sachs.

"Henry got a job with Goldman Sachs," says Ray with a slight giggle. "They were all good friends of mine."

With Henry working as a trainee at Goldman Sachs, what could be more helpful than having a brother, or the nearest thing to a brother, standing beside him as he made his way in the rough-and-tumble world of Wall Street? As anyone who knew the two families well knew, George was the smart one. Henry was always more of a follower.

Ray's assistance did not end there. He also set the two boys up in an apartment, rent free, in the Hyde Park, which was then a residential hotel on the corner of Madison Avenue and Seventy-seventh Street. The mother of a friend of Ray's had died, leaving a lease that had already been paid. The fact that the building was filled with little old ladies with blue-tinted hair, and that it had all the ambience of a St. Petersburg rest home, Ray regarded as unimportant. "It was an old-lady's apartment. I said, 'What's the difference? You're not paying for it,' " Ray recalls.

Henry and George, being good, clean-cut kids who had been raised to be unfailingly polite to their elders, quickly turned the situation to their advantage. Not only did the little old ladies come to dote on the boys, insisting from time to time that they eat some of their good, home-cooked food, but a few would even go down and let them in when they got locked out after eleven-thirty.

Although Henry was used to New York City, having visited the city frequently with his parents and from nearby Loomis, George found Manhattan's pace overwhelming. The crush of people, the noise, the fast pace, was a shock to all of his senses. Even now he shudders as he recalls his first few subway rides that summer in New York.

"Henry and I would leave to go to work, we'd take the Lexington Avenue subway at eight in the morning. And I've never seen such a crush of humanity. It was just wall-to-wall people. You'd fight your way on, fight your way off. And I did that a couple of days and I said, 'You know, there's got to be a better way to do that. If I leave earlier, there's not as many people, and if I come home later, there's not as many people.' " So George did just that, leaving Henry to drag himself into Goldman's offices a few hours later. In those early-morning hours at Bear Stearns, George found he had the place to himself—or almost to himself. "I kept getting in and I kept seeing this nice bald-headed guy walking around at seven-thirty in the morning, too. So I introduced myself to him, and it was Jerry." It's interesting, he said, a solemn look crossing his face, "how fate affects you."

JERRY

Jerry, or Jerome Kohlberg, Jr., worked in a corner of Bear Stearns that few people had much interest in. The heartbeat of Bear Stearns was the trading room floor, where a sea of young men manned rows of telephone banks, shouting into receivers a stream of unintelligible stock and bond prices. Even the firm's senior partner, then Cy Lewis, sat on the floor amidst this hullabaloo, snarling bid and ask prices into his phone right along with the rest of them.

Of course, other Wall Street firms had trading areas, too. But the driving force, particularly at many WASP firms, was the team of well-mannered investment bankers who acted as personal advisers to the nation's corporate elite, many of whom were their former prep school or college classmates. A firm such as Bear Stearns, composed primarily of sons of Jewish immigrants, was not blessed with those social ties. Instead, it attracted people whose gut could tell them in an instant what the price of a stock and bond would be, not just a month from now, not just a week from now, but in the next thirty minutes—or even thirty seconds. They might not have been as cultured or their table manners as perfectly refined, but one thing Bear Stearns traders did know was the value of securities and how to anticipate their price movements.

The area that Jerry worked in, however, was corporate finance, which was about as far away from that go-go trading world as one could get. People in that department analyzed a company in terms of its financial needs, whether it was going to have a cash crunch while it was building a new plant, whether it needed to invite more people to put up some capital in exchange for a piece of the business, or whether it should borrow more money, and if so, from whom and for how much. Increasingly, corporate finance specialists also helped a company decide whether it should buy a competitor, merge with another, or even be acquired itself.

Corporate finance mavens almost invariably thought their business was more important than trading and, certainly, more intellectually stimulating. But by definition, their business took time to develop. It could often take years from the time that a Bear Stearns investment banker raised the subject of selling equity or merging, to the time when a corporate treasurer might actually take that action and give Bear Stearns the mandate for the transaction. It was only at that point that Bear Stearns would earn a decent fee for its trouble. And time and meticulous research were luxuries that Bear Stearns, under the indomitable Cy Lewis, could not, or did not want to, afford.

As the person in charge of corporate finance at Bear Stearns, Jerry Kohlberg was by definition already a misfit. But his manner and demeanor made him even more so. Almost entirely bald and wearing rimless glasses, Kohlberg looked slightly monklike as he skulked around the firm's offices, shoulders hunched, brow furrowed, wearing one of his many bow ties. This extremely correct, professorial-looking gentleman could not have been more of an anomaly amongst a horde of loudmouthed, boorish traders if he had tried.

When Roberts came to work for Bear Stearns, Kohlberg was exploring a concept he liked to call a bootstrap, but which has since become known as a leveraged buyout. Like a mad scientist who comes across a new chemical compound, Kohlberg thought he might have stumbled onto a financial technique that could revolutionize corporate America.

His concept was disarmingly simple. Prior to World War Two, many of the country's leading companies were owned or dominated by the dynamic individuals or families that created them. Whenever one of these companies needed more money to grow, families such as the Mellons, the Du Ponts, and the Carnegies would turn to their banks for money or issue stock to a relatively small circle of interested investors. But they tended to be closely involved and took good care of their companies.

As the economy spurted after World War Two, many companies could not expand rapidly enough by simply relying on family money or a limited investor group. To raise the millions of dollars that were becoming necessary, and to spread the risk across a wider group, they increasingly resorted to the practice of selling shares of their companies to the public at large. Gradually, the ownership of well-known American companies began changing from a situation where ten or twelve individuals owned 80 percent and a few hundred shareholders held the rest, to the reverse, where 10 or 20 percent of a company belonged to a particularly wealthy family, and the remaining 80 percent or more belonged to thousands of individuals, no one of whom wielded any real control. "Going public" became the latest fad in the corporate community.

Kohlberg believed that for many companies, particularly smaller ones, this was an unhealthy development. Not only did many of them not need the money, but it separated the owners of a company from the people who actually ran it. Technically, the shareholders of a company could keep management's feet to the fire through the board of directors, which was charged with overseeing those executives on the shareholders' behalf. And if shareholders really became dissatisfied, they could always vote to replace managers and directors with choices of their own.

But in practice, that rarely happened. Chief executives, the hired hands, were the ones who got to put forward the names of directors to their boards, and the nominees were typically people whose support they thought they could count on. Shareholders, meanwhile—the dentists, lawyers, and proverbial widows who owned stock—rarely knew enough about the innards of the company or had the time or wherewithal to make sure that its businesses were being run effectively. Shareholders' meetings and vote-casting became nothing more than a rubber-stamping exercise. And chief executives, no longer held accountable by a small and committed group of shareholders, were free to embark on empire-building exercises, buying other companies, expanding for the sake of expansion.

"Companies had no guiding overseer, no one to tell them they weren't doing a good job," said Kohlberg. "The chief executive became his own boss, he picked his own board of directors. It was self-perpetuating, in effect. And with that came the fiefdoms and the perks." Today, of course, it is fashionable to criticize managements for the excesses of the past, the carefree way that chief executives fly around in private corporate jets, the decadence of corporate bathrooms filled with pink marble and gold-plated taps. But in the late sixties, when Kohlberg first started grousing, his was a relatively solitary voice. (One of the great ironies is that when the leveraged buyout was originally formulated, it was intended to combat the greed and egotism that today it is often thought to have spawned.)

Though Kohlberg was co-head of the corporate finance department, whose purpose was to help companies raise capital, he didn't want to get too carried away with this "going public" craze, even though the firm clearly would have profited from it in the short term. "He wasn't interested if you could take a company public at fourteen dollars a share and it went to sixteen the next day," recalls Donald Oresman, a lawyer who worked with Kohlberg on some of his early deals. "One of Jerry's great strengths was that tomorrow was much less important than next week, which was much less important than next month."

Instead, Kohlberg thought he had come up with a way to keep managers honest, to help companies grow, *and* to get rich in the process. His idea was to replace the diffused public shareholders of a company with a small group of highly motivated investors. In order to come up with enough money to buy out the public shareholders' interest, Kohlberg's investors would borrow heavily, usually by pledging the assets of the company they were intent upon acquiring. It was the equivalent of getting a mortgage on a piece of property. The lenders would have the land as their collateral. The owner would improve the property and sell it at a higher price.

The concept has always been considered appropriate for a home mortgage because the banks, if they are doing their job, check to make sure that borrowers have enough income to cover their mortgage payments with a comfortable cushion. Generally, the assumption is that a person's income will not fluctuate wildly, but will rise steadily as he or she gains more experience in the work force. By contrast, companies have tended to be wary of assuming large amounts of debt because their earnings do fluctuate with the economy, inflation, and new competitors. Precisely because of this risk, Kohlberg believed his concept could only be applied to certain types of companies: those that were in relatively stable businesses and generated predictable amounts of cash with which they could pay the interest on the newly created debt, and midsize, family-run companies that knew their business backward but could not grow further without tapping a broader market for fresh capital. This latter group generally resisted issuing stock to the public out of fear that they would ultimately lose control of the business.

The object of Kohlberg's bootstrap was not to overburden a company with debt, but to create a new class of owner who would have a large stake in a company's well-being. Here is how it would work. Before a buyout, a company's finances typically might look something like this: $40 million of stock held by a wide group of owners and $60 million of debt. Kohlberg would offer to buy out the stockholders by paying $50 million for their equity, giving the shareholders a profit, and either assuming all of the company's outstanding debt, if the lenders agreed, or replacing it with new loans. In order to finance this $110-million transaction, he would make a "down payment" of $20 million in equity on behalf of himself, Bear Stearns, and the company's top managers, who would then have a direct stake in the company's performance. And he would finance the rest by borrowing from an assortment of banks and insurance companies, whose loans would be secured by the property of the company Kohlberg's group was buying.

Over the next few years, the company's management would concentrate on getting the company to run more efficiently and would use the additional cash it generated to pay off the company's loans as quickly as possible. When it was time to resell the streamlined company, it was the highly leveraged aspect of the deal that would make Kohlberg's profits seem so extraordinary. Since the investors in the LBO had put up so little of their own money to buy the company, the profits would seem gargantuan by comparison. It was really no different from a stock investor's being allowed to play the market by putting up only $10 to buy $100 worth of stock. If that stock then soared to $150, the investor would pay off the $90 of debt and enjoy a $60 return on a $10 investment. In the real world, of course, investors are required, at least initially, to put up collateral for at least 50 percent of the value of their investments, precisely to discourage such speculation.

Kohlberg believed that by requiring top managers to own a significant stake in an LBO, they would be sure to treat his high-risk transactions with great care. The top layer of management, in addition, was expected to alter the way workers were compensated, to link their pay more directly with performance. It was also important to Kohlberg that he and his team have some of their money on the line, too. That would give them a powerful incentive to oversee the company and its executives. It was a way to reunite owners and managers in a way that he thought could prove beneficial to all. If the company's performance improved, it would generate more jobs and growth for the community, and since the profits would be divided amongst a much smaller group of owners, Bear Stearns, Kohlberg, and the managers stood a chance of becoming rich.

Kohlberg frequently referred to these deals as bootstraps, because companies were pulling themselves up by them. But on Wall Street they became known as leveraged, or management, buyouts, because of the debt that was involved, and the inclusion of the company's executives.

The first summer that George Roberts worked at Bear Stearns, he was placed in the firm's research department, an area where he crunched a few numbers, but generally felt underutilized. He was delighted, then, when Kohlberg arranged for him to work in the corporate finance department for his second summer job. By then, Kohlberg had already been quietly experimenting with his bootstrap concept for four or five years. He had persuaded the firm to give him some money to buy a few small companies, and he had thrown in some of his own. Several years later those companies were run so much better and were generating so much cash that each share was worth ten or twenty times what Kohlberg's group had initially paid for it. Kohlberg and his fellow investors would only reap their profits when they sold their companies to new owners or issued stock to the public—a process that could take five to seven years from the time they made their initial investment.

George was fascinated with the deals Kohlberg was doing

and found his boss's quiet demeanor a welcome relief from the noise and confusion that seemed so prevalent in other parts of the firm. Kohlberg, in turn, appreciated the seriousness and dedication with which young George, who was eighteen years his junior, was applying himself. Jerry had always enjoyed working with younger people, watching them absorb things for the first time, and George reminded Jerry a little bit of himself, when he was younger.

Beginning that summer, a bond began slowly forming between the two. In Kohlberg, George had found the model of a quiet, steady, successful businessman so unlike his unpredictable father. Indeed, Kohlberg was about as far removed from Lou Roberts as anyone could be.

Where Lou was loud and self-promoting, Jerry was modest and unassuming. Jerry would painstakingly trace and retrace his options before making a decision about a deal, driving some people mad with his conservatism. Lou was so determined to make a quick buck that he would often cut corners, so much so that he wound up in jail. Jerry, on the other hand, practiced such an acute version of "Do unto others . . ." that he became a symbol of sobriety on Wall Street. He was often referred to as "Mr. Kohlberg," even by those who knew him well. "He had a highly respected name on Wall Street," said Donald Stone, who has known Kohlberg for twenty-five years and is a senior partner in the brokerage firm of Lasker, Stone & Stern and a vice chairman of the New York Stock Exchange.

Kohlberg's straight-arrow character has been hewn since childhood. The early years of his life coincided with the Depression, and though his family was comfortable in their two-story rented brick home in New Rochelle—a bedroom community north of Manhattan—there was little time or tolerance for frivolity. Evenings were usually devoted to homework or practicing his beloved trumpet. On weekends, when it was warm enough, Jerry would play tennis or swim at the Beach Point Club in nearby Mamaroneck, a favorite of middle-class suburbanite Jews. Or he and his pals would sometimes take the train into Manhattan and listen to jazz bands at the Paramount Theater.

Kohlberg will not talk much about his home life. He was not particularly close to his father, a heavyset man who never made it past high school, and who earned a reasonable but by no means exceptional living trading everything from tobacco to feathers to candy. Jerry's mother, Edith, was the warmer, more emotional of the two. College educated and briefly a free-lance writer, she always made it clear to Jerry that she regarded him as holding great promise in the family and that she expected him to do something about it.

In school, he was popular and unusually well respected. Kohlberg is remembered by former classmates at the public high school for his refusal to be drawn into cliques. He spanned all racial and ethnic boundaries; his friends were Italian, Irish, Hispanic, and black. In his senior year he was elected president of his class; at graduation, he was dubbed "most likely to succeed."

Kohlberg's ties to the local Jewish community, meanwhile, were slight. He rarely attended Sunday school and dropped out of the Jewish fraternity group at New Rochelle High School after deciding it was not broad-minded enough. Even in his high school days, "he knew his own mind, his own standards," recalls Leonard Blumberg, a high school classmate and one of Kohlberg's oldest friends.

Kohlberg honed his values even more as a student at Swarthmore College, where he went in 1943. Set on a lush, wooded campus just outside Philadelphia, Swarthmore was established by the Quakers in the mid-1800s. Though by Kohlberg's time the college had relaxed some of its religious formalities and welcomed students of all religions, the school remained imbued with many of the Quaker principles, such as tolerance, selflessness, and humility, all of which Kohlberg found compelling.

Although Kohlberg loved his years at Swarthmore, these were hardly free and easy times. Hitler was storming Europe, the Japanese threat was growing, and the American war effort was intensifying. Swarthmore's pastoral setting was obviously far from the front, but war was nonetheless a pervasive influence on campus. Food was rationed; students attended year-round so they could graduate in three years; and a quarter of the teachers were siphoned off to help with the war effort. By Kohlberg's second year, nearly half the male students on campus belonged to a naval unit, the V-12s. He enlisted in the unit, a step that permitted him to continue his studies. The presence of uniformed men on campus was met with horror by some faculty members, who viewed them as a direct affront to the Quakers' deep commitment to pacifism. But the navy men were ultimately accepted, in part because without them classes would have been decimated. By the time a unit of Chinese navy officers arrived to learn English, there was nary a word of protest.

Those years were a time of sorting out for Kohlberg. A popular student and good athlete, the blond-haired Kohlberg, whose nickname was Swede, was invited to join one of the "better" fraternities on campus. But when he found out that with the exception of him, they had never accepted any Jews, he told them to change their rules or forget it. They refused, and so Kohlberg did not join. He meanwhile became increasingly intrigued with Quakerism, thanks in part to one of his roommates, Philip Evans, who was a Quaker and happy to bring his friend into the fold.

The campus meeting house, where weekly Quaker services were held, quickly became one of Kohlberg's favorite haunts. As those who have attended Quaker meetings know, there is no minister leading the sessions. Those who attend share silence together until someone feels moved to speak, the notion being that "God is in every man." Even the configuration of the meeting house reflects this egalitarian principle. The room is encircled with benches; there is no podium, no single focus of attention.

"The idea is that truth can come from unsuspecting quarters, that each of us has a responsibility for how things unfold," explains David Fraser, the college's current president, who happens to be a Quaker. Minority opinions are encouraged and respected; egotism and self-aggrandizement have no place. The college inspires "a sense of fitness," said Walter Scheuer, who, like his first cousin Kohlberg, attended the school. Those who are steeped in Swarthmore's traditions are fond of saying they share "a same, sweet secret."

Quakerism seemed to fill a spiritual vacuum for Kohlberg that had been left by his own religion. In his family, being Jewish had more to do with ethnicity and family values than any formal beliefs. Years later, when his roommate Phil Evans passed away, Kohlberg endowed a large scholarship program in his name. So determined was he to do this the Quaker way, without any personal recognition, that Evans's widow, Gloria, who had become a close friend of the Kohlbergs, did not even find out about the program until someone from the college asked her if she had any objections to the use of her husband's name. Kohlberg has since offered up to $5.8 million in a fund-raising challenge to the college's board of trustees and alumni.

Even in Swarthmore's highly moral atmosphere, Kohlberg stood out. He was elected several times to the student council—once as its president. And in his yearbook he is described as having "a deep sense of fairness" and "hard-to-beat judgments." He developed a reputation amongst his classmates for being a good mediator; he would constantly probe discordant views until he was able to find that tiny sliver of common ground. "Jerry was often the quieting hand when someone was provoked," recalls Scheuer. "He was the second, sober voice of judgment."

Kohlberg's studies were disrupted by a brief stint in the Navy Supply Corps, during which he was sent to a naval hospital in Panama. But in 1945, after the war ended, Kohlberg was able to take advantage of the GI Bill and pursue a more ambitious academic career. He blitzed his way through Harvard Business School, and just days after finishing that degree, he enrolled in Columbia University's law school.

Three years later, Kohlberg was ready to face the world. He had a business degree, a law degree, and a wife, Nancy, whom he had met through family friends.

A down-to-earth schoolteacher of Russian heritage who grew up in Scarsdale, New York, Nancy both complemented Jerry's character and added still more backbone. She wanted no part of the social climbing that often consumed young couples in Manhattan and was never given to putting on airs. She was perfectly content in their modest apartment on Riverside and 116th Street when he was a young lawyer making several thousand dollars a year and she was a primary-school teacher.

In later years, she would proudly tell her children how she used to go to the market and buy fish heads for fish stew, and how they would stay within their budget by eating liver three times a week. "I remember when we were married, she gave me this little cookbook that was just like that: how to make a casserole with one hot dog," says her daughter Karen. "But you know, the thing I feel that I received from that is that there was so much joy in that. It didn't matter how much money you had." Despite her husband's financial success, Nancy today is as down-to-earth as ever. Her fridge is still stocked with leftovers that she is carefully hoarding for some future meal. And her days are devoted to running the farm she and Jerry moved to in Westchester in 1985. Visitors will find her in blue jeans and a turtleneck as she checks in on her llamas, peacocks, guinea hens, cattle, and sheep, the latter of which she has sheared for the wool she then uses to weave rugs.

Not long after their first child was born, Nancy and Jerry decided to try a life outside New York. They headed for Portland, Oregon, where Jerry had secured a position as a law clerk for one of the state's up-and-coming judges, Gus Solomon. Kohlberg's starting salary in 1952: $4,600.

Solomon, a deeply committed liberal, became an important figure in Kohlberg's life. Long before Kohlberg knew him, the judge had been waging personal, and often highly contentious, legal battles against discrimination. When he heard that local businessmen were refusing to buy the products of a Japanese American farmer who had just been released from an internment camp after the war, for instance, Solomon went to the market and made a personal appeal to the other farmers to cooperate. He initiated boycotts of local clubs that refused to admit Jews or blacks, even to the point of causing important visitors such as Isaac Stern to cancel their guest appearances. During the 1950s, he was labeled a communist for his activities on behalf of labor unionists and in favor of establishing a public power cooperative. Though he vigorously denied the charge, its mere suggestion in the midst of the McCarthy era briefly threatened his appointment as a federal judge.

Once his position was secure, however, Solomon immediately turned his sights on the Portland courtroom. He chastised local attorneys for their delaying tactics and sloppy procedures and ran his courtroom as efficiently as an army platoon. To clerks like Kohlberg, Solomon stressed the principles of fairness, compassion, and ethics. Among the clerks who came under his spell and have since credited him with influencing their lives are Michael Pertschuk, who was the chairman of the Federal Trade Commission under President Carter, and Stephen Gillers, one of the nation's leading law professors, who specializes in legal ethics.

Kohlberg was completely taken with this outspoken but kindhearted judge. To him, Solomon was a living, breathing example of the values he had found so inspirational at Swarthmore. The two became close friends, and many years later, Jerry would visit the judge whenever he passed through the area. After Solomon died in 1986, Kohlberg established a scholarship in the judge's name at the Lewis and Clark Northwestern School of Law.

By the time the young and impressionable George Roberts ran into Jerry Kohlberg, he had been living a life of probity for many, many years. Indeed, Kohlberg had developed it into something of a fetish. Who else would arrive at Bear Stearns lumbered down with shopping bags instead of a fancy leather briefcase that others considered de rigueur? Who but Kohlberg would run around the elite community of Martha's Vineyard with a crumpled red felt hat pulled down over his ears? And then there were his private boycotts. To register his opposition to the John Birch Society, for instance, he refused to buy his children Junior Mints or those butterscotch taffy Sugar Daddys, because the chief executive of the company that made them was an active John Birch Society member. "For a long time after the war, and even now, he won't easily buy Japanese or German products," says Kohlberg's daughter Pam. "He felt these moral issues came into everything."

It was to this stable, principled approach to life that George Roberts was drawn, perhaps as an antidote to the model offered by his father. And the attraction was mutual. Jerry had always been drawn to young people. He was fascinated with watching them grow and learn, and he was always looking for ways to learn more about them, to help them in any way he could.

When it came to George, with his earnest ways and his difficult childhood, Kohlberg was particularly eager to be supportive. And he was gratified when George reciprocated by displaying such a keen interest in the business. When George graduated from Claremont, Jerry arranged for him to continue working for Bear Stearns, even though George remained out in California and did not work for the firm full-time. The Vietnam War was taking more and more of America's young men, and in order not to be drafted, George had to continue with his studies. Kohlberg helped convince George that a law degree would ultimately serve him better than an MBA, and so George applied to several law schools in California. He was determined to remain out west, where his girlfriend, Leanne, resided and where he felt most at home. After his first choice, Stanford, again turned him down, he ended up at the University of California (Hastings) Law School, which had a more liberal admissions policy but then weeded out its weaker students with its rigorous courses. Kohlberg persuaded Bear Stearns to employ George as a consultant for the next three years while he studied law. George worked like a demon in those years, juggling Kohlberg's demands with those of his law professors. Don Stephens, who sat near George in class and became a close friend, remembers George sitting in class looking attentive, while he was frantically working out financial calculations for Kohlberg on the backs of his legal case studies.

Working as a consultant for Bear Stearns in those years was more than just professionally fulfilling to George; it was a financial imperative. In 1967, his first year of law school, he married Leanne in a private, family-only ceremony in her parents' house in Hillsborough, California. Although Leanne's parents were said to be less than thrilled that George's father had been imprisoned over tax problems, they nevertheless gave the couple their blessing. The two exchanged vows in front of the Bovets' living room fireplace and then attended an elaborate reception at the elite Burlingame Country Club. As George and Leanne intended to live a fairly traditional married life, George suddenly had to provide for two people, as well as the hoped-for children. And Lou had always been clear about the fact that once George got married, his financial support would come to an end. "I didn't have any other choice except to work and finish school," said George, "because my father was true to his word—that was it."

After his protégé finished law school, Kohlberg offered him a full-time job in New York, and though George and Leanne were reluctant to leave California, they took up his offer and moved. For the next year, Jerry worked closely with George, schooling him in the finer art of corporate finance, unable to satiate his eager student's appetite for knowledge. Just as he had at Culver, George threw himself into the subject he wanted to master. Business was the realm he was determined to excel at, to dominate, and through Kohlberg, he had an opportunity to do just that.

"Jerry was the person who gave him legitimacy," says Don Stephens. "And I don't mean that as a negative against George, but George was always far ahead for his age, so when George would be working on deals, I think Jerry would help him have the credibility that his mind deserved but that maybe his appearance didn't. So he'd walk into a room and someone would say, 'What's that kid doing here?' and Jerry would say, 'Listen, that kid really knows what he's doing. You'd better listen to him.' "

By this time, the relationship was growing intensely personal. George had become a kind of adopted member of the Kohlberg family, often joining them for dinner in the evenings, spending time at their house over the weekend, or borrowing the Kohlbergs' house on Martha's Vineyard for a vacation with Leanne and their baby boy Eric. In those days, the Kohlbergs lived in an airy, open house right on Long Island Sound next to the elegant Larchmont Yacht Club. Nancy would whip up a simple dinner, and the group would sit out on the porch and eat supper as they watched the sun set. After dinner, George and Jerry would spend hours talking, Jerry patiently explaining the business, George soaking up every detail. "George's father hadn't been there in any perceivable way, so I think my father sort of perceived him as an orphan," recalls Kohlberg's daughter Pam.

George's friend Stephens says that "Jerry so much consumed that father figure position that I don't think he [George] ever needed anybody else." George asked Kohlberg to be the godfather of his second son, Mark. And years later, he wrote his mentor several long letters expressing an outpouring of love and affection for the man who had helped him find himself. "George said, 'You've given me confidence,' " said Kohlberg softly.

George's relationship with Jerry was especially unusual because the young man so rarely opened up to anyone. He had responded to his arduous and traumatic childhood by drawing inward and keeping the outside world at bay while he concentrated on developing his own strengths and a sense of self-worth.

Even today, George Roberts's world is sharply divided in two. There is the external world in which he works, where he exhibits a cold, tough exterior. Those who have encountered him at the few social events he attends often describe him as polite but extremely aloof. After agreeing to be interviewed for this book, he came armed with a tape recorder and a tall glass of plain water. Throughout the meeting he sat motionless, his face barely betraying any trace of emotion. People who have sat across the table from him in business meetings say he is often stone-faced and intractable. His refusal to concede even a hint of self-doubt is often mistaken for arrogance. As if to punctuate his feelings toward this hostile outer world, George told the Kohlbergs that in order to ward off any would-be intruders, he slept with a gun beside his bed.

But there is also an internal world for George, where his family and a handful of close friends reside and with whom he can let down his guard. With them he is tender and caring, even emotional. In the mornings, says Michael Wilsey, perhaps his closest friend, George will come down the stairs and kiss and hug his three children good-bye, as if he is afraid he will never see them again. He will do the same with close friends he has not seen for several weeks.

George's physical appearance seems to demarcate these two worlds. During the week, he is always immaculately dressed in custom suits and crisp, white or blue, monogrammed shirts, and his gray hair is always perfectly combed. He prides himself on his splendid appearance and frequently chastises those whose dress he feels does not live up to his high standard. But on weekends, in the sanctity of his home, George can be found sitting around in jeans and an old T-shirt, unshaven and with a gap in his teeth. The false tooth is reserved for weekdays—for outsiders.

Jerry Kohlberg was one of the privileged few who was granted access into George's private world. But despite the close bonds that had developed between the two, George increasingly wanted to return to California. The shy Leanne was finding New York a trying place to live, particularly with a little baby boy to take care of. And she missed her family back in Hillsborough and wanted to be closer by.

George had no particular desire to stay in New York either. Though he enjoyed working closely with Jerry, there was much about the Wall Street culture he found distasteful. He was never one given to macho behavior and had little patience or aptitude for office politics. Besides, everybody spent far too much time socializing. He persuaded his mentor that he could do just as well, if not better, if he was working in the firm's San Francisco office. And besides, he already had a replacement in mind: his first cousin and good friend, Henry Kravis. It would be years before anyone would understand what an explosive situation was in the making.

HENRY

Like relay runners passing the baton, Henry arrived at his desk at Bear Stearns in August of 1970, and George packed his bags and headed for San Francisco the next month.

While George had been going to law school and building a career for himself at Bear Stearns, Henry had been conducting his own kind of blitzkrieg. In the three years since he had left Claremont, he had gotten an MBA from Columbia Business School, had three jobs, and found himself a bride. Always in a hurry, just as Ray used to say.

Indeed, in Henry's early adulthood, Ray continued to cast a long shadow. Henry was constantly torn between following his father's directions, as he had learned to do so well as a boy, and striking out on his own in order to prove that he could do things for himself. Henry says that after college he decided to seek a career on Wall Street, rather than in the oil and gas industry, because "I didn't want to be known as Ray Kravis's son. I wanted to do something on my own." Yet in picking Wall Street, Henry chose the place where Ray was known best, where he could not turn around without running into one of Ray's good friends.

Henry's feelings toward business school were similarly confused and ambivalent. In deciding to go to Columbia, says Henry, "I talked to my dad about it, and my father didn't have a graduate degree. He had an undergraduate degree in engineering, at Lehigh. My brother didn't have a graduate degree, and I thought, 'Well, it would be nice to be the first in the family to have a master's degree.'"

But unfortunately for Henry, his years at Columbia coincided with the rise of the antiwar movement. And Henry's pin-striped suits, silk ties, and fixation with things Wall Street did not mesh too well with sit-ins and the anti-Establishment ethics that were then so prevalent. As he once told *Fortune* magazine, "I left it to my liberal friends to get arrested. I had my mind on business."[1]

It wasn't long after Henry arrived at Columbia that he wondered if he'd made a terrible mistake. He wanted to get on with his life, learn about business, build a future. School just seemed like a colossal waste of time. Unsure of what to do, he turned as always to his instructor, Ray.

Ray was emphatic that Henry should continue with his studies. He had no doubt that an MBA would look good on his son's résumé. And one could never tell when one might need a credential such as that. "Henry didn't like the rabble-rousers and turmoil at Columbia, the uprisings," Ray recalled. "He was ready to drop out and I talked him out of it. I convinced him that he ought to stay."

So stay Henry did, though he did it his own way. He decided that the only way he could stand it was if he was working at the same time. So he picked up the phone and called one of Ray's good friends, Ed Merkle, who was then running the Madison Fund, a money management group. Henry didn't like his father to do the asking. He always wanted to do it himself. But thanks to Ray's good preparation, asking a CEO for a job was not as hard as one might think. Henry had met all of Ray's friends many times when he was growing up and had always managed to impress them with his bright questions and his enthusiasm. By the time Henry had graduated from Columbia—he went straight through the summer, finishing in a year and a half—Merkle had made him the vice president of a company owned by his investment fund. At age twenty-four, Henry was in charge of expanding the holdings of Katy Industries, which owned one of the oldest railroads in the country, and one which had, in an ironic twist, been one of Tulsa's earliest links to civilization.

Diversifying the railroad's interests was fun—at first. But Henry longed to be on Wall Street. And so he left Katy after a little over a year to join a small firm called Faherty & Swartwood, which invested in newly formed companies. But that job didn't seem to amount to much either. By the summer of 1970, when George was preparing to move to San Francisco, Henry was frustrated and looking for another job. He considered going to Goldman Sachs, where they had encouraged him to become a stock salesman. But Henry didn't think the future for salesmen was all that bright. Besides, salesmen all sat crammed next to each other in a big, open trading room. This was not the future that Henry had envisioned for himself. "When I'm forty-five years old, I want to have an office," he remembers thinking at the time. "I don't want to be at a desk with fifty other people around me. My father has an office—I should have an office when I'm forty-five."

The more that George told Henry about his situation at Bear Stearns, the more tempting it sounded. If Henry was working for Jerry, he'd be in corporate finance, which he found more interesting than sales—and he'd certainly have a desk that wasn't jammed in amongst scores of noisy traders. Cy Lewis, Bear Stearns's ornery senior partner, was only too happy to offer Ray's son a job. After all, his decision to hire Ray's nephew George had turned out well. For Henry it was a no-brainer: "I went to Bear Stearns because I thought I could get to where I wanted to go faster. And George was there."

Henry also needed a job if he was to support his new wife, Helene Shulman, the daughter of a well-established psychiatrist. Henry had met Hedi, as she was always called, on a blind date just after he graduated from Columbia. She was stunning. Tinier than he was, and perfectly proportioned, her long black hair shimmered as it hung down her back. She also had fire in her and Henry seemed to like that. She didn't necessarily have the money or the position that his parents had hoped for, but she was smart as a whip and ambitious. She wanted to make a mark just as he did. Yet she wasn't conventional. There was a wild streak in her that made Hedi unpredictable and untamable, and his old friends say Henry found that aspect of her irresistible.

Hedi, in turn, was said by friends to have been swept off her feet. She was just twenty-one, and here was a man who was everything that she'd hoped for. He was very good-looking, with his chiseled face and good build; and he was so sophisticated and possessed with such an intense personal drive that she was excited by the prospect of being his partner. Together, they could take New York by storm. Raised in a prosperous, upper-middle-class family and the product of Manhattan's fashionable private schools, Hedi had developed a taste for the good life at an early age. And marrying someone with Henry's upbringing and bright future would allow her to indulge even more in fancy clothes, jewelry, and exotic resorts, which she had been brought up believing were her birthright. "Hedi was a Jewish American princess," says one friend who often ran into Hedi shopping at Bloomingdale's, dressed to the nines. "She must have had fifty-two pairs of shoes."

The couple's wedding engagement was announced on July 20, 1969, the day that Neil Armstrong walked on the moon. The two families agreed that the ceremony would be held at the prominent Temple Emanu-El and would be followed by a reception for two hundred at the grand, old-style Pierre Hotel, where Ray and Bessie always stayed when they were in New York.

Not long after they announced their engagement, however, Hedi began to waver. She began to worry that Henry was too remote and cold for her taste. She didn't mind him working hard, but when he was off duty, she wanted him to be involved and affectionate, and she feared that this wasn't in his nature. There was also this mean streak that Henry exhibited every once in a while when he lost his temper that seemed to make her nervous. She told her close friends she had seen it in Ray, too, when he lashed out at Bessie. She feared its origins might run deep. As her own doubts began to grow, some of her friends started telling her they thought Henry was too serious, too straight. One remembers being taken out to dinner by Henry when she was in her senior year at college in New Orleans and he was there on a business trip. Hedi had arranged for the two of them to meet. It was 1969, the height of the tie-dyed shirts and love beads, and Henry arrived on campus in a suit and tie, having made reservations to take her to dinner at the Pontchartrain, an elegant, Old World hotel with a famous restaurant. "He looked like he was forty," she recalled. "He was very old when we were young."

Hedi told Henry the wedding was off on the day that their wedding invitations were delivered. Henry, according to those who knew him then, was absolutely devastated. Hedi was not the first woman who had rebuffed Henry. Shortly after college, he had fallen head over heels in love with a beautiful blonde. Though he had repeatedly asked her to marry him, she had always refused, insisting that she wanted to marry the kind of person who would put on blue jeans and go for a romantic stroll in the woods. "He told her he could put on blue jeans, too," says Renberg, wincing at his friend's lack of sensitivity.

Faced with a second, more public rejection, Henry fled

to Europe for several weeks of vacation with George's friend from law school, Don Stephens. From hotel rooms in great cities across the Continent, the wounded young man wrote long, heartwarming letters in which he declared his love for Hedi and promised her his everlasting devotion. This relentless outpouring of emotion finally got through to Hedi, young and romantic as she was.

When Henry came back from Europe, the two were quickly reconciled. He bought her an even bigger diamond ring, and they announced their reengagement. Hedi's ambivalence, however, continued right down to the wire. In preparation for the rehearsal dinner, Bessie asked each of them to write a few sentences about each other that she secretly planned to have set to music. While Henry's ode to Hedi was pure poetry, Hedi didn't hold back. She wrote that while most people, given a nickel, would buy a stick of gum, Henry would buy a peppermint stick because it's bigger, looks better, and lasts longer. She said she loved him madly and was fiercely proud of him, but that she feared his mean streak. With love, she concluded, she hoped that they could work it through together. It was some ditty. Bessie decided it might be better to keep some thoughts to herself.

The night of the rehearsal dinner, which Ray and Bessie gave at the Ritz-Carlton Hotel, some of the couple's friends showed their disdain for the fancy black-tie affair by disappearing into the bathrooms and passing around some marijuana one of the ushers had brought with him. Hedi thought it was kind of funny, but Henry was not amused.

The next day, in a scene straight out of the movies, Hedi got cold feet again. While two hundred guests waited patiently in their pews at Temple Emanu-El, Hedi's seven attendants, including George's wife, Leanne, fluttered around her anxiously, a blur of navy-blue gowns and straw bonnets, trying to soothe her nerves. When she finally walked down the aisle, she was crying, and she never did utter the magic words, *I do.* "She finally did it," said one wedding guest, "but she was late and in terrible shape. It did not bode well."

* * *

It was just two months after that tumultuous event that Henry showed up in Jerry Kohlberg's office, ready to report for duty. He was determined to do well at Bear Stearns, and to impress Kohlberg as his cousin George had before him. He threw himself into the work, and because of his previous experience at Goldman and the Madison Fund, he was a very quick study. The more work that Kohlberg gave him, the more numbers to analyze, the more companies to visit and scrutinize, the happier Henry was. Finally, his business career was taking off in the way that he had envisioned.

If those early years were fresh and exciting for Henry, they were tough on Hedi. She did not take kindly to his long hours or his obsession with work. He was completely and utterly absorbed by it, and this was not how she thought a newly married couple should live. She tried to while away the hours by shopping, working on charity events, and spending time in sunny Palm Beach with her in-laws. But less than a year after they were married, Hedi told Henry she wanted a separation.

It wasn't a lengthy separation, but it proved to be decisive. Soon after they were reconciled, Hedi became pregnant with their son Harrison, who was born the day before Christmas in 1971. He was followed just over a year later by another boy, Robert, and finally, in 1975, by the Kravises' only daughter, Kimberly. Henry and Hedi asked Kohlberg to be Kimberly's godfather.

These were intense years for the young couple. On the one hand, they were part of a young Jewish community that was trying to "make it" in New York, and they were having quite a bit of success at it. Henry and Hedi had approached the American Jewish Committee with the idea of forming a "youth group" to get people their age more involved. With the organization's approval, they formed the Contemporary Action Division, which Henry chaired for many years. The group hosted lectures and seminars and threw the annual Prize Party, a high-spirited fund-raising event.

The Kravises' circle of friends was an outgrowth of this organization. Among those in the group were Bonnie and Tom Strauss—he is now president of Salomon Brothers; Judy and Lewis Eisenberg, the latter of whom was an executive at Goldman Sachs; and Rodger and Betty Hess, she being the daughter of Goldman Sachs's chairman Gus Levy. Some of the couples would take vacations together at low-budget resorts such as Nassau or Acapulco to play golf, swim in the pool, and complain good-naturedly about their children. It was a close circle of friends—the men all rising young stars at work, sharing their dreams and frustrations, the women all dedicated mothers, fiercely supportive of their husbands' careers and actively engaged in the charity circuit. Within this circle, Henry was always a favorite. Surrounded by such close friends, Henry was finally able to relax and indulge his playful side, which Hedi and his childhood friend Don Renberg had both nurtured. In vacation snapshots he is the one everyone is trying to splash in the pool, or who is always playing the clown. On his thirtieth birthday, his friends surprised him by chipping in to buy him a motorcycle. Never one to miss an opportunity, he surprised them by riding it around the apartment, his flower-bedecked helmet adding a special accent to his tuxedo.

From the outside, Henry and Hedi appeared to be the perfect couple. But Hedi found being home alone with three young children under the age of five trying, if not impossible. Henry was constantly traveling, and when he was home, he wanted dinner ready and the apartment clean. Often, he would fall asleep in front of the television before she could even begin to talk to him. She wanted more from her marriage, she confided to a few close friends; she resented his freedom and felt abandoned. To make matters worse, the young couple did not have much money.

Although Ray had given Henry a small trust, it was not enough to pay for a bigger apartment and furniture that their growing family required. Hedi needed new clothes to replace all her maternity dresses, in order for her to go to all the social events they were expected to attend. And they wanted a home in the country, where Hedi could stay with the children during the summer months and be near the country club that all their friends and their children belonged to. Henry took it upon himself to solve that problem by renting a house in Croton-on-Hudson, but he neglected to consult Hedi first on the decision, and the house turned out to be an hour's drive from the club—no closer than their apartment in Manhattan. Hedi quickly dubbed it "Croaking-on-Hudson."

Henry still remembers with precision the turning point in his life, when his determination to succeed went into overdrive. "I can remember exactly where I was," he says with a slight flinch of his shoulders. "I was driving after we'd played golf up in Westchester. I was on the highway with him, going to our house in Westchester." Henry liked to talk to his father in the car because he knew he had a captive audience; there would be no phone calls, no people knocking on the door.

Henry had been brooding for weeks. Hedi had been pressing him about how badly they needed a bigger apartment. The boys were getting to the point where they each needed their own bedroom. And she had found the place of her dreams, a four-bedroom apartment in a fine old building on Park Avenue. She wanted it badly, and Henry felt under great pressure to give it to her. They had been fighting a lot, and if he could buy her this, maybe their relationship would settle down.

It wasn't easy for Henry to ask his father for help, and before he even dared broach the subject, he'd thought about it long and hard. "I'd gotten my courage up to ask him, because I didn't want . . . I hated him to say no to me if I really wanted something and had got my mind set on it," said Henry. By this time, Henry had come to put his father on something of a pedestal. "The more I learned about him, the more in awe I was of this man," he explained. But now, Henry finally had him—in the car, where he would be forced to listen. The right moment, the one that he had been waiting for, had finally arrived.

"So I asked him for some money for an apartment and he told me, no, he couldn't afford it. And I knew he could. But he said, 'No, I can't, and I'm sorry I can't help you.' I was really hurt. Not that he wouldn't help me, but I was hurt and I didn't understand it. And because it wasn't a question of my always asking him for things, because I rarely asked him for anything. And this I had really thought a lot about.

"I said to myself then, 'Okay, I'm never going to ask him for anything again.' You know, or anybody. I'm going to do it myself. And this was where the independence came back again. And I said, 'I want to get myself into a position where I can give, and I don't ever have to be beholden to anybody.'" It was Henry Kravis's version of that famous scene in *Gone With the Wind*, where Scarlett O'Hara stands holding a radish in her hands against the fire-lit skies of Atlanta, swearing she will never be hungry again.

"I had this drive before," Henry concludes, "but this just really highlighted it for me."

Henry felt betrayed, even humiliated, by his father's rejection. But Ray says he was merely trying to make sure that his son wasn't taking things too quickly. Henry was moving up in the world awfully fast for a boy who was just thirty. And he feared that Hedi, with her social ambitions, was egging Henry on even further, to the point that his son might lose his balance.

To Ray's way of thinking, they did not need a fancy apartment on Park Avenue. "They had no business—they were young kids—they had no business having an apartment like that," he says testily. He thought the one they were in was perfectly adequate. "Henry didn't need any big apartment," said Ray, clearly agitated. "I tried to keep them . . ."

At this point, he holds his hand out flat and pushes down against the air.

Ray had learned the hard way what can happen to people who are in too much of a hurry. Not long after he married Bessie, the bottom fell out of the stock market in the famous crash of 1929. Like many investors, Ray immediately pulled his small savings out. But when the market began showing signs of recovery several months later, he thought he would be smarter than the rest and put his money back in. Unfortunately, the market soon reversed again and began its long, protracted slide down. As prices fell lower, Ray's broker called constantly to tell him he would have to put up more money as collateral. To meet these margin calls, Ray hocked all his furniture and borrowed everything he could from the banks. Before long, his entire net worth was wiped out.

Many of his friends chose to file for bankruptcy, but Ray had been brought up believing that your name was all you had. Rather than take a route that he considered dishonorable, Ray says he decided to dig himself out slowly, paying his creditors off whenever he could. After five years, he finally succeeded, but those five years were difficult, and Ray never forgot what it felt like to lose everything. "It seared him," says Tulsa oilman Elson. "It made him understand."

Ray's experience during the Depression made him cautious, and he tried hard to convey that caution to his impatient son, Henry. Climbing the ladder was okay, but it had to be done carefully, in moderation. He wanted his son to learn that there were certain limits. Take things too fast and you risked losing everything. "When your money goes, your friends go with it," he constantly preached to the young couple.

But to Henry, Ray's warnings seemed to be nothing but irritants, the preachings of an old man. Henry knew what he was doing. He knew where he wanted to go, and he wanted to get there fast. "He was very driven, he wanted to be successful. He set his father up as an objective, a goal," says

Donnie Renberg. What Renberg remembers most about Henry is when he said that "his main ambition in life was to make more money than his dad, to be more successful."

Amazing as it may seem, Henry got off lightly when it came to the indelible impact of Ray. It is Henry's brother, George, say friends of the family, who has really borne the brunt of his father's force. While Henry responded by striving to equal and then surpass his father in the business world, George's way of handling the pressure took him in an entirely different direction.

Ray wanted to be a kind and supportive father to both of his sons, but his instincts constantly betrayed him. It has always been clear to everyone who knew the family that George could do nothing right in Ray's eyes, and that Henry was the one on whom the sun shone. "George? Henry just kind of put him in the corner," said Howard Conhaim, Ray's oldest and dearest friend. "It's hard to compete with Henry."

Now in his fifties, George even walks with a sense of the downtrodden. His feet seem too large for his five-foot-eight-inch body, and he places them down with such deliberateness that it's as if he's trudging through a muddy field. Plump and more pudgy faced than his younger brother and with a pale complexion, George often wears a worried look, as though he is bracing himself for some sign of disapproval.

Ray and Bessie tried to help their eldest son find his way in the business world. In college, George demonstrated an interest in radio. He majored in broadcasting and three times a week had his own jazz program on the campus radio station. After George graduated, Ray went out and bought his eldest son a radio station. With that, George became the youngest radio-station operator in the country, an achievement he still likes to mention to visitors.

To George, however, radio was never a business—it was something to be cherished. He had his apartment wired so that he could summon music into any room at the mere touch of a button. And in his office he kept a collection of old radios that he had picked up over the years at various garage sales and flea markets. "They make me smile," George once told a local reporter. "If I'm having a bad day, all I have to do is look at my Mickey Mouse radio and I can't help but feel better."[2]

Once George had converted his new station, KROM, from religious broadcasting to pop music and built it into a credible station called KRAV, he set out to expand his franchise. With Ray and Bessie's financial assistance, George bought two more radio stations in Florida, and another in Tulsa.

George is the first to admit he does not have the business skills of his younger brother. Today he gently laughs at himself for selling the two stations in Jacksonville, Florida, a growing market, and keeping the ones in Tulsa, where the economy has suffered a virtual depression. And he notes, with more than a hint of self-deprecation, that he's basically abandoned his second Tulsa station because he only acquired the rights to daytime transmission. "At night, if you tune in," he says, laughing, "you'll hear Mexican."

Undaunted, George has tried his hand at numerous other business ventures. In the 1970s, when disco was hot, he opened Casablanca, giving Tulsa a swinging nightspot complete with strobe lights and a huge speaker system. He also tried real estate development, announcing with great fanfare that he intended to build ten of the biggest, most expensive homes Tulsa had ever seen.

In 1984, he turned his attention to photography, one of his childhood hobbies, and acquired Knox Camera, one of Tulsa's long-established photography stores. But his plans for expansion failed, and after losing over $1 million, he sold the stores in defeat in the spring of 1990. "One store, then he opens two others, and now it went busted. He's not the businessman that Henry is," says Ray, clearly frustrated.

Indeed, when Ray heard that George might be interviewed for this book, he became quite agitated. "Why would you want to call him? I wouldn't ask him, no, because he's not the successful one," Ray implored. But what about the radio stations? "Sure, he owns them, but how much are they worth?"

Ray was not good at hiding his disappointment in George. Even later, when the kids had graduated from college and the family would occasionally get together for dinner, the conversation would frequently dissolve into petty bickering, accusations, and finally, a flood of tears. The trouble would often start with Bessie's having too much to drink and expressing an opinion that Ray dismissed as stupid and ignorant. He would bark at her to shut up and then turn on George, picking on him for having committed some petty offense. George would shake his head back and forth furiously like a child, insisting that his father didn't understand. Angry and humiliated, tears would well up in George's eyes until they finally spilled down over his cheeks. Henry would sit there stoically, waiting for the evening's ordeal to be over. "It was a warring family," said one person who knows the Kravises well. "It was just awful."

Ray may have been disappointed with more than just George's lack of business prowess. He may also have shared the suspicions of many others in that small town—that George harbored a sexual preference for men. George was never effeminate, but local townspeople noted that he only seemed to have men "friends." One owned an antique store where George would often hang out. And he was fairly well-known in gay circles of the arts community in New York, where he briefly had an apartment. Friends of the Kravises still like to joke about the bachelor party that George threw for Henry at Manhattan's swanky "21" Club. Among the more curious items of the evening were dinner rolls in the shape of a penis.

"Henry didn't shun him, but I think he was very embarrassed," says one person who was close to the family. "He didn't fit into how Henry wanted people to perceive him to be." Henry wouldn't discuss with even his closest friends whether George was gay. As for George, one of the few comments he was willing to make about his younger brother was that "he always had lots of girlfriends." He said it with a wistful tone.

George tried, in his own simple way, to live up to the Kravis legacy. Ray got him into the Southern Hills Country Club, and like his father, George sits on the boards of a number of nonprofit institutions in Tulsa. George has also done his bit for the local art museums, donating a large painting by Lowell Nesbitt to the Philbrook Museum of Art.

But no matter how hard he tries, it just doesn't seem to work. The Nesbitt painting of an enormous white iris is glaringly out of place in a fine arts museum devoted to eighteenth-century paintings. And George simply does not have the financial resources of his parents or brother, which sharply limits the extent of his involvement. Visitors to the Gilcrease Museum, for instance, which features Western American art, will see George's name on a plaque listing donors to the museum's beautiful gardens. But whereas Ray and Bessie tend to have their names prominently displayed next to the largest amounts, George's contribution gains him entry to only the lowest category: $1,000 to $4,999. Similarly, when George came up with the idea of a Kravis wing at the Philbrook, he got credit for having the idea, but it was Henry who coughed up most of the money.

Over the last few years, George's finances have been drained by an enormous house he has been building for himself just a few blocks from his mother and father's home. Designed by Michael Lustig & Associates, the same Chicago architect who is building the Kravis wing at the Philbrook, George's house strikes some local observers as a colossal monument to bad taste that is badly out of keeping with the conservative residential neighborhood surrounding it. Nestled in a wooded area in an exclusive Tulsa neighborhood, the home is surrounded by fifteen-foot-high white stone walls. Steel spikes jut out from behind the walls at six- or eight-foot intervals, and diamond-shaped skylights rise above the roof. Inside is a 10,000-square-foot, three-bedroom home that looks out over a lap pool. Next to the pool cabana,

George is building a three-car garage in which he can park his car, which, like Ray's, sports his own personalized license plate: KRAV, the name of his radio station.

Ray shakes his head in obvious dismay as he walks around the building site. George tags along behind him, wearing that ever-present worried look. Bessie has been after Ray to help their eldest son out, because George has spent an estimated $3.5 million on the house and has run out of money trying to finish it. George is both excited and nervous that his father has come by to see the house. He says he has been trying to get Ray to make the four-block trip for over four months.

Ray climbs back into his Mercedes and, as he pulls away, says with a somber voice, "I feel sorry for George."

Ten days later, Ray would feel even sorrier. Late that Friday night, George made the mistake of striking up a conversation with a man in his mid-twenties named Mark McCrory in the parking lot of the Fantasyland Adult Video Arcade, an enormous peep-show center and pickup joint located in a particularly sleazy part of Tulsa. After the two had chatted for a while, George invited Mark to follow him back to his apartment to watch some hardcore sex videos. The two watched some videos and George brought out some pictures he had taken of nude boys whom he told Mark he had met at various truck stops. When George proposed that he and Mark have sex, Mark whipped out his vice squad ID card, identified himself as a police officer, and arrested George on the spot. Among the personal items that were later seized with the aid of a search warrant were fifty-one videocassettes with sexually explicit titles, vials with suspected traces of cocaine, some marijuana, and other drug paraphernalia, according to police records.[3]

The Tulsa district attorney charged George with three felony counts: possession of child pornography, exhibiting obscene material, and possession of cocaine, as well as three misdemeanor counts of possession of marijuana and drug paraphernalia, and soliciting a lewd act. Bond was set at $4,500. George, through his attorney, entered a plea of innocent.

The papers had a field day. "Kravis Faces Drug, Pornography Charges," was the headline of *Tulsa World*. George promptly stepped down from his position as KRAV's station manager and voluntarily entered a treatment program. Eight months later, he agreed to plead guilty to felony charges of possessing pornographic photographs of minors and exhibiting obscene material, and a misdemeanor of sex solicitation. In exchange, the government dropped the drug charges.[4]

Family friend Renberg thinks that what hurt George Kravis more than anything "was the pressure, trying to excel and achieve the standards which were expected of him by his family." The terrible irony in all this is that though George may have been perceived to have failed in his father's eyes, to some in Tulsa, he was more appealing than his successful younger brother. George had no pretensions. He would think nothing of going to a charity event sporting a helmet with an oil well on top that even had movable parts. Despite his eccentric ways, most townspeople seemed to regard him as kind and good-natured. In many ways, that may have been George's problem. In the Kravis family that simply didn't count for much.

EARLY DAYS

So this was the background of the three men whose lives intersected, who would go on to form a company named Kohlberg Kravis Roberts that would radically alter the shape of modern American capitalism. There was Henry, the young man driven by the need to live up to and even exceed the lofty standards of his father. There was George, bitterly disappointed by his father's imprisonment and seemingly determined to prove to the world his own worth. And there was Kohlberg, the genial senior statesman, reveling in the role of mentor. Only many years later would it become clear what a potent mix this was.

In the early 1970s at Bear Stearns, however, the three worked well together, extremely well. Although George was three thousand miles away on the West Coast, the time he had spent working closely with Jerry in New York meant he knew exactly what was expected of him and what he had to do. Henry, in turn, was eager to take advantage of the opportunity that he had been given and was more than willing to put in the long hours and log the miles that were required. Kohlberg would tell the two young men whom to call on, what to say, what companies to look into, and they would eagerly pursue his leads. And with the command they demonstrated over a company's financial architecture, and the intensity with which they pursued their work, the two young men made very favorable impressions on almost everyone they encountered. Business executives would often pass along compliments to Kohlberg about the professionalism and caliber of his two young associates.

The trick was to find the kinds of companies that were suitable for a leveraged buyout. They had to be solid companies with dedicated managers in industries that weren't subject to sudden technological changes. Yet they also had to be companies where there was room for improvement. In those days, that often meant two universes. There were family-owned companies where the founders had either died or were having trouble passing their enterprises on to the next generation. These people often resisted taking their companies public because they didn't want to put their life's work into the hands of thousands of unknown people who had no long-term commitment to the company's welfare. The other group of candidates that Kohlberg and his two colleagues avidly pursued were overlooked divisions of huge multinational companies, victims of that great wave of conglomeration that had been so popular at business schools in the 1960s and early 1970s. In those companies, managers were often unable to get the attention of top management or were starved of resources because they were just one of many businesses, and not the central one at that.

To generate leads, Kohlberg and his two colleagues put the word out to anyone who might know of a small to midsize company that might be for sale. And they would pay a "finder's fee" to those who called them first with a good idea. They also pounded the pavement themselves. "George and I would go to see a company in the Midwest," says Henry. "I remember, we'd be driving along, and we'd see names on plants, and it would be an attractive looking plant, and we'd write the name down, and we'd come back, and we'd get a Dun and Bradstreet report. . . .We might call on them, write them, say we'd like to come see them. We were always looking. We had the attitude that if you throw enough stuff on the wall, something will stick." They were helped by the fact that at the time they were scouring the corporate landscape, they had very few competitors. And thanks to a poor economic climate, the prices of corporate assets were relatively cheap.

Once they had a lead on a company, they would analyze it to death. They would examine every piece of financial information they could get their hands on: How much cash was coming in, and how well or poorly were the company's expenses being managed? How stiff was their competition? How efficient were their factories and would they need upgrading soon? How good was the management, how long had they been with the company, how willing were they to put in long hours?

If, after all of their analysis, Jerry, Henry, and George were still interested, they would approach the management of the company, either through an intermediary or directly, and ask them if they wanted to discuss a leveraged buyout. Kohlberg always made it clear at the outset that he was only interested in doing a friendly deal—if the company wasn't interested, he would walk away.

This wasn't just a question of reputation or good manners; it was a fundamental component of Kohlberg's business strategy. He wanted the management of the company—the ones who knew the company best—to feel as if they were his partners. Hiring outside managers meant adding another layer of risk to an already risk-laden deal. To ensure the involvement of the managers who were already in place, Kohlberg insisted that they buy around 10 percent of the shares of the newly configured company. Only then would he feel sure that the company would have the management's undivided attention.

If the management of a company indicated that they were on board, the three men would begin to work out the financing arrangements of the deal. That meant figuring out how much debt the company could support, and how quickly it could generate the cash to pay it off. As Kohlberg explained to *Forbes* magazine in 1978, they were careful not to over-burden a company with too much debt. "We look at a company and ask ourselves in our financing, 'What happens if the earnings go flat; or if they drop back to where they were three years before we bought the company? Is the financing substantial enough to hold the company over a bad period?' If not, then the financing is wrong."[1]

Most healthy companies at that time would have about two dollars of debt to every one dollar of equity, which is the permanent cushion of financing that a company can draw on in hard times. In a leveraged buyout that ratio would change radically, to eight or nine dollars of debt for every one dollar of equity. Since the company can deduct the interest it pays on its debt, but cannot deduct the dividends it pays on its stock, the government indirectly helps subsidize an LBO transaction. Some academics believe that at least a third of the premium over the market price of a stock that an LBO sponsor pays to a company's shareholders is "paid for" by this tax advantage.[2] Besides being attractive for its tax deductibility, debt was the means by which Kohlberg and his partners raised the money to pay for the company: they borrowed it from banks and insurance companies, using the company's assets as collateral for the loans.

Because of the heavy debt burden an LBO places on a company, it is by definition a risky transaction. But when it's done right, and limited to only certain types of companies, a buyout can be accomplished in such a way that a company's earnings grow, it hires more workers, and the community in which it is located benefits. Eventually, the new equity owners and their management-partners get rich.

Kohlberg and his partners are essentially making two bets: that if management has a greater incentive to run a company more efficiently, it will; and that most companies do not manage the cash that comes through their doors very carefully. If they can improve the efficiency of the company's flow of cash, and quickly pay down the debt, they are left with a company that is generating more earnings, which only have to be distributed amongst a much smaller group of stockholders. When the company is eventually resold, Kohlberg and his partners reap 20 percent of the profits as the reward for their efforts.

Consider the case of Vapor Corp., which George, Henry, and Jerry bought with a group of investors in 1972. Vapor, which had been a division of the Singer Company, manufactured door-opening systems for mass transit systems, as well as pumps and valves. To buy the company and have a little left over for working capital, Kohlberg borrowed $33.5 million from a group of banks and insurance companies and put in $4.4 million of his own, Bear Stearns's, and other investors' money as equity to provide permanent capital for the company.

To be sure, with 88 percent of the company's financing suddenly in the form of debt, the interest expenses that Vapor had to pay initially soared to over $2.7 million a year. Net income the first year after it underwent a leveraged buyout was a mere $1.2 million, or less than half of what it had been the year before. But with management improvements, the company's sales jumped from $46 million in 1973 to $86.5 million four years later. Net income, in turn, quintupled, to just over $6 million. At the same time, the company used the cash it was generating to pay off its loans as quickly as possible. By 1977, these had been reduced to $10.7 million.

The crucial thing to understand is what happens to the owners of the company during this process. Each shareholder had paid $2.80 a share to own a piece of the heavily indebted door-opening manufacturer. Four years later, with the debt substantially paid off and sales nearly double their previous level, the company's shares were worth a lot more. In fact, in the fall of 1978, Kohlberg and his partners sold Vapor to the Brunswick Corporation for $33 a share. Investors in the deal, in other words, made twelve times their original investment in just six years. Not bad.

But that wasn't nearly as good as the results they had with Incom—a division of the much larger Rockwell International—which made gears, filters, and other industrial parts. In that case, in 1975 management bought 20 percent of the newly configured company, at $1 a share, with Kohlberg, Bear Stearns, and other investors buying the rest. By controlling its inventory much more carefully, collecting the money owed to it by customers more quickly, and weeding out any investments that weren't absolutely necessary, the company generated extra cash with which to pay down its debt. Five years later, Kohlberg and his group sold the company to a foreign corporation for $22 a share, a shocking twenty-two times their original investment. Nine of the managers in the division became instant millionaires.

Although Kohlberg and his investment partners were reaping the benefits of this financial engineering, they had little or nothing to do with the actual management of the company and did not pretend that they did. Indeed, George once remarked, "If our partners had to rely on us to run anything, we would be in trouble."[3] Management was not their forte and they knew it. What they were good at, or so they believed, was analyzing a company from a financial standpoint, understanding its capacity to generate cash and therefore to absorb larger amounts of debt, and picking managers who could handle the obvious strains that such a financial structure implied. Once a buyout was initiated, the ultimate success or failure of a deal rested almost entirely with the quality of the day-to-day managers. Kohlberg and his two protégés would merely observe from a distance, through their positions on the boards of the companies they acquired.

"They played an absolutely minimal role in management," said Al Dunlap, who was hired by KKR in 1983 to turn around Lily-Tulip, the paper-cup maker, which was flagging badly. "I would talk to them maybe once a month at a board meeting, where we would review the results. Their style was extremely hands-off."

When management couldn't cope with the vagaries of a buyout, the results could spell disaster. That is precisely what happened in the case of Cobblers Inc., a deal that George orchestrated for Bear Stearns in 1971. The company's founder and chief executive, an Austrian Jew who fled Europe after Hitler's rise and set up a shoe manufacturing operation near Los Angeles, never got used to the idea that he was no longer the only person in charge and that he had partners to whom he was accountable. He ended up committing suicide six months after the deal by throwing himself off the company roof. Though the company staggered through another eight years before folding, the equity investors in the company never got back their $400,000 investment.

Of course, that was just the kind of fiasco that drove Cy Lewis and the other partners at Bear Stearns wild. They didn't really understand what Kohlberg was doing, and whatever it was, they didn't really like it. Of course, when Kohlberg's team had their home runs, everyone loved it—since other partners at the firm were investors, they benefited handsomely. But those bursts of enthusiasm were short-lived. In a trading culture such as Bear Stearns, an overnight exposure of an investment position was sometimes considered long; an investment that took four or five years to mature was simply unfathomable.

Cy Lewis and Kohlberg enjoyed a love-hate relationship that made matters even worse. As Cy got older he became more crotchety and vindictive, in the view of many Bear Stearns executives. And Kohlberg grew increasingly restive under his influence. At the same time, Kohlberg felt that he owed Cy some loyalty. It was Cy, after all, who had given Kohlberg the latitude to pursue his ideas in the first place, and he could not have developed his contacts with banks and insurance companies had he not had Bear Stearns behind him. The more convinced Kohlberg became that he was on the right track with his bootstrap idea, the more delicate his position at Bear Stearns became. And the more agitated he grew about his situation.

Eventually, in 1975, Kohlberg resolved to leave the firm. He was fifty at the time, with several million dollars under his belt, thanks to his partnership interest in Bear Stearns. He was convinced that buyouts had great promise and that he would never get a chance to truly develop the concept at Bear Stearns. It was time to risk setting out on his own. The worst that could happen, he figured, was that after several years he would fail and have to set up a small investment business, or something that would supplement his income. Nancy was not the least bit concerned. Her daughter Pam recalls her mother shrugging her shoulders and saying, "Oh, well, we always have the garden. If it doesn't go, it doesn't go."

Kohlberg hoped that he could persuade his two young associates to join him. They knew how he operated, how he liked things done. Training new people would take time and would slow him down. He also recognized that their personal situations—George's in particular—were quite different from his. Roberts had a promising future at Bear Stearns, having been made a partner at the young age of twenty-nine. And since George had no family resources to fall back on, starting up a business that might produce little or no income in the early years was a considerable risk for him, especially with a wife and three young children depending on him. Kohlberg also knew that George would be worried about meeting his mortgage payments. Several years earlier, Jerry had persuaded George that the business was doing well enough that he could afford to buy a house. George didn't have enough money for the down payment, so Jerry lent him $50,000 or so to help make up the difference, money that George, years later, paid back. Kohlberg knew that Henry came from a family that had money—although Henry had never let on quite how much. But Jerry figured that the decision would still be tough because Henry's father, Ray, was such a close friend of Cy's, who was bound to oppose the trio's departure.

To induce George and Henry to come with him, Jerry made the following offer: he would set up the firm with $100,000 of his own money and take 40 percent of the firm's future profits. They would only have to put $10,000 each into the firm, and he would give them the remaining 60 percent to split between them. Kohlberg also offered to guarantee them a minimum salary during the first few years, even if that meant he was unable to take any money out of the firm himself during that period.

Today, now that all three are worth over $500 million apiece, Kohlberg's offer sounds like the deal of the century. In those days, however, it was a difficult decision for both George and Henry. "I agonized over it a long, long time," recalls George. "Because when Leanne and I got married, we had two thousand dollars between us. And that was it. And in 1975, when we first started seriously considering this, I had become a partner of Bear Stearns, made one of the goals, which was to do that before I was thirty. I think I had a pretty good future there. I was not in New York, which was great, because I didn't have all the political hassles to put up with. Jerry was great because he took all that heat for me. And I was sort of free to go do what I wanted to do. Also, we had just bought a house a few years before in Atherton, and whatever savings I had went into that, and we had three little kids."

After months of agonizing, it was Leanne who finally persuaded George to take the leap. She assured her husband that they could manage, and that if she had to, she could always get a job. "In a nice way she said, 'Quit complaining about it and just go do it,'" George recalled.

In the end, says Kohlberg, Henry was the most reluctant of the three to leave, a fact that he now finds humorous in light of Henry's recent speeches espousing the importance of risk-taking and entrepreneurship. "I was on the fence. I was scared," Henry acknowledged to his business school magazine in 1983.[4] "I didn't have a lot of money. I knew I could always get a job, but I didn't want to fail at anything." Fortunately, he said, he had a partner who was older and more established. "Jerry Kohlberg was a great comfort to us," said Henry. In the end, what clinched it for Henry was that he wouldn't have to work for anybody else anymore. He had never really liked working for an organization as large as Bear Stearns, where he was many levels down the pecking order, taking orders from somebody else. At least if he worked with George and Jerry, he would be on his own, with no one telling him what to do.

"I always knew that someday I'd want to do my own thing," he explained as he sat in his offices overlooking Central Park. "I've always liked small organizations. I like shopping in small stores. I'm happier in smaller environments. I went to a small college. . . . I'd rather be a big fish in a small pond."

The reaction to the three men's decision was swift and unpleasant. Though Bear Stearns had shown little appreciation of the men's work while they were there, the firm fought their departure with a ferocity rarely seen in those days on Wall Street. Afraid that the trio might take files and internal papers with them, the top brass promptly had the locks changed on their office doors and posted twenty-four-hour security guards in front of them for good measure. It was an illustrious beginning.

Kohlberg Kravis Roberts & Company opened its doors to the public on May 1, 1976. The three partners took over recently vacated offices of the Tosco Corporation at the corner of Fifty-fourth Street and Fifth Avenue. "A big attraction of the space on Fifth Avenue was that the furniture came free," recalls Arthur Aeder, the new firm's accountant, who was a close friend of Kohlberg's. Never mind that the desks were made of brown Formica.

Their first task was to find a group of investors willing to back them. Kohlberg and his partners wanted someone to cover their overhead so that they wouldn't feel compelled to do a deal just to pay the rent. If their expenses were covered, they would be free to go out and find the best deals, however long that took. Their main financial reward would come from investing some of their own money in their deals, and from their 20-percent cut of the profits they made for their investment partners. Their interests, in other words, would be identical to those of the investors who were backing them. And that, they thought, was the way it should be. To put their idea into practice, they decided to create ten "units" and sell them for $50,000, payable each year for five years, with certain reductions if KKR bought any companies. Kohlberg, George, and Henry bought two of the units; eight other investors, including Ray, took the rest. The deal was that anyone who bought a unit would be entitled to invest with KKR in any future transactions. As it turned out, those early investors got a real bargain.

No one knew, of course, what a gold mine KKR would become. In those days, the trio's aspirations were limited. They couldn't gauge the extent to which their success up until that point had been a result of having the Bear Stearns name behind them. They all hoped they could make a living, but none of them really expected the business to explode the way it did. As Henry told his alma mater's magazine several years later, "We had no idea whether it was going to work or not."[5]

Kohlberg had a clear idea, however, of the kind of firm he wanted KKR to be, and Henry and George shared his views. For starters, it would be democratic—everyone would share in the rewards, from the top partners to the secretaries, a characteristic that remains true to this day. And it would be small and intimate, like a family. Only Henry chose to remain aloof from the support staff.

To cement relationships, every Christmas Jerry and Nancy would have the entire KKR office, including secretaries, and their spouses over to their house in Larchmont for dinner. One year they had a platform built over their indoor pool and set up tables over the water, which was shimmering with light. These were warm, cozy affairs and they made everyone feel that they were participating in something special. All the families knew each other from previous gatherings and would compare notes on their children, marvel at the firm's growth, and look with anticipation toward the next year. Jerry wanted to maintain that family atmosphere and did not envision taking in any new partners. "We want to stay small and not grow just to grow," he told a reporter in a rare interview.[6]

Indeed, Kohlberg rarely talked to reporters. That was another of his bugaboos. Not only did he cherish his privacy, he also thought their business would be best served by keeping a low profile. That way competitors wouldn't learn too much about their business strategy, and their investment partners wouldn't feel that KKR was flaunting itself or that the firm's success was coming at their expense.

David R. Wood, a pension-fund consultant who in later years tried to help KKR market itself to investors, found Kohlberg absolutely adamant on this point. "He abhorred publicity," Wood recalled. "I was telling him, 'Unfortunately, in this business, notoriety is a good thing.' And he said, 'No, it isn't.' " And that was the end of the conversation.

As with so many young firms, life at KKR in the early years was tough. Although they had little trouble identifying good companies worth buying, convincing people to help them finance their deals was another matter. The term *leveraged buyout* was still fairly new, and many people were left scratching their heads after hearing a KKR presentation. The investment returns the three claimed to have generated seemed too good to be true. No one could really figure out how these LBO deals worked. It all sounded too easy, like magic.

Insurance companies and banks were the hardest to persuade of all, coming as they were from a very conservative tradition. "We tried to buy a company for ten or fifteen million dollars, and we would have to make as many phone calls as we would now to make a three-hundred-million-dollar deal," Henry told a reporter in 1983.[7]

But gradually, Kohlberg's quiet, steady demeanor and his years of experience began to win over executives in the staid insurance industry. "Jerry Kohlberg had a record and he was an element of control. And that was very, very important," said Mike Resanovich, who oversaw some investments with KKR when he was a Prudential Insurance executive. In 1977 KKR bought three companies, including their first over $100 million. And in 1979 they created waves with the acquisition of Houdaille Industries, a pump and machine-tool maker that was listed on the New York Stock Exchange. The price KKR paid for it—$355 million—made it the largest transaction of its kind to that date. "When we announced the transaction was going to be done, no one on Wall Street believed we could get the financing put together," Henry recalled.[8]

Although the deals gradually started to roll in, money was still scarce for the three partners. Because they had deliberately structured their business so that they would make money at the end, with their 20-percent take of the increase in their companies' values, those early years were lean ones indeed. Kohlberg guaranteed that George and Henry would earn at least $50,000 a year, and that wasn't far off the mark. To help get by, the three made a great effort to keep their costs down, refusing to hire even a bookkeeper because it was cheaper to have one part-time. They each drew a salary, but it was modest and left little room for anything other than life's staples. George, for instance, found he did not have enough money to invest directly in KKR deals. That was another way for the three to enrich themselves: besides splitting the 20-percent profits that were due to KKR, they could also each buy shares of the companies KKR was acquiring, an investment that would, theoretically, increase in value, too. To help George out, Jerry lent him money so that he could participate in KKR's deals as an investor.

As for Henry, he was so preoccupied with work that he barely noticed his wife's growing frustration with the lonely life she was leading. On those rare occasions when he would be home for dinner, he would spend half his time on a phone he had had installed in the dining room. More often than not, however, he would be out at some business dinner, and while Hedi liked to accompany him and had good instincts about people, it was hard for her to get away three or four times a week with three young children all under the age of eight. Sometimes the only time she would see Henry was when he would come staggering into their bedroom, very drunk, and collapse fully clothed onto the bed. The last straw, say Hedi's close friends, was when she found out that Henry was fooling around with a barmaid at a downtown restaurant. She told him he had to make a choice: his family or himself. They separated again in 1978, got back together for a few months, and then separated for the last time the following year, although they continued to see each other sporadically until early 1981.

If the challenge of starting a new business was putting strains on the two younger men and their families, to Jerry, KKR was the fulfillment of a dream. He was finally free of the dictatorial Cy Lewis and Bear Stearns's stifling political environment. And he was creating an organization that represented the beliefs and ideals that he stood for.

The fact that he was able to share this experience with his two surrogate sons only increased his pleasure. For Kohlberg was moving into a period of his life where he felt he had accumulated considerable knowledge and was eager to begin passing it along. Having had such an unsatisfying relationship with his own father, he longed to be more of a path-clearer for his own children. And his experiences with Judge Solomon had convinced him of the importance of nurturing the next generation. But Kohlberg's own children had not shown an interest in anything as dry and socially unredeeming as their father's business. Kohlberg's two sons, Andy and Jim, were both professional tennis players. (Andy eventually played at Wimbledon.) Kohlberg's daughter Pam had chosen to go into forestry and environmental planning, and his daughter Karen was a preschool teacher. "He really needed to pass this stuff on, and he felt like his kids weren't going to be there," says Jerry's daughter Karen.

With none of Kohlberg's offspring cooperating, George and Henry emerged as a very acceptable alternative. He was genuinely fond of them, particularly George, and he was deeply gratified by the intensity of their response to the opportunities he was creating for them.

Having George and Henry there, whom he could trust to be immersed in the details of the business, also allowed Jerry to concentrate on the overall thrust of the business, and to devote more time to philanthropic efforts. He led a lengthy search, for instance, for a new president for Swarthmore. Kohlberg liked to play the role of captain, standing at the helm of a ship looking out at the horizon, plotting his course, trying to keep his eyes trained not just on the ship's crew, but on the water, the weather, and any bits of flotsam that might suddenly hit his bow. "Jerry did have sort of the chairman-of-the-board approach," recalls John McLoughlin, an attorney at Latham & Watkins, who has worked closely with the three since the early 1970s. "If a deal was six months old, he wouldn't be as attuned as George and Henry were to who's on the board, how many, what's this."

George and Henry, in turn, thrived on their new independence. Jerry was "very good at not getting in the way of anything," says George. "[We would] just go and do what we

do, and I'd call him and talk things over with him." Mc-
Loughlin, who because of his West Coast location worked
mainly with George, says that that arrangement was by no
means a fluke. "I think I know George well enough to say
that if he couldn't have done that, he wouldn't have stayed.
He was bound to be the kind of person he is, running his
own show," he says.

Henry, too, demanded independence. "I was always the
kind of kid . . . let me have the freedom. I've never been
good in . . . a regimented environment. . . . Leave George
and me alone and we'll produce a heck of a lot," he said, his
voice beginning to rise. "I'm just always that way—as soon
as I start to feel cornered by people telling me I have to do
this or I have to do that. I know what I have to do and I
know what's important to get done. And I've always been
that way, and George Roberts is exactly the same way—we
never have had to have people tell us what to do."

George and Henry may have felt that they were up to
any challenge, but there were times when their youth, their
inexperience, or their brash natures tripped them up.

American Forest Products is one case in point. In 1981,
KKR acquired some timber properties from the Bendix Corporation for $425 million. The group that helped them fi-
nance it included some of the nation's top insurance
companies, banks, and other lenders: Prudential Insurance,
Aetna, General Electric's pension fund, Metropolitan Life
Insurance, J.P. Morgan, and Northwest Mutual. Unfortunately, KKR misjudged the market, and soon after the company had been acquired, the price of timber began to fall
and conditions in the industry deteriorated. By the end of
1984, the company had racked up cumulative losses of $159.2
million. To make matters worse, the management spun off
certain assets to a newly formed subsidiary, and some investors began to get worried that there was a move afoot to
siphon off some of their collateral. "There was some question
about transactions with an affiliate of American Forest Prod-

ucts and whether KKR was, in effect, enhancing its position at the expense of other creditors," says Resanovich, the former Prudential executive, who is now president of Merrill Lynch Interfunding.

KKR's investment partners in the deal became increasingly uncomfortable and started exploring their legal options. The level of dissatisfaction depended on how much money each institution had put into the deal and what the purpose of their investment decision had been. Most of the banks that were involved had lent on a collateralized basis. That is, if the company defaulted on its payments, they would have first dibs on the assets—so they were not unduly worried. There was another group of institutions, however, that had lent money on an *unsecured* basis, without any collateral, and they were in a much more vulnerable position. Although, under the terms of their agreement, they charged 11-percent interest on their loan of $90 million, they would only receive it if the company had enough funds to pay it. And since it obviously didn't, they were forgoing about $13.6 million a year in interest and getting a heap of IOUs from the company instead.

Now, certain of the investors did not object loudly because the losses helped them shelter income they had earned on other investments, and the IRS allows deductions for timber depletion. But for two institutions in particular, J.P. Morgan and General Electric, the situation was intolerable. Since Morgan had lent the company money from its investment management subsidiary, which is not subject to tax, and since General Electric had lent the money from its pension fund, which also is not taxed, American Forest Products' losses were real. To them, it was money out of their clients' pockets. They wanted to be made whole, and they demanded that KKR do something about it.

George was KKR's point person on the deal, in large part because the timberlands were located in northern California. Instead of responding to investors' complaints and trying to soothe their angry feelings, George decided to tough it out. He did not want to sit down and negotiate anything and told them KKR would not even consider putting any more money into the deal. That kind of "tough guy" response was how George often responded when he was confronted, say those who have worked with him. Mike Wilsey, a close friend who is also an investor in KKR, says George isn't merely decisive, "you could almost say he's unbending."

While intransigence works in certain cases, in this instance, it only further irritated the already hostile group. They threatened to declare the company in default on its loans, an action that could have forced it into bankruptcy. "Things came to a boil," recalls one lender involved in the transaction. "We as a group decided we were going to sue." They went out and hired Skadden Arps, one of the country's most aggressive law firms. But George didn't budge. His response, according to Kohlberg and others involved in the transaction, was, "Go ahead, sue us. See if we care."

At this point, Kohlberg began to believe that George had let things get seriously out of hand. "George just got so abrasive. There we were about to go into court with five of the largest institutions in the country over the way we had handled it," said Kohlberg. Had KKR been sued by such a prestigious group, the effect on the reputation of such a young firm could have been devastating.

"Kohlberg was very conscious of his reputation, and if there were any signs of concern about his integrity or commitment," says Resanovich. "He took it very seriously and I believe that is why he got Arthur Liman in."

Arthur Liman, of course, is the lawyer who represented Congress during the Iran-contra hearings, and more recently, Michael Milken. Kohlberg asked him to step in and help resolve the situation. But it was not easy and the meetings were frequently heated, with much banging on the table. "By the time Jerry got involved—and Arthur Liman—tempers were really fraying," said one business associate who knows the situation well.

In the end, several of the equity investors realized that if they ever hoped to see any return on their investment, they would have to put more money into the company to help stabilize its finances. Although it was not clear that KKR had any legal obligation to do so, Kohlberg agreed that KKR should make a similar injection of money, reversing George's original position on the issue. In the end, Morgan and GE got paid back some of the money they had lent—about sixty cents on the dollar—and agreed to cancel their loans and relinquish any further interest in the company. While Morgan did not cease doing business with KKR, executives at General Electric were not so forgiving. "This was one of the reasons that GE never invested in a KKR partnership after that," says one person who was involved in the transaction.

There were other differences as well that were becoming apparent in the early 1980s. They were more stylistic than substantive, but they nonetheless pointed to the strains that would eventually cause the firm to splinter. Their offices, for one, reflected the different temperaments. By this time the firm had moved into larger quarters on the fourteenth floor of 645 Madison Avenue. Henry, who in those days hated antiques, had decorated his office in the bold modern design of the moment. He sat behind a wine-colored laminate desk, while visitors relaxed in his wine-colored leather couch behind his smoked-glass coffee table with chrome legs. On his walls were several modern prints that he had purchased with the help of his brother, George, and Hedi. In Jerry's office, the furniture was all covered in black leather, with a country-pine coffee table that served as an accent. On his office walls were the obligatory framed business and law degrees, pictures of his children, and a map of the United States that Nancy had given him.

As the years wore on, disputes over office decor came to serve as a kind of barometer of the tension that was building between the younger men and their older partner. While they were still in the office on Madison Avenue, Henry launched a campaign to bring the office into the age of modern art. One time when Jerry was traveling, an enormous package was delivered containing a floor-to-ceiling, bright-yellow canvas that Henry had picked out with the help of a consultant. The secretaries quickly dubbed it the "Yellow Brick Road." Kohlberg nearly jumped with fright when he opened the door to the reception area on his return and saw it standing there in all its glory. On another occasion when Jerry was away, Henry hung a couple of abstract paintings in the firm's otherwise drab boardroom. This time Kohlberg put his foot down. Mary Lou Murray, Kohlberg's assistant, went into the room one day and found Henry's paintings on the floor, leaning up against the wall. Thinking they might have fallen down, she got some help from another secretary and carefully rehung them. Only later did she learn that Kohlberg, in a pique of anger, had taken them down and wanted them to stay that way. Eventually, says Mary Lou, the paintings disappeared.

By the early 1980s, when the firm began planning its move into its current office space, on the forty-second floor of 9 West Fifty-seventh Street, Henry and Jerry were going at it full tilt. To defend their opposing positions, the two men even insisted on attending construction meetings, where some of the finer details of the new office were being ironed out. "Mr. K thought the office was getting too extravagant," recalls Mary Lou Murray. "In construction meetings he wanted to know how come we had to use gold-plated screws, and not plain metal ones. He was always saying, 'Let's not forget, it's our investors' money we're spending. We shouldn't wear it on our sleeves.' Henry would kind of grit his teeth and look to make his escape," she recalls, laughing.

Mary Lou was a classic example of the two camps that were quietly forming in the office. A bright, middle-aged woman with white hair, she threw herself into her job with abandon and was fiercely protective of her slightly absent-minded boss. Jerry could barely function without her. Henry, on the other hand, liked his secretaries young and beautiful. He also preferred them to have an English accent. His current assistant, Lesley Harrison, fits the bill perfectly. An attractive blonde from Liverpool, she was a *Penthouse* "Pet" before joining Henry's employ.[9]

ROGER

Kohlberg Kravis Roberts could have proceeded at the same pace for years doing midsize deals with managers as their allies, earning good money for themselves and their investors, enjoying their familylike atmosphere and staying out of the limelight. But that would have required restraint. KKR was focused on growth; it wanted to be the biggest, the best. Its marketing documents all emphasized that it had raised the largest fund, bought the biggest company, been the first to take over a particular kind of company. And in searching for vehicles that would help it accomplish that, it tapped into a new vein of financing that would change the lives of its partners—not to mention that of Wall Street and corporate America—forever.

When Kohlberg started doing leveraged buyouts in the early 1970s, his main sources of financing were the large insurance companies: Prudential, John Hancock, Met Life, for example. They had a long-term investment perspective, they were looking for high returns, and their natural conservatism made them good at analyzing risk. To be sure, they would quibble over terms and insist on all kinds of restrictive clauses that would weed out overly risky or unsound deals. But they would give a credible LBO firm, armed with a sensible deal, a fair hearing. And Jerry's years of experience and "gray hair" factor gave KKR a natural edge with these institutions.

In the beginning, the insurance companies were all that KKR needed. But as the firm's deals grew larger, it needed to develop a bigger and more diverse pool of financial backers. In 1979, the three men raised about $32 million in equity from wealthy individuals and one bank and got insurance companies to finance the rest of what they needed. The following year they managed to wring about $75 million in equity out of a slightly larger group. But as they started to consider larger, publicly traded companies, they needed to move into the next tier of financing. They wanted several hundred million dollars' worth of equity. If they then leveraged that amount—at ten dollars of debt to every one dollar of equity—they would be able to buy $2 billion or more worth of corporate America.

To make that leap, KKR avidly began to pursue commercial banks and pension funds. Banks were interested in KKR for a number of reasons. First of all, their traditional lending business was doing poorly. Corporations were increasingly bypassing the banks and raising money directly from lenders by issuing their own, short-term IOUs. Auto companies had figured out that they could make their own low-interest-rate car loans. And just about anybody seemed to be able to issue credit cards. On virtually every front, banks suddenly seemed to be facing intense competition for all of their best customers.

High returns on KKR investments could help make up for the shrinking profits in their basic lending businesses. At the same time, banks that put some of their own money into the equity funds that KKR raised every few years to make acquisitions were naturally among the first that KKR would turn to when it was seeking debt financing for its deals. And since the banks viewed KKR as one of the nation's premier dealmakers, they figured that their close affiliation with the firm would ensure that they ended up financing the best (and they hoped, the soundest) deals. Furthermore, when they financed LBO deals, because of their size and greater risk, they got to charge a wide array of fees—as many as they could come up with names for, one banker liked to joke. There were annual fees, commitment fees, syndication fees, administrative fees, and they added up to a lot of money— usually between 1 and 2 percent of a deal. Between the higher fees and interest rates they could charge on these loans and the returns on their equity investments, banks could do well by aligning themselves with KKR. Bankers who were able to get KKR's business had themselves a one-way ticket to the top.

When the dust had settled after KKR's 1982 fund-raising effort, banks had signed up for almost 30 percent of the $316-million total, a proportion that has held fairly constant ever since.

The other source of funding that KKR was starting to tap were the pension funds, those of corporations as well as those of states and cities, which pay the pensions of firemen, policemen, and teachers. In the early 1980s, the corporate pension funds were considered the obvious ones to go after by those with an investment idea looking for backers. The corporate funds were regarded as sophisticated enough to consider such an idea, and they had money. Their retirement funds were growing at the rate of about 11 percent a year.

The public funds, by contrast, were considered too sleepy to waste time on. Many state funds were not even permitted to invest in the equity of companies, since many state legislatures regarded stocks as too risky and bonds a safer bet. State and city legislators had a direct interest in making sure that public pension funds did not get themselves into trouble, for if there was ever a shortfall and they didn't have enough money to pay the promised retirement benefits, the only way to make up the difference was to raise taxes. And everyone knew how politically unpopular that would be. Of the handful of public funds that were allowed to invest in equities, most were considered too risk-averse and too conservative to bother with.

There was one public pension fund expert who was different from the rest, however, and George Roberts managed to find him.

In 1974, when Roberts was still working in Bear Stearns's San Francisco office, the head of that office, a stockbroker named David B. Cranston, offered to introduce his young officemate to a man named Roger Meier. Meier, then in his forties, was wearing two hats. The fourth-generation offspring of a prominent Portland family, Roger was an active investor, managing several million dollars of his family's money. At the same time, Meier was also the chairman of the Oregon Investment Council, which had around $600 million in its coffers—money that represented the future retirement benefits of thousands of Oregon's state employees.

Cranston had been trying to sell Meier stocks for years and knew him well. But George was more interested in Meier's role on the Council and hoped to interest him in helping to finance a leveraged buyout of an Oregon brewery that he and Kohlberg had identified as an attractive acquisition candidate.

In those days, the chance that a public pension fund might consider investing in anything as new and complex as an LBO was slim indeed. But Roger Meier was anything but typical, and George could hardly have found a more receptive audience.

Roger and the Council's staff member, James George, listened as George Roberts described the concept of a leveraged buyout. Although the staffer had reservations about the political risks of investing in a company that produced alcohol, the two were sufficiently interested to hear more. "We went down to the taproom, which doubles as the boardroom, to listen to this young guy, George Roberts, describe a buyout," recalls Jim George. "And when Roger got outside on the sidewalk, he said, 'You know, that sounds like a pretty good investment. Let's think about it.' "

The deal never went through because the family that owned the brewery decided they could do a buyout by themselves and did not need help from Jerry Kohlberg or George Roberts. The contact having been made, however, George, Jerry, Roger, and Jim stayed in touch. Oregon, after all, was a logical market to cultivate. Kohlberg's close ties to Judge Solomon, who by then had become something of a local hero, were helpful in persuading skeptics that he was a man of honor and integrity, a man to whom one could sell one's family business.

In 1979, Kohlberg and his colleagues made a bid for Pay-Less Drugstores Northwest. Again Roberts talked to Roger Meier about the deal, and again Roger was game. But again the company went off and did its own buyout without KKR. It would not be until 1981 that George's efforts with Roger Meier and Jerry's efforts with the local business community would finally pay off.

In the early days, one of the first places that Kohlberg would visit when he passed through Portland on a business trip was the office of Fred Meyer. Fred Meyer was a legend in Oregon. He started out peddling coffee in 1909, and with his wife, Eva, by his side, forged a retail shopping empire that at last count had 120 stores in seven states. Shoppers at Fred Meyer could find everything from clothes to toothpaste to shoes. It was the original one-stop-shopping concept, and it was so successful that Fred Meyer grew to be the largest private employer in the state.

Meyer was an inspirational founder who worked seven days a week out of a ramshackle office with his wife and scores of other devoted executives. His business strategy was to keep prices so low that competitors could never afford to come into his territory. While he was alive, he was successful: no K mart, Sears, or JCPenney ever bothered to come any-where near Fred Meyer country.

Whenever he was in town, Kohlberg would stop by to chat with Meyer, pass the time of day, see what was new, and politely ask the old man once again if he was interested in selling his store. Meyer would always hear him out and then just as politely say he'd ask his fellow executives in the com-pany, which was as good as saying "not on your life."

After Meyer's death in 1978, however, a dispute broke out among the trustees of the company's stock, with one side wanting to sell the company and the other viewing a sale as a desecration of Meyer's name. Sensing the internal strains, Kohlberg pressed Meyer's successor, Oran B. Robertson, to meet with him about selling him the company. When Kohl-berg showed up at a board meeting to make his case, Rob-ertson was so appalled by the dealmaker's brazenness that he stormed out of the meeting without another word. "I can tell you, our relationship was not very good at that time. No, no, no, it was like two wildcats in a cage together," said Robertson, now in his seventies, recalling the episode.

Robertson had never even heard of KKR, and he was not about to turn over his mentor's dearly beloved company to a band of nobodies. He dispatched one of his employees to Washington, D.C., to see what she could find out about this mysterious KKR in the Library of Congress. She turned up almost nothing.

Judge Solomon, meanwhile, prevailed upon another trustee of Fred Meyer's estate, Gerry Pratt, to meet with his close friend Kohlberg. "Gus encouraged me to bring Jerry Kohlberg into the deal," said Pratt, recounting the deal years later. "I met Kohlberg over breakfast one day. My perception of him was that he was meticulous, guarded, and careful. I finally persuaded them to meet with Kohlberg privately, and he made them an offer." It took well over a year to come to terms, during which Robertson briefly flirted with the idea of selling the company to a French supermarket chain. But in the end, Kohlberg's reputation and perseverance paid off.

George Roberts, meanwhile, had been busy pursuing Roger Meier about helping with the financing of the deal. Initially, KKR had offered $45 a share, a substantial increase over the $18.50 level at which the 20 percent of the shares that were public were trading. After some lengthy negotiations, KKR and the board finally settled on a price of $55. Out of the $420 million that it took to finance the deal, Oregon's public pension fund provided $178 million.

At the end of the day, even Robertson, who had been bitterly opposed to the sale, came around to appreciating KKR. After signing the three volumes of acquisition documents, he discovered that some of the terms he had gotten KKR to agree to had somehow been overlooked or left out. Neither he nor his lawyers had caught the omissions in their frantic dead-of-night reading that had preceded the signing of the deal.

"I knew that we had screwed up in some places, both for the company and for some of my people at the company," Robertson said. "And they knew that it wasn't their intent either. And I'll be damned if they didn't come forward and say, 'Let's revise this thing, let's do it the way it was supposed to have been done,' even though it was done. You know, I don't know of anybody that really would do that," said Robertson, still amazed that a Wall Street group would volunteer to fix something they didn't have to, which would cost them money. Robertson says the decision was made by Kohlberg. Not only was this Kohlberg's deal, with his two partners clearly the more junior players, but "he's that kind of a guy. He just is," said Robertson.

Looking back on it, Robertson, who still sits on the Fred Meyer board despite a recent quintuple bypass, says he doubts that he would ever have done the deal if it had not been for Kohlberg, whom he ultimately came to respect. "I liked the way that Jerry did business," he said. "That was *my* way of doing business."

When KKR's acquisition of Fred Meyer was announced in December 1981, it took the financial world by storm. To be sure, the firm had done a number of other buyouts, so their name was not entirely new. The $355-million acquisition of Houdaille, the first buyout of a publicly held company, had caused quite a stir. And the purchase a few months earlier of the Marley Company, which makes air-cooling systems, for $354.5 million was also considered an impressive feat.

But Fred Meyer was a departure of a different kind. At $420 million, it was the largest leveraged buyout KKR, or any other buyout firm, had ever done. It was also a highly complicated transaction. KKR split the company into two entities: one for the real estate assets and the other for everything else, and designed separate financing packages for each. The sheer complexity of it drew oohs and aahs from other dealmakers and earned KKR respect for its ingenuity. But it was also a breakthrough from the standpoint of the financing. For KKR had acquired the company with a large slug of public pension fund money, courtesy of the State of Oregon, and more specifically, Roger Meier.

"I think that set KKR," observed Charles Swindells, the head of a Portland investment company who sat on the Investment Council for several years with Meier. "I think that it would have taken them ten years to get where they are [if not for Fred Meyer]. That just catapulted them into the driver's seat. The combination of KKR and Roger. That's where it started, that's how it got going."

Roger Meier was a real find. The man lives and breathes money. Those who know him well say that no subject gets him so animated. Of medium height and skinny as a rail, Meier springs forward from his chair like a missile when the subject of stocks and bonds comes up, glaring at you intensely through large glasses that give him an owlish cast.

Roger's family had owned and run one of the largest department stores in town, and Roger's father had made him aware from his earliest days that someone in the family had to learn about the stock market in order to diversify the family fortune away from retailing. Ever since he was a teenager, Meier has devoted himself to that task, first as a hobby and later as a full-time occupation.

Meier desperately wanted to be on the cutting edge of investing. And since the subject was more than just a job—it was his first love—he applied himself with a fervor usually reserved for romance or sports. He longed to know the country's top money managers, hear their latest theories, be part of that circuit that passes along ideas for up-and-coming stocks. Roger, says Cranston, will "sit and try to figure out how to make a dollar all day long."

Meier's family wealth was not so great that his portfolio would be of anything more than passing interest to the country's top money managers. The Oregon Investment Council, on the other hand, with its hundreds of millions of dollars, was a much better calling card. In the late 1960s, he submitted his name for consideration to the governor, who every year had to appoint thousands of citizens to various state commissions. And in 1970, the governor asked Roger to join the Council.

Unlike other states, Oregon had the foresight to realize that there were sound investment reasons for public pension fund money to be invested in equities. The state treasurer in the midsixties, Bob Straub, lobbied the legislature for three years and finally got them to pass the first law in the country that would allow such investments. But the legislators were not stupid. They realized that if the state fund invested in stocks that turned out to be losers, they would never hear the end of it. Their solution was to require that the Council hire independent firms to manage the state employees' equity investments. All of which meant that in the early 1970s, Roger

Meier was in the enviable position of being able to go around the country in search of money managers, with the right, indeed, the *obligation*, to scrutinize their investment practices.

Although George Roberts was out selling a financial technique that few had ever heard of and that had barely been tested, Roger was personally inclined to give him a hearing. He was in the market for hot Young Turks, the kind of people who, as he likes to say, "have the touch." Accompanied by the quiet, unassuming Jim George, Roger was engaged in a nationwide search mission.

Throughout the seventies, the two men would spend days climbing back stairs to offices in the middle of nowhere, in search of some disheveled man buried underneath stacks of financial documents who they had heard through Roger's ever-growing network was "hot." Jim George would explain the size of the Oregon fund, its growth possibilities, the kind of investors they were looking for. Those being interviewed would then explain their theories, their views of the economy, their wonderful track record. And then Roger would go in for the kill, pressing them until they handed over the list of stocks they owned at the time. Just by looking at that list he could immediately size up their investment style and determine whether they were sticking to it. That was how familiar he was with stocks of all kinds.

Meier says that he got so good at understanding the differences between various money managers and their investment approaches that after he had hired them, just for fun, he used to take the Council's list of stocks, lay his hand over the names of the money managers, and just by looking at the stock, identify which money manager had bought it. He was almost always right.

Once they had checked out a money manager to their full satisfaction, Roger and Jim would return to Portland and report at the monthly Council meetings to the other members. Meier would inform them that although the state treasurer or a senator had recommended a reputable old-line firm such as Brown Brothers Harriman, he was keen on hiring a guy no one had ever heard of who he thought had an interesting theory.

Most states would not have allowed so much power to be so concentrated in the hands of one person. They would have insisted that rigid—even stultifying—procedures be followed to ensure that any investment decisions could later, if needed, be justified as sound. Meier's attitude was, to hell with procedures, let's go for the high returns. "Roger was not a big believer in having notebooks full of administrative rules. It was a one-man show," says Council member Carol Hewitt.

Fortunately for Oregon retirees, Roger knew his stuff. His approach was not scientific, or even necessarily well thought out. And he would often violate cardinal rules of investing, such as the wisdom of diversifying one's portfolio. But Meier relied on his instincts for people and his knowledge and appreciation of money to carry him through. And sure enough, under Roger's watchful eye, Oregon ended up hiring some very astute people—such as Ralph Wanger and Sam Zell, two Chicago investment managers who went on to become very successful. Under Meier's stewardship, the Oregon fund earned a return of about 18 percent a year on its equity investments—an extraordinary record for a fund of its size, and one that often surpassed those of AT&T, General Motors, IBM, and Xerox, Roger's most worthy "competitors."

"Roger has a very good head for people, and he's intuitively a good investor," says George Roberts. "He's just got very good instincts. And his goal was to take the state's money and let the best people he could find go manage it for him."

Thanks to Meier and Jim George's pioneering efforts, Oregon was one of the first pension funds—corporate or public—to buy foreign stocks, one of the first to dabble in more exotic securities, such as futures and options, and of course, the first public fund to invest in a major way in leveraged buyouts. The two would stop at nothing—they even tried to launch their own hostile takeover of a company listed on the New York Stock Exchange, until the owners raised such a ruckus that they were forced to back off.

Roger chortles with joy as he recalls the incident, which involved a real-estate investment trust named Hubbard. The company had about 4 million shares outstanding, and its stock was selling at around $17 or $18 a share. "I said, 'Let's buy the company!' " recalls Meier excitedly. "I said, 'Jim go write a check for eighty million dollars.' " The next thing Meier knows, his phone is pulsating with blinking lights. The chief executive is one of many calling to demand that Meier withdraw the offer or face an avalanche of lawsuits. More alarmed by the prospect of endless political flak from the Oregon legislature, Meier promptly withdrew his offer. Still he says, "I loved that idea, I'll never forget it. Oh, God, did that phone light up!" Compared to that episode, investing with KKR seemed tame.

Meier loved his newly elevated position in the financial community that had come with being asked to sit on the Council. He relished his new association with his handpicked investment hotshots, and the friendships he subsequently developed with many of them. "How else could a poor little ex−rag merchant in Portland, Oregon, meet these guys?" he says, arms outstretched, exclaiming at the wonder of it all.

Meier's growing prominence as the chairman of the Investment Council caught many in Portland by surprise, and not everyone was entirely happy about it. Roger's family had been an important economic and political force in Oregon almost since the time of their arrival in 1857, two years before the state was incorporated into the Union. Roger's great-grandfather founded the Meier & Frank department store chain, which grew to be the third-largest department store chain in the Northwest. And one of Roger's great-uncles, Julius Meyer, became the state's first Jewish governor, in 1930.

Although the Meier & Frank store prospered, the rewards were not evenly divided between the two families, who

had become related through marriage. Over several generations, the Franks came to own more stock and to play a
larger role in running the company. And they were not shy
about displaying their wealth. One branch built an enormous
country estate called Fir Acres, in English Tudor style. The
mansion sported a ballroom, conservatory, and library, while
the formal English gardens were manicured by a force of
thirty-four full-time gardeners.[1]

Roger Meier's father, by contrast, never rose above the
level of secretary-treasurer of the corporation, a position that
sounded good but in actual fact was rather menial. Thus,
although Roger grew up in relative prosperity and was sent
to Hotchkiss, an expensive New England boarding school,
and the Ivy League Yale, he inherited the Meiers' resentment
toward the Franks' material success.

"I guess I always looked at them . . . and thought to
myself, well, why couldn't . . . why weren't we there?" said
Roger in a lengthy interview in his office atop a downtown
Portland skyscraper. "I think that was part of my motivating,
driving force."

As a boy, for instance, Roger longed for a Caphart phon-
ograph, which had the amazing feature of being able to turn
over a 78 record after one side had been played. "I remember, I liked music, and thinking to myself, 'Jesus, why
couldn't . . .' Well, they were a thousand dollars. And we
didn't have it, but . . . Uncle Aaron had one," he said. "These
were just anecdotal incidences that I think really put a burr
in my butt."

Roger got a chance to wreak his revenge many years
later. In the 1960s, the department store became the subject
of one of the country's earliest hostile takeovers. The May
Company persuaded some of the two families' offspring to
sell it their stock in Meier & Frank, a move that unleashed a
bitter and divisive battle for control of the company that
dominated the Portland papers for months.

Not only did Roger sell his family's Meier & Frank stock
to May, but after the hostile takeover was finally consum-

mated, he embraced the enemy by accepting an offer from the new owners to run the branch in Salem, the state's capital. In doing so, he replaced his cousin Gerry Frank, who had endeared himself to down-home Salem residents by uprooting himself from the more cosmopolitan Portland and building an impressive home in their town. He was later named "First Citizen," an honor that the town bestows once a year on the person it deems most civic-minded.

Roger refused to move to Salem. Instead, he hired a driver and was chauffeured the one-hour drive to Salem every morning in a large town car. Locals said he would go into the store and shut himself behind closed doors all day, from whence many suspected he did little more than read the *Wall Street Journal* and call his brokers. And then about three or four o'clock in the afternoon, he would make his grand exit back to Portland, walking through the store's ground floor, nodding to the clerks, the driver trailing dutifully behind.

In Oregon, where populism is still a way of life and pretension is abhorred, Roger's behavior stood in sharp contrast to the beloved Gerry Frank's and earned him no fans. "People in Salem learned to hate him; anyone with a chauffeur is hated," says one local businessman who watched the whole saga from the sidelines. "The biggest insult they could have done was to send Roger Meier to Salem."

Many in Oregon's insular business community never quite forgave Roger for his behavior during the May takeover. And they were less than thrilled to see his position on a little-known investment council turning into yet another personal launching pad.

"He's not a particularly nice man. People don't like him very much," said Jerry Drummond, the Council's new chairman, who is also the chief executive of NERCO, a Portland-based energy company. Another prominent resident of Portland who knows the Meier family well says that "money is their god." Although some in Portland's business circles simply disliked Meier's personality, others complained bitterly about how a man as wealthy as he was could be so stingy when it came to local charities. "He's not charitable, and in this community, that is taken very seriously. It's viewed as a measure of one's importance," said Drummond.

But if Roger was building up antagonisms in the Portland business community, he either did not realize it or did not care. He did little to disguise the fact that he viewed the money he was charged with overseeing as if it were his own, and that Oregon was lucky to have him take such an interest. He was also unapologetic about using his position on the Council for his own benefit. It would have been hard for Roger to act any other way. He had a high opinion of his own financial skills and considered the work he was doing for the Council to be an act of generosity—since he was not being paid for it. He was also so taken with the investment managers that he was meeting that any other attitude would have been quite out of character.

The "real brownie points" from his job, Roger explained, came from getting to know top investors on a personal basis. "Listen, they're fascinating people to me! And often I can have lunch or dinner with them on the side. Through the years, I became very, very friendly with them," he said.

Roger would play tennis with George Roberts, for instance, and entertain visiting money managers at the Arlington Club, Portland's most exclusive private club, which, for many years, excluded Jews, blacks, and women. Among those Roger became friendly with were Sam Zell, the well-known Chicago investor who waits for companies to falter and then buys them at bargain-basement prices, and who has recently gotten Oregon to invest in one of his funds, and Fayez Sarofim, the secretive Middle Eastern money manager based in Houston.

"You have to understand," said Swindells, who sat on the Council with Roger for four years and often sparred with him during that period, "Chairman Meier likes big names. He likes high-profile names. He can be attracted by who's getting the big print in the financial journals."

Roger's new friends, of course, were not merely fun, interesting, and worldly, especially compared to those whose life experiences had been limited to Portland. They also had great investment suggestions, which Roger used to help enlarge his own family's portfolio, which is now close to $30 million. "Roger and Fayez got to be best friends," recalls Dave Wood, who helped market KKR to state pension funds. "Fayez would find an interesting side investment for himself personally; he'd call Roger. Roger would find something for Fayez, and they would both go in on it. They talked daily."

In addition to his personal contacts, as a member of the Council Roger would receive a list of the stocks that the money managers he had hired for the state were buying. "This whole time, people would wonder why I would spend so much time with it," Roger said, showing considerable surprise. "Because I loved it! And it helped me! It made me a better investor! I don't want to say this was complete, unadulterated altruism. I didn't have any inside information, but obviously, if Fayez Sarofim was going to buy, say, Westvāco, I could look at Westvāco and think, 'Gee'—this is ten days or two weeks later . . . 'maybe I ought to look at it,' " Roger explained. What better way, he insisted, to ensure that the state's money was being carefully and diligently invested? "If I'm going to do it for the state, I'm going to put it right there," said Roger, indicating with his hands that he meant side by side.

Roger thought it was improper, however, for members of the public to be privy to the same kind of information that he was. When he saw several stockbrokers rush to the phone once after a money manager had given his report at a Council meeting, Meier tried to cancel all future meetings. "To let a broker sit there and find out what one of the great money managers in the country . . . was doing, that this is what he thinks interest rates will do, was unfair," Meier said, bouncing agitatedly on his beige couch in his all-beige office. And when the governor tried to appoint a discount broker to sit on the Council, Roger was outraged: "Because they're privileged to confidential information, or information that the state's paid for. I can't say that ninety or sixty days later it shouldn't be made public. But [when you're on the Council] you get it right away."

Some local businesspeople questioned the wisdom of allowing a man with Meier's intense pecuniary interests to have such extensive exposure to top money managers and access to their nonpublic investment decisions. Jerry Drummond, the Investment Council's new chairman, seems to share some of those concerns. A serious, careful man with an officious air about him, Drummond said quietly, "There's some sense that Roger Meier got as much out of his involvement as the state did. In managing his own portfolio, he obtained access to some of the better money managers and thinking in this country. And that wouldn't have happened if he hadn't been on the Council."

But if people found Meier's position distasteful, no one did anything about it. Indeed, for many years, other Council members generally deferred to their energetic, devoted, and extremely knowledgeable chairman. Virtually all the other members had full-time jobs elsewhere and could not afford to run around the country with Roger and Jim for weeks on end. When Meier came to the meetings and said, "Here are the decisions we've made," no one was really in a position to challenge him.

"He would do a lot of screening, of ideas, concepts, and products; he would make a determination that we would not be interested," said Carol Hewitt, who sat on the Council from 1981 until 1990 and was chairwoman for the last two and a half years of her term. "He was moving along and kind of didn't pay any attention to the fact that there were other people on the Council, at times."

Many Council members were retired business executives who knew a great deal about corporate law or logging, but were neophytes when it came to dividend payments or stock options. And Roger had little patience with those less knowledgeable than himself. "Roger became a very strong leader within the Council," says Jim George. "A majority of the members of Council through most of the years you would characterize as senior businessmen, and almost none of them were what you would call investment professionals."

Looking back on it, Roger says somewhat ruefully, "I'm sure I didn't try them [ideas] on the other members, and they may have felt offended that I didn't consult them. And I would present them and say, 'Look, here's what we should do.' You know, I had been doing this a long time, and I didn't want to have to educate everybody of what was a stock and a bond."

Swindells, a Council member in the mid-1980s, remembers being in a meeting when Roger announced that it was time for the fund to invest in convertible bonds. Well, some of the Council members had never even heard of that type of security, which is an offbeat hybrid between a stock and a bond. "Of course, we didn't even know who the managers of convertible bonds were, and Roger says, 'Well, I've got a firm, Froley Revy, out of Los Angeles.'

" 'Well, who are they?'

" 'Well, you're going to meet them in fifteen minutes because they're outside in the next room.' " And that, says Swindells, was that.

No one ever wanted to take Roger on. "There were other people on the Council. But he dominated it. He really dominated that Council. Now, that's going to be tough to swallow for some of the Council members. But he had so much time to devote to the research of this," said Swindells. "It was his agenda. He didn't really share. . . . He controlled it lock, stock, and barrel. He was a benevolent dictator is really what he was."

When this "benevolent dictator" decided to invest $178 million—8 percent of the state fund's entire portfolio—in the Fred Meyer deal, all hell broke loose. In those days that was a lot of money, and leveraged buyouts were still not well known or well understood. Many investors regarded Oregon's investment as extremely risky and thought the state Investment Council had been ill advised to place such a big bet on one company using such an untested financial technique.

Roger Meier thought the skeptics were nuts. Having spent a lot of time evaluating real estate for his family's own portfolio—they owned a number of warehouses and properties in downtown Portland—Meier viewed the leases on the Fred Meyer stores alone to be hugely valuable. The old man had never charged his stores much rent, and so they were severely undervalued in the market. Just raising the rent would make his investments sound, Roger thought.

But if Meier was supremely confident, he faced a lot of criticism in the community. He found he couldn't even go to the men's room at the Arlington Club without being accosted by some local businessman who criticized him for his decision. Indeed, so vitriolic was the response that the Portland Federation of Teachers, whose retirement funds were among those being used by the OIC, filed a lawsuit in conjunction with several of Fred Meyer's competitors, challenging the OIC's authority to make such an investment.

During the course of the lawsuit, one detail emerged from the proceedings that struck a chord with many local citizens. It was a memo written by the then deputy treasurer, Fred Hansen, to his boss, the state treasurer, Clay Myers. Calling the proposed transaction a "serious mistake," Hansen concluded that the Council's investment in Fred Meyer violated its long-standing policy to diversify investments and warned that investing such a large sum of money in a low-cost department store located in one geographic area was "way too risky.

"The rate of return is good, may be even very good," he continued, but that "does not justify exposing the pension fund to this kind of risk." He then placed the blame for what he considered an ill-advised proposal on Meier's personality: "Roger Meier's infatuation with the deal is a function of who he knows through the old-boy network of Portland. I am convinced this type of deal would never be contemplated by OIC, even if the terms were as attractive, if it did not involve people Roger knows personally."

The suit was eventually settled out of court, with the state agreeing not to participate in the management of Fred Meyer and the company agreeing not to take advantage of the state pension fund's stake in the company in soliciting business. As Roger Meier predicted, Fred Meyer turned out to be a successful deal: the state has gained over 53 percent on its original investment.

THE CIRCLE WIDENS

O regon has always been something of a trailblazer. It was the first state to pass a "bottle" bill to encourage recycling; it is the only state on the West Coast to insist that all of its beaches be public; and it was the first to try to limit the state's Medicaid expenditures by ranking medical problems by their severity.

So it is not entirely surprising to find that Oregon is also a leader in the arcane world of public pension fund finance, even though the state is far from the glitz and glamour of the nation's top financial centers. It was the first state in the country to give its trustees more leeway in making investments—they have only to prove that they acted prudently. And it was the first state to allow its fund to plunge into stocks. The proportion of the state's pension fund money that could be invested in equities rose dramatically, from 10 percent in 1967, to 35 percent in 1973, and finally to 50 percent in 1983. Because stocks do better than bonds over long periods of time, that policy change alone resulted in impressive improvements in Oregon's track record and made other states sit up and take notice. Oregon became such a star that at pension fund conventions—yes, there are such events—representatives from Oregon would find themselves besieged by strangers eager to learn the secret of their success.

Unfortunately for them, Oregon's secret was Roger Meier, or more precisely, a chairman who did not care one whit what anyone else thought of him, who trusted his instincts entirely to place big bets on new ideas, and who so cowed the rest of his board with his energy and his knowledge that he had no opposition.

Those ingredients simply did not exist in any other state. On the contrary, at most state funds, board members have little time to devote to their investment responsibilities and may have little investment expertise. They are usually a motley crew: political appointees of the governor, publicly elected officials such as the state treasurer, prominent businesspeople with busy careers of their own, and retired schoolteachers or policemen representing the group whose funds are being invested.

Board members have often had no more investment experience than balancing their own checkbooks. Yet they are suddenly thrust into a position of approving the investment of billions of dollars of state employees' money. At the better-run state funds, board members are required to attend seminars that will at least help them understand the language of investing. And many of them are extremely diligent in trying to understand the magnitude of their responsibilities. But there are plenty of state funds at which being a board member is nothing more than a boondoggle. They meet once a month for half an hour and then take themselves out to long, liquid lunches often paid for by the fund's beneficiaries. And they spend their time roaming from one investment "conference" to another that money managers, interested in getting their hands on more investment funds, have thoughtfully sponsored in some of the most fashionable resorts around the world.

Picture an assortment of board members and their staff counterparts, often with their spouses in tow, staying in top-notch hotels in Hong Kong or touring the vineyards of France while ostensibly learning about international real estate or stocks. At the more serious gatherings, sessions start early and end in time for participants to get in at least nine holes of golf before dinner and the evening's planned entertainment. At the more relaxed meetings, the day's scheduled activities often end promptly at noon. For fund managers on limited salaries or retired busdrivers, these seminars are often one of the few perks of the job. And they certainly beat taking the family to Disney World.

At most state funds, it is the staff—not the board members—who make the real decisions. And they are generally overworked and underpaid. The task before them is impossible—to decide how to allocate billions of dollars of other people's money in such a way that they and their board members are insulated from any political heat. For this honor they are paid a fraction of what their counterparts in the private sector earn, and they are given almost no resources with which to work. Many public funds have just three or four people to oversee $10 billion or more, while a fund of similar size in the private sector might have thirty or forty people on its staff.

With salaries that range from $50,000 to $70,000—about what a twenty-six-year-old lawyer or investment banker makes the first year out of graduate school—the state funds are generally assured of getting second- or third-tier candidates. Typically, they are graduates of local state colleges with little or no postgraduate training. Staff officers may be dedicated and hardworking civil servants, but their financial knowledge is often limited to what they gleaned from working their way up through the personnel-benefits department or a local accounting firm or bank trust department. Unkind as it may sound, they are often no match for the money managers they are being asked to select and then monitor. And the result is that once they make a decision to go with a particular money manager, they have little choice but to hope that that investment manager handles that money responsibly. Staffers have little incentive to subject their money managers to close scrutiny because if they find something wrong, it will only be used against them: they will have to explain why they were foolish enough to have selected that errant money manager in the first place.

Being a staff officer of a state pension fund, in other words, is a thankless task. And there is virtually no incentive to take risk—it can only lead to trouble. Better to stick with a tested investment idea.

All of which meant that until George Roberts, who was trying to expand KKR's investor base, was able to get one person in the staid state-pension-fund world to sign up with KKR, he would not be able to get any others. On the other hand, once one took the leap, it would be much easier to attract others. And the fact that KKR was able to snare Oregon as its first state fund would prove to be an enormous boon. For, as one of Oregon's former state treasurers, Bill Rutherford, likes to say, getting Oregon as a client is "like getting the Good Housekeeping seal of approval."

When word of Oregon's investment in Fred Meyer made the rounds, other state pension fund managers wanted to know what on earth that crazy Roger Meier was up to. Happily for George Roberts, there were one or two other funds that wanted to follow in Oregon's footsteps. John Hitchman was determined to be next. The sandy-haired head of the State of Washington's Investment Board was cynical about many of the ideas that Wall Street investment bankers brought him to consider. He always felt that by the time he was told about them, any opportunities that had been there had already been picked over like a dead carcass. KKR interested him for several reasons. Leveraged buyouts were a new concept, so the potential to get in early was still there.

He liked the firm's philosophy and shared the view that many of America's largest corporations had become unwieldy and inefficient and could benefit from some restructuring. And he knew and respected Jim George, Roger Meier's trusted right-hand man. The two of them had worked for the same employer once, in the trust department of the First National Bank of Oregon in the 1950s, now a part of First Interstate Bancorp.

"Jim just said, 'Hey, you ought to talk to these guys.' And I said, 'Okay, I will.' And then he called George and George called me, and we set up a meeting, and I was immediately very favorably impressed with not only George as a person, but him as a professional and what they were all about," Hitchman recalled many years later from his perch at a well-appointed money management firm in Los Angeles. Hitchman managed to squeak Washington into an LBO fund that KKR was just finishing raising in 1982, with a small commitment of about $10 million. When KKR had nearly exhausted that fund and came back for more two years later, he upped the ante to $150 million, making Washington the largest investor of KKR's by far, with about 15 percent of KKR's total $1-billion fund.

As KKR invested that money over the next few years and the companies it bought seemed promising, Hitchman decided to turn his friends on to the KKR bonanza, too. "Some of the people out there, my counterparts that I kind of like . . . I would call them and say, 'You know, you really ought to talk to these guys.' Just like Jim George did to me," said Hitchman. Whom did he call? "I think, um, Utah, and Minnesota. A lot of them didn't bite—I guess I shouldn't say that. Minnesota, Utah, and Michigan. I didn't go too far east. Michigan was about as far east as I got." (All of those that he mentioned subsequently signed on.)

Hitchman didn't stop there. In 1983, he invited George and Henry to speak at a meeting of the National Association of State Investment Officers, a group of his peers that gathered every year in different states to discuss issues that were confronting them. Although Hitchman's actions helped his friends at other funds, they were also of enormous benefit to KKR. The setting was a fund manager's dream: to be invited to address a roomful of potential investors, with no competitors within miles. The marketer of a competing fund still grouses years later about the unfair advantage he felt that entree gave KKR. "That was unprecedented, to allow anyone to sell their wares," he said.

But the unprecedented happened a second time. Roger Meier and Jim George did the same thing several years later, when it was their turn to chair the meeting. "We kind of gave them a double whammy," said Hitchman, who now works for a money-management firm that was hired when he worked for the state. "You get involved in your own programs, you get excited about what you're doing." And unlike private funds, who guard their successes jealously, "the thing that's interesting about public funds, public funds communicate," Hitchman observes.

How important was Oregon's involvement to getting KKR started? "It was absolutely necessary," explained Dave Wood, who introduced George Roberts to several state fund managers. "Because nobody likes to be the first guinea pig. And Oregon was willing to be the first guinea pig, not only in this arena but in other arenas, and that lets everybody else off the hook. People need endorsement in life. Especially people that are paid a lousy salary to run a lot of money and who don't get paid for their performance."

Roberts seems to concur with Wood's assessment. "The success we had in Oregon helped us get in the door with the people in Washington, and then eventually, the people in Michigan, and it's grown from there."

Once the camel's nose was under the tent, there was a headlong rush for the public funds by just about every investment group that was trying to raise money. It wasn't just that a few state funds had shown they were willing to be more daring. They were also quickly becoming the only game in town.

By the mid-1980s, the wave of mergers had shrunk the ranks of middle managers, and therefore the pool of employee benefits. That, and the booming stock market, meant that most corporate pension funds were growing at a much slower pace. They therefore had less to parcel out to investment managers in the way of new funds.

The situation at most state funds could not have been more different. Since so few states had been allowed to invest in equities and instead had been chalking up single-digit returns usually associated with bonds, they were far behind in terms of having enough money to cover their future obligations. And unlike the corporate funds, their pool of retirees was still growing: the states were hiring more teachers and policemen, and many public employee unions had negotiated better retirement packages in lieu of higher salaries, which would put still more pressure on state funds. The result was that many state funds were getting more and more money to invest each year, and they were desperately in need of high returns to help compensate for their previous lackluster performance. By the early 1980s, many state funds had followed Oregon's lead and were shifting as much as 50 percent of their investment pool out of bonds and into equities. That meant that billions of dollars were suddenly becoming available for investments in equity. Ripe territory, in other words, for a firm seeking people with lots of money to invest.

"The big state funds, that's really where the money in this country is," said George. "And it's certainly where the money in this country in the future is going to be."

Of course, KKR was not the only one to figure this out. Other investment firms started targeting public pension funds, eager to get in on the action. State fund managers suddenly found themselves besieged with calls from people they had never heard of, insisting that they had the next "hot" investment idea. The dilemma of Thomas E. Flanigan, the chief investment officer of the California State Teachers' Retirement System, is typical of many fund managers. He presides over $50 billion in funds from his maroon leather chair in an office on the third floor of an office building on the outskirts of Sacramento. When he took the job in 1988, he found a fund that had been sorely neglected. After signaling to some consultants that he was interested in increasing the proportion of his fund's money that was invested in stocks, he suddenly found himself swamped with proposals from dozens of firms wanting to make his life easier. Does he feel besieged? Flanigan lets out a loud laugh and then points his finger at the entrance to his office. "A thousand ideas come through that door," he says, grinning from ear to ear.

To fend off the hordes, many state fund managers turn to consultants. Not only can consultants take some of the heat off by taking responsibility for sifting through the scores of applications from interested money managers, but they can make staff members' relations easier with their boards. It's much harder for a board to blame its staff for a decision that turns out to be poor if that decision is based on the recommendation of a third party who is considered competent by the rest of the industry.

"What's important is not how well you do, but to avoid mistakes and have no controversies," says one investment banker who has tried to interest state funds in his ideas. "There's little upside in doing new things and lots of upside in maintaining the status quo. That's the whole reason consultants exist. It's covering your ass, laying off decisions on somebody else." John Carroll, who is responsible for the pension fund at GTE Corp., has observed the same phenomenon. "Public funds use consultants more, and they need them more," he says. Not because they're dumb, but because "they act as insurance with board members."

In the early eighties, most consultants knew the universe of stock-pickers, but were unfamiliar with leveraged buyouts.

They were still viewed as newfangled financial inventions, and no one had really taken the time to study them. Besides, consultants like track records. Just like the fund managers who hire them, they, too, need to be able to back up their recommendations by pointing at lines on a graph.

Into this vacuum came Douglas Le Bon. With the build of a football quarterback and a raspy voice, Le Bon was a real go-getter. Born in Rapid City, South Dakota, he and his parents moved to California when he was a young boy. Le Bon adopted the laid-back manner and surfing skills that seemed to be a requirement for young California boys. But Le Bon's father was a businessman, and Doug always found his work intriguing. So despite the antiwar protests and the hippie movement that were sweeping the country, Doug went to college and majored in business administration. He got his bachelor's degree and his MBA from California State University at Dominguez Hills, a virtually unknown college that Le Bon says gets a laugh every time he mentions it. To help pay his way through school, he joined the Teamsters and started driving a Coca-Cola truck through some of L.A.'s worst gang-infested neighborhoods. After graduation, he was offered a job working for a company that did valuations of companies and their assets, and over the next few years, he learned a lot about the way that companies work and are financed. Before long, he was hired by Wilshire Associates, one of the largest pension fund advisers in the country.

Le Bon was intrigued by leveraged buyouts from the start. From his previous job, he knew that many companies had assets buried in their bowels that were undervalued by the stock market and by their owners. Clearly, if he could get in early on this investment trend, and make a name for himself, he could do very well. "I had this world pretty much to myself," recalled Le Bon. "People have started to come in just in the last year or so. I was probably one of the only ones in the field. None were advocating that clients do it. Wilshire was pretty much alone."

But first he had to convince some of his clients to go

along, and given their horror of anything risky or new, that was not going to be easy. "You have to understand, at the time I was just twenty-nine or thirty years old and I was trying to convince these people to invest in LBOs. So I actually found somebody who was investing in LBOs who could be a role model."

The person he "found" was Roger Meier. To Le Bon, Roger Meier was a godsend. "Roger Meier was a businessman and he had real business reasons for investing, and he became an excellent role model," said Le Bon as he sat in a fashionable Santa Monica restaurant overlooking the Pacific Ocean. "I could say, 'Look at Oregon, they're doing it.' I could come up with all my empirical and anecdotal evidence, and I could point to someone who actually did it." Although it was not until several years later that he finally met Roger Meier, "wherever I went, I pointed to him," Le Bon said.

Armed with his numbers and his role model, Le Bon crisscrossed the country talking to potential and actual Wilshire clients. He told them about KKR's track record up until then—the 40-percent-plus returns. And people would scratch their heads in disbelief that such returns were possible. But since Wilshire was known for its number-crunching, and since Roger Meier was already in on it, many were willing to lend an ear.

There was another important angle to Le Bon's pitch. He thought KKR offered state funds a way out of another dilemma: size. Many funds were by now growing at such a fast clip that they were faced with the daunting prospect of investing several billion dollars a year. In the investment world, that's the equivalent of an avalanche. Many money managers oversee only $200 million or $300 million in total. And since most state funds rarely like to represent more than 10 percent of any one person's business, that meant the most they could put with a stock-picker was $20 million. It would take a lot of those little bets to get rid of all that money they were faced with investing. No sooner had they invested last month's inflow—which in the larger funds could amount to as much as $45 million—than they were faced with yet another wave of money that had to be put to work. Although it may sound like a luxurious position to be in, it's actually hard work.

"A twenty-million-dollar investment doesn't get you anything," explains Le Bon. "I wanted a fund with a good track record, decent size, where I could put a meaningful amount of money to work where it could impact the portfolio. So that's why KKR was a natural choice."

John Hitchman, of Washington, says that size was one reason that he was so enthusiastic about KKR. "I perceived that one of the major problems that public fund managers had was a problem of size. How are they, with all the cash flow they had and how big they were going to get, how in the hell were they going to invest all this money?" When he began to consider KKR, Hitchman said he didn't really give much thought to the returns. Instead, he says, "I saw this as a vehicle to place a lot of money."

Happily for everyone concerned, the public funds' need for a place to stash a lot of money dovetailed neatly with the direction in which KKR was going. Other competitors had started to crowd the field. The firm needed a way to shake its new competitors off, and going for size was one way to do it. If they had billions of dollars at their disposal and others had only hundreds of millions, as was more typical, they would be able to bid for huge companies and face little or no competition.

Hitchman remembers having a long talk with George Roberts about this one day in early 1982 or 1983. He and George were kicking around the idea of how Washington and KKR could take over a major international oil company that they thought looked undervalued, and whether such a feat could be accomplished. "At that time," Hitchman recalled, "no really big deals had been done." But George had a sense that as other players came onto the field, KKR's turf would get crowded. "What George was searching for was another new niche," said Hitchman, seated in his red leather chair in his sumptuously appointed Los Angeles office. "It was just a personal conversation, it didn't go anywhere. I gave him some views, but I could tell that George was interested in size and bigness."

George was not to be disappointed, for the combination of forces he had helped unleash was potent. With Roger Meier happily leading the way, other states following right behind, Le Bon ratifying their decisions, and KKR ready and willing to take as much money as the states would give them, a money machine of vast proportions was in the making.

By 1986, when KKR was shooting for the $1-to-2-billion mark in its third formal fund, the steamroller was moving under its own momentum. The number of state funds that signed up jumped from three to eleven: Washington and Oregon, of course, but also New York, Wisconsin, Illinois, Iowa, Massachusetts, Montana, Michigan, Minnesota, and Utah. "Representatives from other state pension funds kept telling me how great they were," was how Robert Harmon, the former director of the Illinois State Board of Investment, explained his decision to a *Crain's Chicago Business* reporter.

One year later, when KKR raised the largest fund ever—a stunning $5.6 billion, much of which is now invested in RJR Nabisco—those same eleven states provided 53 percent of the total. It took sixty-seven other institutional investors to make up the rest. Of the eleven state funds, four were Doug Le Bon's clients.

One might expect people who are entrusted with investing other people's money to keep some distance from a money manager whose performance they are expected to evaluate objectively.

Over the years, however, KKR and the state funds came to be more like partners. Each side helped the other, and both profited from the arrangement. In the case of Oregon, for example, when the Investment Council and KKR were being sued by Fred Meyer's competitors for the Council's decision to become one of the largest owners of the company, it was KKR's lawyers, Latham & Watkins, who came to the rescue and drafted a settlement that was acceptable to all parties. KKR, meanwhile, got tips from its friends on the Oregon Council about companies in the state that might make good LBO candidates. Council members would even make personal appeals to executives they knew and try to persuade them to sell their companies to KKR. That was one reason KKR came to buy the Red Lion Inn, a chain of motels in the Northwest. And Roger Meier worked hard to persuade the management of Hyster Co., a fork-lift truck company, to let KKR acquire it. Several years later, Meier referred to KKR as "one of the most successful partners the State of Oregon has ever had."[1] He liked to say that LBO really stands for Let's Build Oregon.[2]

KKR also became a way for lowly state officials to become involved in the glamorous takeover game that was beginning to seize Wall Street, capturing the hearts and minds of executives and investors across the country. Washington's John Hitchman, for example, viewed his ties to KKR as a way for the state Investment Board to amass a pool of companies of its own. Hitchman's fund ended up buying the Red Lion Inn and a forest products company in conjunction with KKR. He even tried to orchestrate a secret takeover bid for Seafirst Bank and ended up competing against Bank of America for this local bank, which had gotten caught in the Penn Square debacle and needed a buyer to rescue it from collapse.

"I brought in George," said Hitchman, "and we really kicked it around." The group got to be a serious contender until the press got wind of it and the political reaction to the state pension fund's owning a bank was so heated that they had to back down.

But if Washington and Oregon viewed KKR as their silent partner, the feeling was mutual. Whenever KKR needed one of its investors to contribute a little more equity than its share of a fund would normally dictate, Washington was one of the first places KKR would call. At one point, said Hitchman with not an inconsiderable note of pride, Washington was the single largest owner of the Beatrice Companies, a Fortune 500 company that KKR acquired in 1986 for $8.2 billion.

Not surprisingly, when other leveraged-buyout groups realized the extent to which KKR had succeeded in tapping into the state pension fund network, they wanted in, too. And had they succeeded, KKR's competition would have been much more intense. But KKR's competitors found states such as Oregon and Washington intensely loyal to KKR. When Theodore J. Forstmann of Forstmann Little & Company, KKR's main competitor and chief nemesis, tried to interest Oregon in one of his funds, he ran into a brick wall, despite the fact that he could also point to equity returns in the 40-percent-plus range. His rebuff was even more surprising because one of his top associates, who accompanied Forstmann to his meeting with Meier, came from a prominent Oregon family and was the grandson of a former governor. Jim George, reporting to a monthly Council meeting in May 1984 on Forstmann's visit, is quoted in the minutes as saying, "he didn't feel the council would be interested in it because of the large amount already committed in this area." Meier said he heard Forstmann out, but just couldn't understand his performance numbers, an odd comment from a man who prided himself on his number-crunching abilities. When it came to other LBO firms, the irrepressibly diligent Meier became unusually passive. His view, he said, was that "we had hired KKR and we should stay married. In other words, why chippy around and get somebody else?"

Competitors of KKR who tried to tempt other states to invest in their funds ran into similar roadblocks, a response that was stiffened by the hostility they encountered when they met Doug Le Bon. By this time, he had become the leading pension-fund consultant on LBOs in the country and counted among his clients at various times during the 1980s Iowa, Massachusetts, Oregon, and New York. His early endorsement of KKR netted him handsome fees from his happy clients and a reputation for being a heavy hitter who had clout with KKR. Le Bon's fortunes soared. He rose from his position as a midlevel employee in 1983 to the head of an entire division, as well as a member of Wilshire's board of directors. The Coca-Cola truck was replaced by a Mercedes, which he drove to work every morning from his apartment in fashionable Marina Del Rey.

Le Bon was now in a position that unless he endorsed other LBO funds, many of his clients amongst the state funds simply would not climb on board. And that is exactly what happened. Time and time again, when competitors of KKR tried to interest Le Bon in their investment funds and could demonstrate that they had returns that were at least as good as, if not better than, KKR's and that they charged lower fees, they say that Le Bon would not even give them the time of day. The firms he spurned were not fly-by-night operations—they were some of Wall Street's most highly re-garded institutions and individuals. Yet several major LBO sponsors say that Le Bon would not return their calls or, if he spoke to them, would be so rude and arrogant that they would refuse to go any further, convinced that they would never get a fair hearing. When one of Le Bon's clients spe-cifically asked him to review a particular fund, Le Bon sent a junior person from Wilshire and after a brief once-over gave the investment proposal the thumbs-down.

"Wilshire was the only outside consultant that didn't bless our deal," said one fund-raiser. "We were meeting with enor-mous success in the institutional investment market. And it's inconceivable to me that he would turn us down with such short shrift." He continued, clearly agitated, "He wouldn't return our phone calls, I wrote him letters. All I can see is behavior that is very strange." Despite Le Bon's lack of in-terest, this fund sponsor ultimately succeeded in raising a large amount of money, which suggests that Le Bon's judg-ment was not shared by others.

Many industry consultants and LBO fund managers are mystified as to why Le Bon, who has since left Wilshire to start his own firm, would develop such a loyalty to KKR and treat its competitors with such disdain. Especially since his clients might have earned more money if they had invested with some of KKR's competitors, paid less in fees, and diversified their risk. "The issue of favoritism is one that many in the industry have raised, that he's very biased, particularly towards KKR," says one pension fund consultant.

Le Bon says he didn't want his clients putting money with entities that might compete with investments they had already made. He acknowledges that he did, however, encourage clients to commit money to a number of midsize LBO firms that frequently ran into each other in their own market niche.

Le Bon says the perception that he is unaccommodating might stem from his skepticism of Wall Street firms with LBO units. They might be tempted, he feels, to do deals for short-term fees and the ancillary business they could generate for other parts of their firms. The only Wall Street-based LBO groups he has endorsed, he says, are those that split their fees with their investors, a practice that KKR, by contrast, has fought long and hard to resist.

To many public pension fund managers, it doesn't matter how one investment performs relative to another. As long as a decision doesn't backfire on them, they are generally content. "What counts is the process, not the conclusion," said one KKR competitor. All Le Bon had to do was explain that KKR's returns were better than could be obtained in the stock market and were consistent over time. The fact that there were other LBO firms out there offering as good results or better and charging less in fees was not necessarily relevant. "He could justify it in terms he knew his clients would understand," said this LBO sponsor. "These aren't investment professionals, they're process professionals."

REWARDS

Doug Le Bon was not the only person whose fortunes came to be closely aligned with those of KKR. The firm seemed to make a practice of helping people put themselves in accommodating positions.

Consider what happened to Roger Meier. By the mid-1980s, he had helped put more than $500 million at KKR's disposal and been influential in getting countless other hundreds of millions of dollars committed to KKR's funds through the public fund network. Yet here he was a supremely successful investor who had to sit by and watch other people's money explode in value based on *his* insight and knowledge. Roger says that he would really have liked the opportunity to buy stock in Fred Meyer, which he was convinced would be a winning investment. Kohlberg says that Meier went so far as to approach KKR several times with the suggestion, although other KKR executives and Roger firmly deny that he did so. Kohlberg says he vetoed Roger's idea immediately. For a public official to be given special treatment by an investment firm he was charged with overseeing on behalf of beneficiaries would constitute an appearance—if not an actual—conflict of interest.

"Roger kept bugging us. I said, 'Roger, we can't sell you the stock. My God! You're working for the state!' He said, 'Yeah, well, don't forget me,' or something like that. George was willing to do it, but I was not," Kohlberg said. "We told him [Roger] once he gets free [of his job], he's free to invest."

In the meantime, KKR put Meier on the boards of two of its companies. Since it controls the companies it acquires, KKR can nominate whomever it wants to those positions, although in practice it hardly ever put in anyone other than top managers and its own executives. In 1983, however, Meier was made a director of Norris Industries, the building and industrial products company that KKR had acquired in 1981 with the help of the Oregon Investment Council. In addition to the prestige and excitement that came with being a director, Meier received an annual director's fee of $15,000. And in January 1985, without a word to most other members of the Council, Meier accepted a position on Fred Meyer's board. The remuneration for that position was $18,000 a year.

Meier maintained that his presence on the boards was a good thing for the Council because it allowed him to monitor its investments. But when his dual role was revealed in the local newspaper, many Oregonians were outraged. To whom did Roger owe his loyalties, the retirees whose money was at stake, or his buddies at KKR? What if he learned of something on the board that might hurt Oregon's economy, but was the correct step for the company to take? Would he vote for or against it? And why was he on these boards to begin with? Because of his business experience, because the Council was a major investor, or because of his personal ties to KKR? If it was the last consideration, would this influence his future decisions on investing with KKR?

Meier insisted at a Council meeting in February of 1985 that he was invited on the Fred Meyer board because of his retailing experience—which was then fifteen years out-of-date. It was an assertion that the attorney general's office, which looked into the propriety of Meier's board seats, seems to have accepted at face value. "It is our understanding that Mr. Meier's appointment to the Board had nothing to do with his role as an OIC member," an assistant attorney general wrote to the Council stating that he found no fault in Meier's conduct.[1]

His response was striking because it was, and still is, a violation in Oregon for anyone to use his or her public position for private gain. As the current state treasurer, Anthony Meeker, explains it, "If the person acquired that board membership because of their position in state government or on a pension fund or whatever, it's prohibited by law; it's an out-and-out illegal act." Meeker says he would never accept a board seat simply because the perception would be bad.

It is impossible to prove that Meier was given the directorships by KKR *because* of his position on the Investment Council. However, there is a curious pattern: Meier has served as a director on four corporate boards. One is that of a bank that built its headquarters on land that Meier owned, in return for which he also received an equity stake in the building. The other three have only one thing in common. They were all owned by Kohlberg Kravis Roberts and were investments in which the Oregon Investment Council had a major stake. Only one of them, Fred Meyer, involved retailing, the reason that Meier gave for KKR's interest in him. And he was only asked to join the retailing company two years after he became a director of the machine tools company, Norris Industries.

The controversy over Meier's board seats caused the governor to appoint a commission to examine the rules that covered such behavior and to make recommendations. The scope of the commission went well beyond directorships, however, to include many other issues that Meier's conduct had raised.

Should Council members, the commission wondered, be allowed to make the same investments in their personal account as the state? Was there any conflict there, either in appearance or in fact? Meier, for instance, freely acknowledged that his personal stock holdings overlapped with the state's, a position that only grows more complicated when he is also a director of a company in which both he and the state fund own shares. After Norris Industries sold some stock to the public in 1983, for instance, Meier says he bought $20,000 worth of stock, and when Fred Meyer did the same, he bought 7,000 shares.

His actions, again, raised questions of where his loyalties lay—as an individual shareholder, or as the watchdog for Oregon's state retirees. In the case of Norris, for instance, Meier was ready to vote against a $20-a-share takeover offer for the company from Masco Industries that would have given Oregon's retirees a fabulous return on their initial $2.75-a-share investment. As a relatively new *individual* shareholder, however, Meier says he felt that he personally hadn't received enough dividends yet to make it worth his while and that other public shareholders might feel the same way. He told George Roberts in the board meeting that he would vote against the takeover offer. The deal that was finally approved gave KKR, Oregon, and other original shareholders $20 a share, and public shareholders such as Roger $22 a share.

Partly as a result of the thorny issues that Meier's actions had posed, the governor formed a task force to draw up an ethics code for the Council. The proposals it finally presented ruled out or placed limits on many of the activities in which Meier had previously engaged. The proposed code would have prohibited Council members from sitting on boards of companies in which the state had made an investment without first obtaining approval from other Council members. To dilute the effect of any one person on the Council, it recommended that members not sit on the Council for more than two four-year terms, and that the chairman not be allowed to hold that office for more than eight years either. (Roger was chairman for thirteen years.) The proposed code also suggested that anyone running for the state treasurer's office not be allowed to accept campaign contributions from any investment management company doing business with the state.

An ethics code very similar to this proposal was finally taken up by a new state treasurer in 1990 and passed by the Oregon Investment Council. The treasurer, Anthony Meeker, said that the reason he worked so hard to make the codes come about was that "the bigger the pot gets the bigger the temptation to do something with the pot. . . . It's important how we conduct ourselves."

In March of 1986, about a year after his fellow Council members had expressed their concern over his decision to accept the board seats, Meier resigned from the Council. The Council's success had made it more visible, and appointments to its board more prestigious. Meier was no longer getting his way as much with his suggestions to the governor's office. More strong-willed individuals were getting appointed to the board and beginning to question Meier's decisions, an intrusion he sorely resented. At the end of one of the Council's monthly meetings, Roger informed the other members of his decision.

The timing of Meier's resignation turned out to be fortunate. KKR was completing its takeover of Beatrice, the largest single corporate takeover yet, and the financial press was writing glowing stories about the financial rewards that the deal would bring to KKR's investors. According to Kohlberg, Meier knew that if he retired, he would be able to become an investor in KKR's funds.

Several months after he resigned, Meier became an investor in certain companies in KKR's portfolio. "It only was after I resigned from the Council that I was able to participate in KKR," Meier explained. "They said, 'Look, Roger, you did a super job for us.' " After all, Meier had directly or indirectly provided an important part of the equity of many of KKR's financings, and he had worked hard to convince managements of local companies to sell their companies to KKR. "A little reward, for Christ's sake," said one financial industry executive familiar with the arrangement. Yeah, added a second, "you helped us once, now we'll help you."

In addition to becoming a KKR investor, a privilege that many would like to have been able to enjoy, Meier was also offered stock in one KKR company at a price that leads one to wonder whether it was a sweetheart deal.

The case involves a company called U.S. Natural Resources, which produced coal and lumber milling machines, that KKR acquired in 1977. Eight years later, in 1985, KKR offered to buy back 225,000 of the company's shares from its investors for $100 a share, or twenty times their original $5-a-share investment.

While that sounds like a nice, tidy profit, in fact, investors who sold their shares back to KKR did so at an inopportune moment. For soon after KKR had completed the transaction, USNR's earnings spurted upward. In 1986, although KKR had projected to investors that the company would earn $3.1 million, it instead earned $7.5 million, in part because of a windfall from a legal settlement.

The following year, KKR changed USNR into what is called a Subchapter S corporation. That meant that instead of the company paying tax on its income and then the shareholders paying tax on their dividends, they would only have to pay tax once, at the individual level. By eliminating one layer of taxation, the earnings generated by USNR were that much more valuable. In 1987, the year that change was made, the company's earnings were $15.5 million, a far cry from the $4.5 million after tax that KKR had projected to its investors at the time that they sold their stock back.

When a company is generating two or three times as much in earnings, and its dividends only have to be distributed to half as many stockholders, the result is a pretty nifty investment. Which is why Roger Meier must have been so happy when Henry, George, and Jerry each sold him 1,000 of their shares in USNR in the fall of 1986 for the bargain-basement price of $100 a share. True, that was the price that KKR had paid to buy the stock back from its original investors in 1985, and as a result of the stock buy-back the company had more debt on its books. But by the fall of 1986, when the three men sold their stock to Roger, it was becoming much clearer that USNR's fortunes had improved, and that because of the impending change to Subchapter S status, its higher earnings would be worth much more. Today, even in a weak economy, a share in USNR could be worth as much as $400, or four times what Roger paid for his investment. That would give him a profit, on paper at least, of $900,000.

Jim Long, an investigative reporter at *The Oregonian*, got wind of Roger's USNR investment in early 1989. When he phoned KKR seeking an interview, his request was denied. Undeterred, he sent George a detailed set of written questions about the USNR transaction. When KKR first responded, it referred only to the "selling shareholders," not making clear that it was, in fact, the firm's three founders who had sold the stock to Meier. In a May 17, 1989, follow-up response to Long's questions, KKR said it was preposterous for anyone to suggest that they would sell stock to Roger for less than they believed it was worth.

"We believed then and believe now that the price was fair and appropriate and there is substantial basis for that belief. It is always difficult to 'value' an illiquid minority interest in a leveraged private company in cyclical industries, but in this case, that relative uncertainty, which is natural, is in danger of unfairly being used to raise questions about entirely proper behavior."

KKR had wanted to state also that Meier's investment could in no way be construed as a "payoff" because he had never asked for anything beforehand. An early draft of the firm's response to Long stated that "we have checked with Messrs. Kohlberg, Kravis, Roberts and Meier. We all emphatically and categorically deny that Mr. Meier ever asked to buy stock in Fred Meyer or any other private KKR company."

Kohlberg, who by this time had separated from his partners, was furious when he learned that George and Henry were planning to commit the three of them to that position. He says he reminded them that Meier had not only asked for Fred Meyer stock while he was still on the Council, but had positively badgered them. In the final memo that Long received, the phrase about checking with each of the three founders was dropped. The response stated simply that "we emphatically and categorically deny . . ."

"The really bad part about this—to put it baldly and succinctly—is that we've given him a windfall," says Kohlberg today. "As I look back on it, it looks like it was compensation for helping KKR get on the map. That's what bothers me about it—and about my part in it."

When Roger Meier resigned, he nominated Bill Rutherford to be his successor as the Council's chairman. Rutherford, a pale-faced Oregonian with an earnest look about him, was then the state treasurer, a position that automatically granted him a seat on the Council. Meier felt that Rutherford was the right person to fill his shoes, but other Council members were not quite so enthusiastic. Although Rutherford eventually won the election for chairman, the 3–2 vote was hardly a ringing endorsement. Carol Hewitt, a powerful Portland attorney, and Charles Swindells, a local trust company executive, both resisted Rutherford's appointment.

Meier's support for Rutherford stemmed from the two years or so that they overlapped on the Council. Rutherford was a man after Meier's own heart. He, too, was thrilled to wake up every morning and find himself suddenly playing in the big leagues. He was no longer a lowly state representative, or an attorney in the town of McMinnville who also helped run his family's store. He was a person sought after by some of Wall Street's finest. He was a player in a world that he would otherwise never have been given access to. He had a cellular telephone installed in his car long before it was fashionable, and by the time he arrived at work in the mornings, he had often checked in with the Council's brokers in London, Frankfurt, and Paris. Among the projects he looks back on with pride are a huge marina and restaurant complex along Portland's riverfront that he persuaded the Council to finance, and the box-office hit *Stand by Me*, which he helped back with Council money.

Like many other state pension fund managers, Rutherford came to view KKR as a partner, an ally. And just as Jim George and John Hitchman had done, he did his best to help his friends at other public funds get involved. He called his good friend Paul Quirk, the executive director of the Massachusetts pension system, for instance, and talked to him about LBOs and KKR. Shortly after, George called on Quirk, and the Massachusetts Pension Reserves Investment Management Board became a full-fledged investor in KKR's 1986 fund, with a contribution of $25 million.

Rutherford liked being a player, but he didn't really have the money to do it properly. His personal finances were limited, and the Council's limited expense account kept him on an extremely short leash. A divorcé who had been left with two kids to raise, Rutherford was finding it increasingly hard to make ends meet on his $52,850 salary. Money started to get tight when his son began attending Stanford, but when his daughter got accepted to Yale, the situation got even worse. "When your kid calls in the middle of winter term and asks if he will be coming back to college next year, it tears at your heart," he told a reporter.[2]

The problem, as he saw it, was that the state did not appreciate or reward those who were doing a good job of managing public employees' money. "We have $12 billion under management and last year we earned $2.25 billion on that money. Ninety-nine percent of the people don't know and don't care. And we're paid less than traffic judges in this state. Who cares? Who notices?" he asked a reporter.[3]

When KKR held one of its annual conferences in New

York City, for instance, and Rutherford got word that it would be held at the ritzy Helmsley Palace Hotel, he realized his per-diem expenses would never come close to covering the hotel bill. In order for Jim George and him to attend the meeting, KKR kindly offered to pay everything over the $100 a day that the Council would cover. In the end, Rutherford's tab for the four days came to $1,323.56. Three weeks later, the Oregon Investment Council voted to commit $600 million to KKR's next fund. Asked several months later by an ethics commission whether he thought his acceptance of KKR's generosity suggested any possible impropriety, Rutherford said no. No one has suggested that Rutherford's vote could be bought for $923.56, but the cozy relationship that had developed between KKR and Rutherford certainly did not make his vision any clearer.

With Rutherford's finances growing tighter and tighter, he began to look for a way out. It didn't take him long to see that his position on the Oregon Investment Council could be a real launch pad. Oregon's $12-billion fund had a great reputation, and he was one of the key players charged with overseeing it. Through his work on the Council, he had developed contacts with some of the top money-management firms in the country, if not the world. Certainly many more than if he had remained a legislator in the state's sleepy capital of Salem, that much was for sure. Rutherford began quietly circulating his résumé and letting people know that he was interested in job offers. Among those he approached for a job, according to Kohlberg, was KKR.

In May of 1987, Rutherford flew from London to West Germany. The trip was at taxpayers' expense, since Rutherford said he was pursuing European investment opportunities on behalf of the Council. Two weeks later, he announced he was resigning from his job to become executive vice president of ABD International, a West German investment-management subsidiary of the large German bank Deutsche Bank. ABD was well known to the Oregon

Council, since it was then under contract to manage $155 million of the Council's money.

The reaction to Rutherford's conduct was swift. "Is he working for us or is he working for them? Is he upholding his fiduciary trust or is he feathering his own bed?" asked Grattan Kerans, a Democratic state senator from Eugene who had opposed Rutherford in the treasurer's election.[4] An investigation was immediately launched by the state ethics commission. It concluded that Rutherford did make employment inquiries while he was state treasurer, but that he had violated no laws. Even so, the appearance that Rutherford had used his position to get a job in the private sector servicing his previous employer was more than other Council members could stomach. Eight months later, the Council fired ABD as one of its money managers. Although several members, when asked by local reporters, declined to link Rutherford's position there to their decision to fire ABD, some were less reticent. "I don't think there's anything in Mr. Rutherford's business background that would qualify him for this [ABD] job," said Council member and former governor Bob Straub. "Therefore I feel there were motives that were less than laudatory in why he was hired."[5]

Another Council member put it even more strongly. "It didn't take all that long to terminate that snake," growled Jerry Drummond immediately after the vote.[6] Rutherford's latest employer is Touche Remnant, a small subsidiary of the London-based insurance and investment firm. Today he sits at the end of a long, linoleum-lined corridor in a small office in Rockefeller Center behind a spotless desk, looking somewhat forlorn.

The Oregon Government Ethics Commission, meanwhile, voted 5 to 1 in favor of proposing legislation that would add the office of state treasurer to the state's revolving-door law. That law requires certain state officials to wait a year after leaving government before they accept a job with a company they had previously regulated.

* * *

Bill Rutherford's tale illustrates the basic vulnerability of many public pension fund managers. He was not venal, he was simply an ordinary public servant thrust into a position of enormous power with no financial rewards to go along with it. He was asked to play in the big leagues on Wall Street, to cavort around Europe's and Japan's fashionable resorts with some of the world's smartest and richest money managers, to taste the good life that four-star hotels and fancy restaurants can offer. Yet he was expected to do so without ever letting it get to him, without starting to feel that he had more in common with those cosmopolitan money managers than he had with thousands of faceless firemen and teachers whose retirement money he was charged with overseeing.

In this environment, a firm that systematically goes around offering to help those who help it, in a manner that is hidden from view, can undermine the integrity of public officials and institutions. The Roger Meier–USNR transaction is not the only example of this. KKR contributed $6,000 to Bill Rutherford's 1984 campaign for state treasurer, according to state election records, when he was running against a Democrat who proved to be an opponent of the state's investments in LBOs. Large though that contribution was, it paled beside the $10,000 given by a little-known entity called DAW Forest Products, a limited partnership controlled by KKR. If one factored in the $5,000 contributed by US Natural Resources and the $5,000 contributed a few days later by PacTrust—both of which were entities also controlled by KKR but whose donations were not necessarily coordinated—the LBO firm would rank as the largest contributor to Rutherford's campaign by far. When Rutherford was asked about KKR's $6,000 contribution, he told a reporter that the donation came late in his campaign and that he was unaware of it until many months later.[7] Rutherford won the election with 677,714 votes, nearly 200,000 more than his opponent.

When the governor's task force was trying to devise its

guidelines on ethics, one principle it settled on was that candidates for state treasurer should not be able to accept campaign contributions from any investment management firm doing business with the state of Oregon. The chairman of that task force, former governor Robert Straub, who helped pass the original "prudent person" investment standard for the Council, said that the commission felt very strongly about that particular recommendation. The fund is so large and has such great economic power, he told the Council, that they felt the treasurer's office should be insulated against any suggestion of a conflict of interest.

Largely through George's efforts, KKR became even more entwined in Oregon politics. The firm seemed particularly keen to finance candidates for the governor's office, which happens to be the source of appointments to the Council board. In 1986, KKR seemed at first to be enamored with Neil Goldschmidt, a mainstream Democrat. State election records show that the firm gave him $6,000 in the primary and followed up with a $10,000 check in the general election, which made KKR one of his top twenty supporters. However, somewhere along the line KKR switched sides, for it and its top executives began actively supporting Goldschmidt's opponent, a conservative Republican named Norma Paulus, who Bill Rutherford helped solicit money for, including hosting a fund-raising dinner in New York City, which was attended by many Wall Street brokerage firms.

Other Wall Street brokerage houses such as Salomon Brothers and Shearson Lehman Hutton wrote out checks to Paulus for sums in the $5,000-to-$7,000 range. But KKR's backing was breathtaking. The firm contributed $10,000 toward her campaign, but George personally gave her $5,000 and a top executive in the San Francisco firm, Michael W. Michelson, wrote a check for $2,500. Once again, DAW Forest Products got involved, giving a generous $20,000. With that latter contribution, KKR and the companies under its umbrella became one of a handful of Paulus's largest supporters.

When some of these contributions surfaced in the local press, Rutherford offered a strong defense. "George Roberts," he told a television reporter, "feels very strongly that he has the right under the First Amendment to make contributions to candidates he supports."[8]

Interestingly, KKR's generous campaign contributions in Oregon were not matched in most other large states from which it got funds. The only notable exception is New York, where KKR turned its attentions on Edward Regan, the state comptroller who has sole authority to oversee New York's public pension funds. In June of 1985, KKR began trying to secure commitments for its next fund. That same month, the firm gave $25,000 to Regan, who was facing an election the next year. In the months preceding the election, KKR gave Regan another $25,000, making the firm the second largest contributor to his campaign. (The largest was Milton Petrie, the octogenarian philanthropist.) After Regan won the election, KKR gave him another $15,000.

Regan committed $55 million of New York's pension fund money to KKR's 1986 fund and $370 million to its 1987 fund. In the fall of 1988, the *Daily News*, a New York newspaper, revealed that a special assistant to Regan had written a memo in 1985 outlining an aggressive fund-raising strategy for the comptroller and cited the concept that "those who give will get." Regan told the paper that he never saw the memo and that it was a breach of everything he stood for. Though the issue has continued to dog him, and his opponent in the 1990 election tried to make much of it in her campaign, Regan was reelected to the comptroller's office by a narrow margin.

Perhaps it is merely coincidence that KKR would show such an interest in the public fortunes of a little-known state legislator named Bill Rutherford, whose accession to the treasurer's office gave him a seat on the all-important Council. Or that they would want to contribute heavily to Oregon's governor, who appoints the four other Council members. And perhaps it really does not matter that Roger Meier has probably made millions on his investments in KKR deals. Or that John Hitchman, like Roger Meier, was *also* invited by KKR to invest in deals after he left the Washington Investment Board. It is certainly possible that the investment decisions they made were not influenced in the slightest by their personal ties to KKR or the fact that they later received financial rewards from KKR. But no one will ever know for sure.

FRENZY

As 1983 drew to a close, a year during which KKR bought three more companies and launched its effort to raise a $1-billion fund, the largest ever, Jerry Kohlberg began to have excruciating headaches. He finally went to his doctor, who ran a few tests, and several weeks later Jerry and Nancy got the bad news: Jerry had a tumor called an acoustic neuroma.

In lay terms, that meant he had a growth on his acoustic nerve, which is near and intertwined with those that govern hearing, cheek muscles, tear ducts, and balance, among other things. Although Kohlberg has frequently been described in the business press as having had a brain tumor, the term is misleading because it sounds like cancer. In fact, acoustic neuromas are by definition benign; that is, they are not cancerous. So although the operation to remove the growth was serious because it involved surgery on his brain, Nancy and

Jerry were more worried that he might suffer side effects, such as not being able to move parts of his face afterward.

Kohlberg's assistant at the time, Mary Lou Murray, remembers her boss as being calm and matter-of-fact about the whole thing. He spent the few weeks before the operation going over his work load and dividing it up amongst his partners. Kohlberg's doctors had told him he would have to stay away from the office for several months recuperating, so he was trying to make the transition as orderly as possible. On the day of the operation itself, January 19, 1984, the fifty-eight-year-old Kohlberg came into the office as usual and worked until noon before walking over to Mount Sinai Hospital and admitting himself as a patient.

The day after the operation, Jerry was extremely pale and frail looking, as are most patients who undergo major surgery, but his spirits were high. The operation had been pronounced a success, although he did lose all of his hearing in his left ear.

About six weeks after the operation, when he seemed to be recovering nicely, Jerry and Nancy decided to go down to their vacation house in St. Croix, so that he could spend the rest of his time convalescing in that wonderfully warm and sunny climate. On the plane on the way down, however, Jerry suddenly developed a severe pain in his chest. When they arrived at the airport, Nancy called a friend of theirs who was a doctor and described the symptoms to him. He told her it sounded like a pulmonary embolism and said she'd better get Jerry to a hospital fast. A pulmonary embolism is a blood clot that forms in the lung and constricts the free flow of blood to other parts of the body. Had Kohlberg not gotten to the hospital in time to obtain medication that dissolves such clots, the episode could easily have been fatal.

Oddly enough, it was the embolism, rather than the tumor, that really set Jerry back. It drained him of his energy and stretched his recovery period to close to a year. Jerry had always been something of a fitness freak—playing endless sets of tennis, swimming, and running. He found his sudden inertia and frailty thoroughly depressing. Worst of all, he was still having those debilitating headaches.

On top of his physical troubles, Jerry was growing increasingly concerned about his partners. The day after his operation, Henry had come by to see him. But he never came again, and George, whom Jerry had befriended since he was twenty-one, never visited his ailing mentor once. He and Henry rarely phoned either. Mentally and physically, it was one of the most depressing periods of Jerry's life.

George and Henry were busy. The business was changing—new people were coming on the scene and challenging their turf. They didn't have the time or inclination to sit at the bedside of a sick man. They had to figure out how they could stay on top.

Ironically, the business was changing in large part because of KKR's own actions. The firm had made so much money that others finally sat up and started taking notice. When KKR first started out, it had the field largely to itself. Sure, there was Clayton & Dubilier, a merchant bank that had acquired companies such as Stanley Interiors and a unit of the Harris Corp. And there was Gibbons, Green, van Amerongen, which went on to acquire Budget Rent A Car and the Kash n' Karry food stores. But they were off on their own, buying small to midsize companies and minding their own business. When KKR started to buy, for half a billion dollars or more, well-known companies that were traded on the New York Stock Exchange, *that* became something to talk about.

Up until that point, the trio had worked in relative obscurity. Thanks in part to Kohlberg's extreme reluctance to be interviewed, they had been the subject of only a few short articles in the business press. But just before Jerry went in for his operation, the three decided to cooperate on their first full-blown profile. The article, which ran in *Fortune* magazine in January 1984, was a thoroughly complimentary piece. Entitled "How the Champs Do Leveraged Buyouts," it referred to the three as the leading LBO specialists and trumpeted their 62-percent annual investment returns. Their track record seemed phenomenal. The editors wanted to run the article on the magazine's cover, but at the last minute Kohlberg refused to have them sit for the photo.

Even without their *Fortune* debut, people on Wall Street were beginning to study how the firm made its money. KKR had several different sources of income above and beyond its 20-percent cut of the profits from its investments. The firm charged a 1.5-percent management fee on any money that was committed to it. When Oregon committed $100 million to a KKR pool, for instance, the state would have to pay $1.5 million a year for the privilege of having that money invested by KKR on their beneficiaries' behalf. The money helped pay for such things as rent, salaries, and travel.

But KKR had other sources of funds. It charged the companies it acquired a "retainer" fee for monitoring their performance, and it charged directors' fees for the time its executives spent on those companies' boards. But much bigger than either of those were the investment-banking fees it charged for structuring the terms of a deal and helping to arrange the financing. Historically, that amount came to about 1 percent of the total cost of the transaction. In the case of PT Components, for example, which makes power transmission products, KKR received $2 million for organizing the 1981 acquisition, $200,000 a year for acting as a consultant to the company, and $20,000 a year for each of the four KKR executives who sat on the board as directors.

KKR always noted that it would charge a 1.5-percent management fee in its sales documents, and it frequently stated that it would also charge retainer and directors' fees, but only once, in its 1979 sales document, did it mention that it would be charging the companies it acquired an investment-banking fee. Investors often only learned the dollar amounts of those fees when they were disclosed in financial documents that KKR-controlled companies filed with the Securities and Exchange Commission, as in the above example, or when reporters mentioned the fees in subsequent articles.

At that time, Kohlberg saw nothing wrong with charging an investment-banking fee. In the early years, before any of their deals had been in the pipeline long enough to generate profits, money was tight. The 1.5-percent management fee covered their basic overhead, but it didn't leave them with any money to cover all the legal and accounting fees they incurred on deals that ultimately did not go through. And it left them with no money of their own to invest in the companies they were buying. The 1-percent investment-banking fee was supposed to bear some relation to the expenses KKR incurred in researching and exploring transactions, many of which were discarded before one finally went through. And it was supposed to leave them with a little capital left over.

Investing in deals themselves was an important Kohlberg tenet. He viewed it as a way to ensure that KKR executives had the same interest as their investing partners. He loved to sit before a skeptical investment committee and say, "We make our money with our partners; we have our own money on the line." Indeed, the firm made this point in its marketing literature. It bragged in its 1982 sales pitch that "KKR's approach is different than most of these other funds in that KKR will be investing $5 million of its own capital in the fund, while others invest little or no money of their own." Public pension fund managers devoured that kind of stuff. Staff directors could assure their boards that KKR would be disciplined in its investments since its own money was at stake, too. "This is what gives me respect" for them, Roger Meier said. "Their feet are in the fire! They don't go chipping around with other companies. They put their *own* money in their deals!" But the only way they could get enough money to invest in deals was by charging investment-banking fees.

As KKR's deals began to grow larger, however, that 1-percent investment banking fee came to have less and less to do with expenses and capital and more and more to do with easy money. When KKR bought Dillingham in 1983, for instance, it invested less than a million dollars of its own money alongside the $50 million of its partners' money. Its fee on the $442-million transaction was $4.5 million pretax —enough to pay the expenses of deals that were never culminated and have some left over. By 1985, however, when KKR acquired Storer Communications for $2.4 billion, the numbers were starting to go off the charts. It invested about $2.5 million of its own money, or about three times the amount that it put into Dillingham despite the fact that the Storer deal was five times Dillingham's size. But the fee it charged on Storer was a cool $23 million, far higher than any "dead deal" expenses the firm could possibly have accumulated. According to *Fortune* magazine's annual ranking of biggest deals, it was then one of the largest advisory fees ever charged for an acquisition.

No one ever stopped to question the logic of whether it really took ten times the brainpower to orchestrate a $3-billion deal than it did a $300-million deal, or whether KKR's expenses could really be ten times as large simply because the assets of the company being acquired were ten times the size. As one Columbia University law school professor, Louis Lowenstein, once observed, "Wall Street is about the only place in America that never has to sell its product cheaper by the dozen."[1]

Most observers seem to have just blindly accepted the 1-percent explanation. After all, the money never really seemed to come out of anyone's pocket. It was the company being acquired that wrote the check, and while that company was technically owned by KKR's investors, they never missed it. All they knew was that another investment had just been made on their behalf that would, they hoped, yield still more fabulous returns and make them look even better with their constituents.

It didn't take Wall Street sharpshooters long to figure out that KKR had found a way to make almost obscene amounts of money, with little risk to itself. They started asking themselves some basic questions. Couldn't they do what KKR was doing? Wasn't that their specialty, after all, to see which companies had unrealized values buried within them that could be more valuable to someone else? When a Wall Street firm acted as an adviser on a merger, it might earn a $4-million or $5-million fee, or even $8 million or $10 million if it was a very large deal. But $23 million, that was a *lot* of money! If they did an LBO themselves, they, too, could charge whatever fee they wanted, since the client was essentially captive. Moreover, they would be the ones to share in any upside gain if and when the equity of the company became more valuable.

Many firms on Wall Street started thinking about setting up or expanding their LBO units. The idea had certain risks: for several firms, KKR was their largest single client, their most important source of investment banking fees. Competing with the firm might hurt them badly in the short run. And there was the dicey question of conflicts with their clients. Suppose their LBO group decided to make a bid for, say, a company that made paper cups, and that company turned out to be a favored target of one of their clients. How would they explain themselves?

The event that tipped many firms over the edge was the 1985 bidding war that erupted over the Beatrice Companies, a Chicago-based conglomerate that made everything from Samsonite luggage to salad dressing. Beatrice was a watershed for a number of reasons. In the first place, it marked a significant departure from KKR's previously friendly-only approach. Until then the definition of a friendly as opposed to a hostile takeover was pretty straightforward. If KKR sent a letter to management offering to buy a company and was politely told to get lost, it would get lost. KKR always assured its investors that it would never do a hostile takeover. That was for the likes of gunslingers such as Carl Icahn or Ronald Perelman, not a class act like KKR. And it was certainly not for state pension funds, sensitive political animals who don't want to have to explain why the group they have invested with is behaving in such an unseemly fashion.

In the case of Beatrice, however, KKR rewrote the definition of *hostile*. When management rebuffed its offer, it made it known that it only would accept a no if it came from the company's board of directors. Some who were involved with the deal remember that George wanted to go even further and launch a hostile tender offer for the company's shares without any apologies. But Kohlberg, who was by this time peripherally involved in the firm's activities, nixed the idea, and the three men arrived at this compromise. Still, their new definition significantly changed the takeover landscape. Since most chief executives tend to want to keep their jobs, few were likely to hand over freely the reins to an uninvited outsider. Directors, on the other hand, are in an entirely different position. They are bound by duty, if not by law, to consider virtually any offer that might enhance the value of a company's shares. By persuading people that the directors' acquiescence was the new test of friendliness, KKR managed to alter the rules of the game such that few large companies would be off-limits.

By promoting this new, broader interpretation, KKR vastly expanded the universe of companies for which it would be acceptable to make unsolicited bids. Until then, making a takeover offer for a Fortune 500 company whose management was certainly going to resist was simply not done. Not, that is, if the would-be acquiror did not want to be dismissed by the Establishment as overly aggressive and gauche. Suddenly, KKR was saying it no longer had to wrap itself in the mantle of management's closest ally. It was okay to be the aggressor, the force that had come to keep management honest, the savior of the embattled shareholder who was being taken for a ride by greedy, self-serving managers. KKR had moved a long way from one of its founding principles, which George Roberts had summarized to a reporter in 1979. "We do not do takeovers," he said.[2]

Although it has the appearance of being a philosophical point, KKR's shift had enormous economic implications. For in making Fortune 500 companies targets, KKR had tilted the game decidedly in its favor. Who else, after all, had billions of dollars at its disposal? "Lots of firms can do smaller deals," George boasted to the *San Francisco Chronicle* as the firm was stalking Beatrice, "but over $1 billion, we don't have any competition."[3]

And since bigger transactions meant bigger fees, KKR had positioned itself to become a money machine of vast proportions. When KKR finally acquired Beatrice for $6.2 billion and assumed $2.0 billion in debt, it charged a $45-million investment-banking fee. That was actually a little shy of its usual 1-percent fee, but KKR decided it shouldn't seem greedy. Still, the gasps could be heard in corner offices of Wall Street skyscrapers for days. After all, KKR had had the temerity to go after a Fortune 500 company in what only a few years ago would have been considered a hostile deal, and it was making $45 million pretax before it even did anything with the company. It was more than some investment bankers could bear.

"You don't sit there and watch fees of that magnitude for too long before you say, 'Hey, I can do that,'" says Thomas Saunders III, who was the chief fund-raiser of Morgan Stanley's leveraged-buyout fund. "KKR's success and the fees associated with it were a key reason that many firms on Wall Street decided to go into the LBO business."

To firms that had been wrestling with the thorny question of loyalty to clients or concerns about conflicts of interest, the issue seemed to suddenly become clear: the profits that could be derived from the LBO business clearly outweighed any of those considerations, which they decided, anyway, could be contained. In the heated atmosphere that began to develop in the mid-1980s, those kinds of concerns became secondary. Merrill Lynch had been one of the first to see the potential of LBOs and by 1985 had raised a $400-million fund. It later stepped on the gas and raised $1.5 billion more.

Prudential-Bache Securities got its parent, the insurance company, to give it $800 million to play with. Morgan Stanley was not far behind. Although its first effort in 1985 netted it just $30 million, by 1988, it was up to $1.6 billion, and by 1989, it had topped $2 billion. Shearson Lehman Brothers wanted desperately to get into the game, too. It persuaded its parent, American Express, and an employee fund to kick in a total of $700 million, and Shearson raised another $500 million on top of that. Later entrants included Wasserstein, Perella with $900 million, and the Blackstone Group, with $750 million. And there was always KKR's biggest competitor, Forstmann Little & Co., which kept raising larger and larger funds. When the dust finally settled, about $20 billion had been parceled out amongst ten or fifteen firms for equity investments in LBOs. The academic community, meanwhile, embraced this burgeoning new industry as something akin to the Second Coming. In a widely circulated article that was published in the fall of 1989, Harvard Business School professor Michael Jensen praised the disciplinary force of high leverage and credited LBOs with signaling the eclipse of the ineffectual public corporation.[4]

But while Henry and George's actions had a lot to do with the burst of activity, the new arrivals made their lives vastly more complicated. Gone were the days when KKR could circle around a company, carefully inspect its financial details, make an offer, and then negotiate a final price with management and directors that would be slightly higher than its original offer but not significantly so. Now, every time KKR bid on a company, two or three others would try to muscle in, too. KKR went from dictating its own terms to being just one of many bidders in an auction.

As anyone who has ever been to an auction knows, the person who has the most money and is willing to spend it wins. In the mid-1980s, thanks to its carefully cultivated ties to the public pension funds, no one had more money to invest as equity in companies than Kohlberg Kravis Roberts. George's days of courting the Roger Meiers, the John Hitchmans, and the Bill Rutherfords of the world had really started to pay off.

George and Henry did have a choice. They did not have to throw themselves into the takeover frenzy with such abandon. There were, in fact, some people who felt it made more sense to hang back and wait for others to get carried away, make their inevitable mistakes, and be forced to retreat to the sidelines. Then, still armed with incredible firepower, they would be ready to come in for the kill. William Simon, former treasury secretary, did just that. He dropped out of the LBO market altogether in 1986, complaining of too much competition and excessive prices, and only announced his return in 1991, after the frenzy had subsided. In the intervening years, he made a nice fortune bobbing in and out of the unstable market for savings and loan institutions. KKR's chief competitor, Teddy Forstmann, followed a similar strategy. He was frequently criticized in the business press for refusing to engage in bidding wars and, as a result, for not buying a company for two years. However, when the dust finally settled, his was one of the only large firms left standing. In 1990, Forstmann Little was able to acquire two major companies—General Instruments and Gulfstream Aerospace—with virtually no competition, and find the financing to complete the transactions—a major feat considering the banking industry's newfound wariness of highly leveraged transactions.

Everything about Kohlberg's behavior suggests that he, too, would have chosen this more conservative strategy. However, Kohlberg was still out of action, distracted by headaches and unable to work a full day. He kept trying to come in to the office, but he'd missed so much and was still feeling so drained and physically unwell that he would often have to leave around lunchtime. Left to their own devices, his two young stallions were inexorably drawn in the opposite direction.

Instinctively, these two men had spent their lives priming

themselves to win. And they were not about to change now. Though they would later deny it, doing deals became much more important to them than doing *good* deals.

Winning had always been something of an obsession for George. Even his close friend Mike Wilsey is amused by how tenaciously George clings to victory, or at least the appearance of victory. George likes to make bets, not on horses or dogs, but casual bets with friends over obscure facts or predictions. He'll bet you that Saddam Hussein will be killed in a coup by such and such a date, or that the Mets will win the World Series. But if he's wrong, he will go to great lengths to reconstruct the bet in such a way that he still comes out the winner. If Saddam survives a coup attempt, he'll say that he had only predicted he would be attacked. Or if the Mets lose, it will be because a certain pitcher twisted his arm and George had only said they would win if he was on the mound, or some such modification designed to extricate him from having to admit that, heaven forbid, he had lost.

"He's lost bets with people, and even with me, and he manages to rationalize in his mind that he hasn't lost it. And he doesn't pay it," says Wilsey, unable to suppress a giggle at his friend's somewhat juvenile behavior. "If he lost the bet, his understanding of the bet will vary or the circumstances will vary, or he'll get back to me and I'll never hear from him. One sign of an intensely competitive person is that it's important to win, and betting is one indication of it."

George is always trying to find a way to manufacture a victory out of a defeat. John McLoughlin, his lawyer, remembers the frantic bidding war that KKR got into for Gulf Oil in 1984. The firm was still regarded as somewhat new to the game and perhaps a bit out of its league. After round-the-clock strategy sessions amidst intense competition with the other bidding group, Standard Oil of California, which was staying at the same hotel, George was finally asked to make his twenty-minute presentation to the board. Afterward, he, McLoughlin, and the rest of the KKR team retired to a conference room in Gulf's Pittsburgh headquarters.

Over the next several hours, Marty Siegel, their investment banker, played cards with some of his team from Kidder Peabody, while George and the rest sat and stewed. Finally, they received a call from the chairman of the board summoning them to his office. They figured the news would be bad, since the chairman had not indicated that they would be meeting with the special committee of directors on the board, as the winner almost certainly would do. The chairman made some remarks about how impressed the board had been with their presentation and the quality of their analysis, but in the end he said he was sorry but they had decided to sell the company to the other bidder.

The chairman finished by saying he was so impressed, he'd like to shake George's hand. George, never skipping a beat, grabbed the man's hand and immediately informed him that since the Federal Trade Commission would almost certainly force the new owner to shed some of the company's divisions to avoid antitrust violations, he'd like to put in a bid for those divisions right away. The chairman, his hand still being pumped by this intense young man, was completely taken aback. "He wins well, but he does hate to lose," says McLoughlin, laughing as he recalls the incident. "George spares no effort if a deal hangs in the balance. He never stops thinking. He never stops thinking."

Indeed, if you ask George what companies he's most proud of having helped grow, he'll tell you that what he really cares about is not so much the company's operations but the kick he gets from proving that a deal can get done when skeptics say it can't.

George prides himself on his persistence, on never giving up. He enjoys telling a story about KKR's purchase in 1983 of Golden West Broadcasters, which owned KTLA, a large independent television station in Los Angeles. A friend introduced him to the company, and after taking a close look, he decided KKR should buy it. Negotiations for the company ensued over the next several months.

Just when George thought he was close to completing the deal, he got a phone call from KTLA's top lawyer thanking him politely for his interest and hard work, but informing him that the company had decided instead to do a deal with Capital Cities, the media giant run by Tom Murphy.

George was incensed. "I said, 'You can't do that.' He said, 'What do you mean?' I said, 'Look, we've invested a lot of time and effort and money in this.' I said, 'You can't sell it out unless you at least listen to me.' And he said, 'Okay, we owe you that.' And literally, Tom Murphy was down in L.A., ready to sign the deal with him. So we went down and I stayed there till eight o'clock that night, and we worked out a deal. We wound up making a deal to buy it for much better terms for them, the sellers, than we had originally [planned]," George says with a hearty laugh. "But we at least worked it out."

George left the meeting elated. It was one of those crisp fall days that can make any urban jungle seem so much more civilized. As he was walking to the garage to pick up his car, he decided the evening was so nice and his news so good that he would stop off at a pay phone and call his cousin Henry. "I said, 'I've got good news and bad news for you.' He said, 'What's that?' I said, 'Well, the good news is, we've got a deal to buy KTLA.' He said, 'That's great!' I said, 'The bad news is, we've just paid a record price for any single television station ever sold, and,' I said, 'the only asset we have is some antenna on top of a mountain, because they don't own anything else.' "

The two cousins laughed heartily at the seeming absurdity of it all. But after he hung up, George got to thinking. Not about how he had just thrown around a lot of somebody else's money for an asset that was hard to nail down, but about how different the outcome might have been if George had not been George. "What would have happened if I had said, 'Well, okay, we lost.' If I hadn't been incensed enough to insist on a meeting?" George thinks one reason KKR has been so successful is that he and Henry have always refused to back down in the face of long odds.

Winning is paramount, and George will work and work and work at it until he finds a way. His greatest asset is his ability to remember and manipulate numbers. Friends say he will sit through endless meetings and never take a note. But ask him three years later about the interest due on a particular 16-percent note, or the research budget for a particular product at one of the seventeen companies KKR owns, and he will give you chapter and verse. Guests arriving at his home will often find George sitting alone in a room, staring out into space. He is not daydreaming, he is engaging in mental juggling: trying to figure out if he can take one figure from this column and move it to another, increase the equity, take out some debt, cut capital spending in this company and increase the marketing campaign, anything that will enable him to stretch the limits just that much further. "We're not afraid to go try something," says the indefatigable George. "We're not afraid to try to bite off, a lot of times, more than people think that we can chew."

Henry is no different. "I've always been the kind of person, as is George," he says, "that the word *can't* isn't even in our vocabulary. You know, I tell my children exactly the same thing. I say, 'Just take that out of your vocabulary, just forget about it.' " The more Henry thinks about it, the more wound up he gets. Suddenly, it's as though he's been transported into a meeting with other KKR executives. " 'Don't tell me you can't do it, don't tell me the market's not big enough! We're going to figure out how to do that.' . . . We were prepared to push and be creative and create new securities and just take the attitude, don't take no for an answer. Other firms may not have been that way. Look at what happened to Gibbons Green. They bought a few companies, and sort of, so what? Look at Clayton, Dubilier—yeah, they made some nice money, but sort of, so what?

"We always took the attitude we want to be on the cutting edge," said Henry. "We were the *first* ones to do a tender offer of a public company as an LBO. We were the *first* ones to do a billion-dollar deal. When we bought Houdaille in 1979 for $350 million, everyone said, 'You can't get that done.' . . . I say, 'I don't know till we try, but we're going to try, we're going to find it somehow.' We had senior bank debt, we had senior notes from an insurance company. We had senior subordinated, subordinated, junior subordinated, two classes of preferred stock, two classes of equity, and warrants. And if we could have thought of another class of security, we'd have come up with that one, too."

George and Henry approach life with totally different styles and personalities, but they both end up at the same place. "We'll go skiing and George will always go with the instructor," says Wilsey, who knows both men well. "He will ski the whole day, the whole time with the instructor. He'll never leave the instructor. He follows him. He does whatever he says. He's a great perfectionist. He's dedicated and he's a great learner. He'll take instruction. And he's controlled when he skis. Henry, on the other hand, goes like hell. It's very important to be pushing a little bit, pushing the limit. And George is very controlled. He wants to master it."

Wilsey saw the same patterns when they went fishing. "Everyone else went off and did their own thing. And George stuck with me and I taught him how to fish. He's very patient, trying to learn. Now I'm going to go fishing with Henry, and I'm sure Henry's going to charge off, and I'm sure it's going to be important to catch the most fish."

Henry wants to be the biggest, the best, the winner, and he will risk a lot to achieve it. George will study the problem to death, until he figures out how to dominate it. George would face far fewer challenges were it not for Henry's hell-bent nature always putting the two on the line. But Henry might fall flat on his face if his cousin were not always standing there right behind him, rooted to the earth, ready with the sure, clever answer. Separately, the two might not have succeeded to nearly the same degree; together, they present a powerful, unified front.

"It has been the most wonderful relationship—I wouldn't trade that for anything," says Henry of his cousin George. "He is closer to me than anybody in the world."

George's mother, Carolyn, thinks that "their relationship is one of the most unusual I have ever heard of or read about. It is almost unreal. Leanne [George's wife] and I have talked about that. And my daughter and I have talked about it. They tell each other things, and it's like putting money in the ground and covering it up. I mean, it never goes any further. They are close, not just in business, but in talking about their personal problems." Neither she nor her daughter-in-law, Leanne, ever get anywhere when they try to discuss Henry's personal life, or if they make the mistake of weighing in with even the mildest of criticisms. George will rise to Henry's defense with such fury that they quickly realize they have trespassed into some forbidden territory. "Henry feels the same way about George," says Carolyn. "They're closer than most brothers."

Wilsey thinks they're even closer than that. " 'Brothers' doesn't do it justice, because a lot of brothers don't get along. George [Kravis] and Henry are not a lot alike, they hardly ever get together." A better way to describe Henry and George's deep bond, their almost eerie intuitive closeness, says Wilsey, is that they are like twins.

With Jerry still out of commission, the "twins" were left to figure out how to respond to the whirlwind of takeover fever that was starting to encircle them. Corporate raiders were becoming a commonplace phenomenon; names such as Ivan Boesky and Boone Pickens were dominating the headlines. More and more companies were being whispered about as takeover targets, and there were other leveraged buyout groups out there with other people's money to fling about.

George and Henry had a choice, but they could not stop themselves from entering the fray. And if they were going to play, they had to win. They were fortunate in having the largest pool of equity with which to make bids for companies. But they needed more than that. Takeover financing generally consists of three parts. The foundation, a company's permanent capital, consists of equity, which is the riskiest because investors only make money if a company is successful and generates earnings, which it then distributes to its stockholders in the form of dividends. Thanks to the public pension funds, equity was not KKR's problem.

Another component of financing is senior bank debt, which is usually considered the least risky because it is secured by the assets of the company and is therefore senior to the claims of other lenders. Banks in those days were so keen to engage in any kind of corporate lending—anything that would diminish the impact of all those soured third world loans—that it was relatively easy for an LBO firm to get billions of dollars of bank loans. It was *particularly* easy in KKR's case because the firm had aligned itself early on with some of the country's biggest banks, which were investors in its funds.

The hardest piece of financing to come up with was the slice in between the equity and the senior loans, called subordinated debt. Its name stems from the fact that the subordinated lenders' claims on the company are lower or subordinate to those of other lenders; they only get their money back if the others are repaid first. In exchange for taking on that greater risk, the subordinated lenders receive a higher interest rate on their money than other lenders do.

Historically, insurance companies rather than commercial banks tended to be the main source of subordinated debt. The scarcity of subordinated lenders put the insurance companies in a strong position vis-à-vis buyers; they were able to impose restrictions on the way a company was financed or the way it used its cash to make sure that those acquiring companies would behave conservatively.

Up until the mid-1980s, Wall Street financiers figured they had no alternative but to rely on insurance companies because it would be too difficult to interest investors in the general public to provide funds for such a risky purpose. But that was before Drexel Burnham Lambert and Michael Milken came along. They persuaded the public that this form of debt was really no more dangerous than any other. Milken argued that if enough different companies issued subordinated debt, and a big enough market developed, there would be sufficient diversity to minimize investor risk. If there was a downturn at a fiber-optics company, for instance, it wouldn't necessarily mean that a new sneaker manufacturer would have problems at the same time. Enticing investors with 16-percent to 18-percent returns on "junk" bonds, as they came to be known, Drexel's salesmen started pushing their concept. Over time they found enough savings and loan associations and mutual fund managers who were hungry for high-yielding bonds that they were able to promulgate an entirely new market. By the end of the 1980s, that market had grown to $200 billion. In effect, what Drexel had done was uncover a vast and untapped source of investment dollars over which it exercised virtual control.

KKR may have had access to plenty of equity and bank debt, but the firm could not have been the highest bidder in a corporate auction without the help of Drexel Burnham Lambert. Over the next few years, an important alliance developed, in which Drexel helped raise an estimated $20 billion for KKR, making Henry and George one of if not *the* most important of Drexel's customers.

Through its control over the junk bond market, Drexel was at the center of two distinct hubs. Off on one side were a group of investors who profited from companies that were about to be taken over: men such as Carl Icahn, Ivan Boesky, and Saul Steinberg, who raised money in Drexel's junk bond market, some of which was used to buy stock that they considered undervalued. On the other side were the institutions that actually bought the junk bonds—the mutual funds and savings and loan institutions that were looking for high-yielding investments. Milken's genius lay in uniting these two groups using Drexel as the conduit. It may have seemed as if Carl Icahn bought TWA, for instance. But deals such as that were often possible only because high-flying thrift institutions like Columbia Savings and Loan stood ready to buy the junk bonds used to finance the transaction.

Just as a factory needs parts to keep coming down the assembly line, so, too, Drexel needed takeovers to keep the system it had erected running at capacity. The picture that emerges from the government's lengthy investigation of Drexel and Milken is one where Milken worked in concert with arbitrageurs such as Ivan Boesky in a way that helped put companies "into play." As the government states in Milken's presentencing documents: "The Boesky Organization presented Milken with the opportunity unlawfully to influence and manipulate the equity securities markets, particularly in mergers and acquisitions, and thereby enhance Drexel's ability to consummate and profit from such transactions."[5]

It cited as an example Harris Graphics, a printing company that Milken and other Drexel employees owned shares of through a Drexel partnership. In May 1985, the government alleged that Milken encouraged Boesky to start buying shares in the company. "Milken told Boesky that he wanted the Boesky Organization to buy more than 5 percent of Harris Graphics' common stock, that he would guarantee Boesky against loss on the position, and that he would share any profits with Boesky 50%-50%." Meanwhile, the firm's junk bond department acted as an informal adviser to another company, AM International, that was considering making an offer to buy Harris.

In September, the government continues, "Milken directed Boesky to increase the Harris Graphics position to more than 5 percent and to file a Schedule 13D." (A 13D is the document investors have to file with the Securities and Exchange Commission when they acquire more than 5 percent of a company's stock.) By October, Boesky owned about

8.4 percent of the company's shares. And by May of the following year, Harris and AM International had decided to merge. The government's conclusion: "Milken used the Boesky Organization to effect the corporate destiny of Harris Graphics. Because of Drexel's client relationship with Harris Graphics' management, Drexel could not take overtly hostile steps to force the sale of Harris Graphics. Through his illegal arrangement with Boesky, however, Milken was able to 'put Harris Graphics into play,' and create an opportunity for undisclosed trading profits."[6]

In November of 1986, Boesky pleaded guilty to one felony count of manipulating securities and agreed to cooperate with the government in its investigations. Milken pleaded guilty in April 1990 to six felonies, one of which was a conspiracy to commit illegal trades with Boesky. In his guilty plea allocution, Milken acknowledged only that "there were other accommodations of a similar nature between the Boesky Organization and Drexel, some of which were wrong." At the time, he did not offer any details, but prior to his sentencing, Milken admitted that he had committed unlawful acts with regard to Harris Graphics.

Clearly, to the extent that Milken and Drexel encouraged certain investors to accumulate large amounts of shares in companies threatened by takeovers, they helped make deals happen.

That was good business for Drexel, but it was also good business for KKR, since the mere rumor that an investor with ties to Drexel was skulking around the periphery of a company, buying its stock, was often enough to make a chief executive run for his poison pills and other self-defense mechanisms. The latter often included falling into the arms of a friendly "white knight"—which was where KKR came in.

Unfriendly takeover situations provided some of KKR's best opportunities. As Henry once explained, "There are several ways that KKR will find companies. . . . One way is we do our own in-house analysis of companies that we think are attractive; undervalued situations that could become an attractive takeover candidate. The second way is that many companies are put into play by hostile raiders, and the managements will come to us as a white knight to try to keep the company independent."[7]

Because of its ties to investors such as Boesky, Drexel was in a pivotal position as far as KKR was concerned. And because of the intensive use that KKR made of Drexel's services, many people in the Wall Street community have wondered about the relationship between the two firms: was the alliance an unholy one?

Certainly, the pattern of transactions between KKR and Drexel is interesting. It is clear that KKR benefited from Drexel's relationship to Ivan Boesky and Martin Siegel, whose interest in companies seemed to coincide with takeover activity. And it is clear that Drexel enjoyed financial rewards from its KKR relationship that exceeded Wall Street norms. Milken, in turn, passed some of those outsize rewards on to particularly loyal bond-buyers, many of whom kept them for their personal benefit, rather than the benefit of the organizations they were managing. Far from objecting to this apparent reward system when it came to light, KKR seemed almost nonchalant.

The best example of the Drexel-KKR relationship involves Storer Communications, a Florida-based cable TV concern. In early May of 1985, KKR made an unsolicited offer to buy Storer for $75 a share plus a package of other securities. At around $2 billion, it was the largest leveraged buyout deal ever proposed. KKR immediately turned to Drexel to help line up the financing. By July 1, while all the details were still being ironed out, rumors began circulating that another company had decided to make a run at Storer, too. The interloper turned out to be Comcast Inc.

According to the government's indictment of Milken, from about July 8 until about July 16, Milken caused Ivan Boesky's organization to buy about 124,300 shares of Storer stock, with a secret agreement that any profits or losses on those shares would belong to Drexel.[8] On July 16, Comcast did indeed come in with an offer to buy Storer for $82 a share plus additional securities. Several days later, Boesky filed a disclosure document with the SEC stating that it had purchased more than 5 percent of Storer's common stock. One could certainly speculate that the arrival on the scene of an arbitrageur—whose business is to speculate on the outcome of takeovers—simultaneous with a competitor interested in swallowing Storer whole, would help persuade Storer to come to terms with KKR, a friendlier bidder that might leave Storer's management in place. At the end of the month, Comcast raised its bid to $83.50 plus other securities. Determined not to lose its prey, KKR immediately countered with an offer of $90 a share, plus securities, and shortly thereafter, upped its bid again, to $91 a share, plus other securities. Comcast said enough and withdrew, leaving KKR the undisputed victor.

The fact that KKR had gone from $75 a share to $91 a share in a matter of weeks didn't seem of much import. In those days, no one worried much about whether a company could actually support such high debt levels. There was always some analyst who, when asked, could generate a new set of financial projections that would show that a company could make enough money to meet its interest payments. In reality, however, as prices for companies were bid into the stratosphere, it became harder and harder for companies to generate enough earnings to meet their interest payments. At the start of the decade it was rare to see a company with earnings that were less than two times its interest payments. By the end, it was considered normal for companies to be acquired with so much debt that they could not meet their interest payments without selling assets.

Even in the overheated atmosphere of the mid-1980s, KKR's $2.4-billion price tag for Storer was considered steep. It amounted to about $1,000 per cable subscriber, a figure that a KKR executive, commenting later on the transaction, acknowledged was "clearly pushing the market at that time." When asked whether he was concerned that KKR was paying too much for the company, the executive, Theodore Ammon, replied, "I was concerned. I think it's fair to say a number of people in the firm were concerned."[9] But not so concerned that they weren't willing to give it a try.

After all, KKR had Milken. And he viewed it as a creative challenge. Undeterred by the prospect of financing the largest LBO ever, Milken and his team came up with a smorgasbord of securities: there was equity, senior subordinated bonds, senior zero coupon bonds, and "pay-in-kind" preferred stock, which meant that instead of getting dividends, investors would receive more preferred stock. Storer was the first occasion on which Milken and his team decided to try and sell such a huge quantity of pay-in-kind preferred stock to the public at large.

The deal was a stretch, as everyone involved in the transaction knew. And so Milken told Ammon and others at KKR that they would also have to offer some form of additional inducement if they wanted to make sure they had takers for all these billions of dollars of securities. It was the same idea as a bank's giving their customers a toaster every time they invested $10,000 in one of the bank's certificates of deposit. The inducement that Milken proposed were warrants—securities that Drexel would sell for the nominal price of 7.4 cents a share, which could later be converted into Storer shares at $2.05 a share. The idea behind this was that Storer's shares were worth much more than $2.05 a share, and that the higher the stock went above that price, the more each warrant would be worth. In the financial industry, warrants are sometimes known as an "equity kicker." In layman's terms, they could be thought of as a souped-up, high-octane version of stock that was being sold to particularly cooperative bond-buyers for a song.

In the end, Drexel persuaded KKR to offer warrants for 32 percent of Storer's stock, which meant a corresponding reduction in the amount of the company that KKR's own investors were getting for their money. Initially, KKR agreed to sell these warrants for the nominal sum of $10 million, but Milken called at the last minute and said that actually it would be nicer if they gave them away for free. Ammon balked and they settled for $5 million. Still, provided the company didn't go under, the owners of those warrants got an awfully sweet deal. (As it turned out, the company did well and Storer was sold three years later, reaping KKR's equity investors an annual return of around 50 percent.) KKR and its investors had paid $218 million for 51 percent of the company's equity. The warrant holders were paying $5 million for 32 percent. Asked several years later why KKR would have given Drexel total discretion over the disbursement of such an important piece of the company, Ammon acknowledged that the priority was to get the deal done.

And that was precisely what Michael Milken proceeded to do. Milken by this time was held in awe by many dealmakers for his ability to finance virtually anything and the maniacal intensity with which he pursued every detail of every deal. Most observers assumed that the financial reward that he and Drexel received for their hard work came solely from investment-banking and underwriting fees.

But beginning in late 1987, it became clear that their remuneration was much more complicated. Several SEC disclosure documents filed then and in 1988 showed that most of the high-octane warrants that had been issued to induce bond buyers to finance Storer, as well as Beatrice, had ended up in the hands of Drexel executives and, more particularly, Michael Milken. Most of the warrants that weren't held by Drexel executives, moreover, had ended up with particularly loyal Drexel bond buyers. And, according to testimony given during the Milken hearings, several of them had not put the warrants into the accounts of their customers, whose money they had used to buy Storer securities, but into their own personal accounts. The government's prosecutors tried to suggest that this was a deliberate system of rewards, while Milken's lawyer, Arthur Liman, said they had not proved that there was any quid pro quo. Shortly after the hearings ended, two of the individuals who were said to have kept warrants indirectly for themselves pleaded guilty or settled SEC charges relating to violations of securities laws.

When the news of the warrants' whereabouts first broke, KKR executives let reporters know they were furious with Drexel's behavior. Their dismay was certainly not surprising, for in keeping most of the valuable warrants for themselves instead of distributing them to buyers of the company's hard-to-sell securities, it appeared that Milken and other Drexel employees had taken KKR—one of its most important clients—on a very expensive ride. Since Drexel did not seem to need the warrants to sell the Storer securities, KKR and its investors could have kept that 32 percent of Storer for themselves and been at least $225 million richer. That was the amount that Drexel executives were estimated to have garnered in profits from the Storer warrants. Even now, George appears to become enraged when asked if he feels betrayed by behavior like this. "You're damn right we do," he exclaims. "It's unforgivable!"

During Milken's sentencing hearing, however, evidence was given that suggested KKR executives were not quite so ignorant of the warrants' whereabouts as their comments implied. A pension fund manager at General Electric, Aubrey Hayes, was called to the stand to testify on conversations he had held with Drexel executives during the financing of Storer. In front of a packed courtroom, he described a meeting at GE's headquarters that was attended by both a representative of Drexel and a representative of KKR, whose name he could not recall. At that meeting, he says he told them that GE would consider buying some of the Storer securities, but that he would be much more inclined to do so if some warrants could be made available.

"I asked specifically during this meeting if there would be equity participation [warrants] for the bondholders in this deal," said Hayes under oath. "Do you recall what response you received?" asked the government prosecutor. "I was told that the deal was going along very nicely and there would not be any equity available."[10] In other words, shortly before the Storer deal was to be financed, a KKR executive sat at a meeting and listened to a Drexel representative tell an investor who might have bought more of the securities that were proving difficult to sell that no warrants were available. Yet that same KKR executive, even if he were only moderately familiar with the deal, surely should have known that Drexel had secured 32 percent of the company from KKR for precisely that purpose.

Ammon, the KKR executive who was in charge of the Storer deal, said on the stand, when it was his turn, that he only began to suspect that Drexel executives might own Storer warrants when he learned in mid-1987 that they ended up with over 80 percent of the warrants in the Beatrice deal. (It was a similar situation to Storer—KKR had offered to sell 24 percent of Beatrice in warrants for the nominal sum of $7.9 million, in order to provide a "sweetener" to bond buyers. The profits on those warrants were later estimated to be worth over $275 million—most of which ended up in the hands of Milken and a few of his closest allies.)

"What did you do when you made that surmise?" asked the government attorney about Ammon's suspicions regarding Storer. "I can't recall if I specifically did anything other than just raise the question with some of the people at Drexel as to where the warrants went and where they went in Storer," said Ammon. It was a surprisingly bland reaction from someone who had just learned that he and the investors who had entrusted their money to his firm had been deprived of hundreds of millions of dollars.

Later, Ammon said he discussed the issue with Milken's right-hand man, Peter Ackerman. Ammon said Ackerman told him that Drexel executives deserved the warrants because they had risked some of their own money to make the deal happen by buying a large portion of the preferred stock and holding it for several days. "What was your response to Mr. Ackerman?" the government attorney asked Ammon. "We had a fairly vitriolic exchange, and at the end of the day we agreed to disagree. He saw it one way and I saw it slightly differently," he said. Again, a seemingly relaxed way to resolve a dispute over $225 million that went to Milken and his circle of favored investors.

If KKR executives were mad at Drexel and Milken for having received $500 million in profits that might instead have gone to themselves and their own investors, they did not show it. Long after the revelations about the Beatrice and Storer warrants, KKR continued to use Drexel Burnham for all its financings—indeed it *insisted* that Drexel be used in RJR Nabisco, over other investors' strenuous objections. "We continued to use Drexel because they were the best at what they did. There was nobody that could come close to them," said George. KKR also continued to pay Drexel hefty underwriting fees for its services. But most important, Ammon confirmed in his testimony that KKR continued to give Drexel large equity interests in companies KKR was acquiring: 5 percent of Jim Walter, 7 percent of the recapitalization of Marley, and 25 percent of a company called IDEX, of which Drexel kept only 6.5 percent.

Indeed, Frederick Joseph, Drexel's CEO, testified during the Milken sentencing hearings that KKR did not seem at all upset over the issue of the warrants. He recounted a conversation he had with Henry in December of 1989, long after the warrants controversy had surfaced. According to Joseph, Henry "said to me that some people think he should be troubled, or he should do something about Drexel's affiliates' purchases of as much equity as they ended up with on Storer and Beatrice, but in substance that he thought that was baloney and sort of waved it off."

Storer and Beatrice were not the last transactions that aroused suspicions on Wall Street, or that saw the confluence of these same personalities. In mid-1986, KKR began sniffing around Safeway Stores, the supermarket chain in California. According to news reports, George told Safeway's chief executive, Peter Magowan, that the firm was interested

Ray Kravis in his office. (SARAH BARTLETT)

Henry Kravis (*far left*) in his junior high school
yearbook.

College yearbook photo of
George Roberts.

Jerry Kohlberg (*far left*) when he was in the Navy,
but off-duty at the Copacabana.

Nancy and Jerry Kohlberg
at their wedding.
(RAYMOND K. MARTIN)

The Kravis family on vacation
in Hawaii. *Left to right*:
Henry, Hedi, Bessie, George,
and Ray, seated.

Henry on his thirtieth birthday,
with his gift—a new motorcycle.

Henry, in the middle, wearing hat,
with friends on vacation:
(*lower left*) Charles Rubinger,
Victor Greene (*standing*),
and Thomas Strauss, president
of Salomon Brothers.

Roger Meier (*left*) and
Houston-based investor
Fayez Sarofim (*right*).

Leanne and George Roberts.
(PETER SIMON)

George Roberts in his
San Francisco office.
(*San Francisco Chronicle*,
ERIC LUSE)

Carolyne and Henry
on their way to a wedding.
(ROBIN PLATZER/TWIN IMAGES)

Henry Kravis and Carolyne Roehm at their "Gone With the Wind" theme party in their Manhattan apartment. (*W*, Eric Weiss)

Left to right: Nancy Kohlberg, Jerry Kohlberg, Michael Michelson (another KKR executive), Henry Kravis, Sen. Bob Packwood, and an unidentified woman, celebrating the completion of a documentary film on the Kennedys that aired on a KKR controlled television station. (Robert L. Knudsen)

Left to right: Richard Beattie, George Roberts, Henry Kravis, and Paul Raether, another KKR partner. (*New York Times*, Chester Higgins, Jr.)

Richard and Diana Beattie on vacation.

Nancy and Jerry Kohlberg at their farm in Westchester.

Henry Kravis in his office. (JONATHAN LEVINE © 1988)

in making a bid, but Magowan said the company had no interest in selling. George pressed further, but Magowan again said no.

Soon after, Boesky began buying Safeway's stock, building up a 4.9-percent stake. The next thing that Magowan knew, the Hafts, a Washington, D.C.–based family investment group, announced that they had decided to make a bid for Safeway that would be financed by Drexel. One of their Drexel advisers was Marty Siegel, who later pleaded guilty to an unrelated securities fraud charge. Safeway filed a lawsuit in which it accused the Hafts of working in concert with arbitrageurs and other takeover artists to force the sale of the company.[11]

Magowan later told a *San Francisco Business Times* reporter that "when the Hafts started buying stock, they [Kohlberg Kravis] asked again. We said no again. At some point I changed my mind. . . . I became convinced that the company would fall into the hands of the Hafts if we did not arrange something else."[12]

KKR ultimately succeeded in taking over the company, but shocked everyone on Wall Street by offering to share its prize with the supposed enemy, the Hafts. KKR agreed to sell the Hafts a warrant for $1 million that would give them the option to purchase 20 percent of Safeway for $2.50 a share. The Hafts sold that option back to Safeway several months later for $59 million. Drexel, meanwhile, was given the go-ahead to arrange the financing for KKR's acquisition of Safeway, even though KKR had been advised throughout its negotiations by Morgan Stanley, and Drexel had backed its opponents, the Hafts. Two *Wall Street Journal* reporters who queried this arrangement were told by Drexel and KKR that Drexel was given the assignment because it offered better terms than any other firms. But, the reporters noted in their article that "the Kohlberg Kravis spokesman acknowledges that Kohlberg Kravis didn't approach any other firms."[13] For its underwriting services on Safeway, Drexel earned an $80-million fee, according to IDD Information Services.

* * *

The Securities and Exchange Commission took testimony from both George and Henry in the course of its Drexel investigation, but no charges were ever brought against anyone at KKR or the firm. An initial request for access to that testimony under the Freedom of Information Act was immediately denied. Five months after an appeal was lodged, however, the agency's general counsel finally decided to release portions of George's testimony that were taken in July and October of 1987. The SEC is continuing to withhold transcripts of Henry's testimony on the grounds that "they are presently being utilized by another governmental agency in an ongoing law enforcement proceeding."

The SEC gave KKR an opportunity to justify why George's transcripts should not be released, and after KKR's initial response was perfunctory, the SEC offered the firm a second chance. At that point, the lawyers at Latham & Watkins seem to have taken the issue more seriously, for they filed a more detailed reply and then sought an oral hearing to better state their case. When they were told that such a meeting would have to be on the record and in the presence of a court reporter, they decided not to pursue the idea. In any event, their arguments must have been at least partially persuasive, for although the SEC gave out portions of George's testimony, it agreed to exclude information concerning KKR's "underwriting and financing arrangements" and "reasons for structuring transactions in certain ways," as well as testimony in which George mentions other KKR employees and Drexel personnel who were not investigated or charged with violating federal securities laws.

Despite those limitations, the testimony is interesting, for it shows the agency apparently suspected KKR of compensating Drexel for helping to make the Hafts go away.

In early October 1986, several months after KKR had agreed that the Hafts could have a warrant for 20 percent of the company's shares, the Hafts wrote George a letter making it clear that they were unhappy with their financial arrangements and that they were considering suing Drexel. Indeed, the letter was accompanied by a draft complaint the Hafts had already prepared.

A summit meeting was held in George's office on October 17, with the Hafts, KKR, Drexel executives, and various lawyers in attendance. The session lasted for seven hours, but by the end of the day, two important decisions had been reached. KKR agreed to sell Drexel warrants for 15 percent of the supermarket company. And Drexel agreed to buy back the Hafts' remaining shares in Safeway that they had purchased during their run at the company. Only, the price that Drexel agreed to pay, $66 a share, was quite a bit higher than the $61.60 in debentures and warrants that other Safeway shareholders were going to receive in the second step of KKR's offer.

The SEC officer asked George several times whether he was aware, at the time that KKR offered to sell Drexel warrants for 15 percent of the company, that Drexel had agreed to repurchase the Hafts' shares—the implication being that there might have been some linkage between the two. "Did you have any understanding that it was necessary to reach that agreement with him in order to resolve the problem with the Hafts?" asked Thomas J. McGonigle. "No, I did not," answered George. "You saw it as completely independent?" asked McGonigle. "Right," said George.

The next day, however, the Hafts lawyer sent John McLoughlin, George's lawyer at Latham & Watkins, a copy of the agreement between the Hafts and Drexel in which they agreed to buy back the shares. George continued to insist to the SEC officer that he had no knowledge of the Hafts' arrangement with Drexel.[14]

Drexel ultimately purchased over 90 percent of the Hafts' shares at the agreed-upon price of $66 a share. Interestingly, the transaction took place in London and, as a result, did not have to be disclosed in the marketplace as it would have had the trade occurred in the United States. KKR never disclosed the Drexel-Haft arrangement in its merger documents, a point that seemed to concern the SEC officer.

One other detail emerged during George's testimony that raises further questions about the relationship between Drexel and KKR. The SEC officer told George that Drexel financial records indicated that the firm expected to receive a fee of at least $5 million from a KKR entity for profits relating to its repurchase of the Hafts' remaining position in Safeway. George denied having any understanding of such a payment.

Legal experts said that if KKR did engage in so-called green mail to make the Hafts go away, it would not have been illegal, but KKR might have been obligated to disclose such an arrangement.

At the time of this writing, there was no evidence that the SEC had followed up on either the fee arrangement or the disclosure issue.

HEDI AND CAROLYNE

During the years that Henry was gradually transforming himself into a high-powered dealmaker, he was also undergoing some significant changes in his personal life. Beginning in 1981, he and Hedi started talking about getting a divorce. By this time Henry had been living on his own for about a year in an apartment at 132 East Seventy-second Street. And although the couple had continued seeing each other and occasionally flirted with the idea of getting back together, they never succeeded in overcoming their underlying frustrations with each other. Still, the idea of divorce didn't thrill either of them, according to those who knew the family well. Hedi didn't relish the idea of being a divorced woman in her early thirties with three young children. And Henry was pained by the idea of becoming an absentee father and didn't like having to admit that his marriage had been a failure.

But by the summer of that year, Henry wanted the situation resolved. He made his first concrete proposal: $66,000 a year in quarterly installments for nine years, plus 20 percent of whatever he eventually earned from his share of KKR's 20-percent take of the profits of companies KKR had acquired. He also offered to make child support payments of about $20,000 a year, and to pay the insurance and tuition costs of his kids' private schools and summer camps. In writing to Hedi's attorneys, Henry's lawyer said, "This goes well beyond what Henry had considered doing for Hedi in the past." From their side, this was "a very generous settlement."[1]

But Hedi was not convinced. She would read almost every month about another KKR deal and knew the firm was doing well. And she knew the expense of maintaining an apartment in Manhattan with three children would be considerable. With the concurrence of her well-known divorce attorney, William Zabel, she decided to hold out for more. Sure enough, by the middle of next year, Henry had increased his offer to $84,000 a year for Hedi, with the rest of his previous proposal remaining the same. Hedi still did not consider this sufficient. During the eight years they were living together, she had endured his lengthy absences, attended endless business dinners, and accepted their lack of financial wherewithal while they were building up equity in companies. She refused to accept Henry's offer, and the negotiations turned increasingly bitter. In the fall of 1982, Henry's lawyer, clearly exasperated, wrote to Hedi's lawyer begging that he get his client to turn down the volume.

"Apparently your client has made a conscious decision to burden three small children [seven, nine, and ten] with the terrible charge that their father has totally abandoned them," Angelo Cometa wrote. "Please speak to her again and direct her to have no further contact with Henry. If Hedi will simply stay away and not telephone Henry, she will be advised in advance by others, if necessary, of arrangements made to provide for Henry's visitation. To give the children play-by-play descriptions of Hedi's interpretation of her husband's actions can only lead to disaster. The children know that their father loves them, and contrary to the assertion of their mother, that he is paying all of the expenses of this family."[2]

Instead of being toned down, the battle between the two just kept escalating. Negotiations eventually broke down altogether, and Hedi sued for divorce just before Christmas of 1982.

That must have been too much for Henry. For he retaliated by cutting Hedi off. Despite the fact that she had no other source of income and was staying home with their three young children, Henry simply stopped paying the bills. The food bills from Gristede's supermarket started mounting up; the telephone and utility bills went unpaid until both Con Edison and New York Telephone cut off her service. Dunning letters started coming through the mail; then people started leaving notes on the door to Hedi's apartment. The garage wouldn't let her take her car out because Henry had let the payments lapse. The tactic seemed to work—friends who saw Hedi during this period say she became a wreck.

By early spring, the two were closing in on the final terms of an agreement, according to court documents obtained independently of either party. Henry agreed to raise his annual payment to Hedi to $150,000 a year, not including the annual child support payments. He had also agreed to pay the mortgage on their country house in Westchester, New York, and to give Hedi title to the Jeep they kept there. As for Hedi's share of his stakes in the companies that KKR owned, that was raised from 20 percent of his share to 30 percent.

Hedi was appreciative of Henry's decision to raise her share of his stakes to 30 percent, but she wanted a guarantee that those stakes would amount to something. After discussions with her attorneys and financial advisers, she suggested a floor of $3 million. Henry was willing to agree to that, but asked, in exchange, that she agree to a maximum payment, which he suggested should be $4 million.

As he explained in an affidavit several years later, "I

asked that if she was to have the security of a minimum payment, creating risk for me, since I could not know when and for how much profit, if any, any acquired company would be sold, she correspondingly accept a maximum."[3]

Hedi wasn't sure what to do. She and her divorce team had tried to estimate the value of those stakes, but since they were private companies—and therefore did not publicly disclose their financial status—and since many of them had not been owned for very long, it was hard to come up with realistic estimates. In the end, she told others, she relied on the advice offered by Henry's lawyer, Richard I. Beattie, Jr., a partner at Simpson, Thacher & Bartlett, whom she regarded as a close friend of the family's. She said he assured her that the amounts were fair, and that her share of Henry's stakes would never come to more than $4 million.

Hedi finally decided to accept the agreement. And with the broad brushstrokes finally settled, the two went about dividing up their personal belongings. Henry wanted several paintings and prints, including those his brother, George, had given them. And he asked to keep the Jensen silverware that his parents had given them as a wedding present, a set of cuff links, and his Piaget watch.

Hedi, in turn, had her own wish list. She wanted Henry to lease her a Mercedes-Benz comparable to the one he was then driving. And she wanted to be able to use his Century Club membership until she could get one of her own. Henry agreed to extend her membership for a year, provided she use the club only in the company of their children. He did not want her bringing her guests to his club. Indeed, the club membership was something of a sticking point. Henry had already scuttled Hedi's attempts to join the Republican Party's elite Inner Circle. Although she had been sponsored by Ronald Lauder, a prominent Republican multimillionaire, and Sen. Bob Dole, and had received a welcoming letter inviting her to a dinner on Capitol Hill, she got a very apologetic call from Ronald Lauder several weeks later saying that he would have to withdraw her membership because he now believed her presence would make things too uncomfortable for Henry, who was also an active member. Having been burned once, Hedi insisted that the divorce agreement stipulate that he could in no way oppose her application, either directly or indirectly, to the Century Club or any other club or association.

Relative to this and other issues, their agreement on visitation rights was fairly standard: Henry would be able to have the kids on alternate weekends and share school vacations. And on the basis of these terms, the two finally signed their separation agreement on June 20, 1983.

With his marriage finally behind him, and the traumatic negotiations with Hedi finally over, Henry could get on with his personal life. As a handsome, wealthy, and charming young bachelor, Henry found himself a popular member of Manhattan's swinging social set. He began cutting a wider and wider swath through the glittery round of dinner parties, concerts, and ballets that had become such a mainstay of New York society life. Although he dated a number of beautiful young women, his life took a turn for the better when he met a tall, long-legged brunette named Carolyne Roehm at a Christmas party. Roehm was single, too, having recently divorced her first husband, Axel, a German aristocrat who was a descendant of a chemical-products dynasty. At the time, Roehm was in the midst of launching herself as a serious fashion designer, and nobody's fool, she quickly latched on to a catch as appealing as Henry. "I've had women say to me, 'How do you meet such wonderful men?'" said Roehm, laughing as she explained her secret to a reporter. "You let life happen," she said with a flutter of her hand.[4]

The two made something of a comical couple: at five feet ten and thin as a reed, Carolyne towered over Henry like a gawking heron. To accentuate her long neck and show off her strapless dress designs, she always seemed to stand with her shoulders arched back and her chin jutting forward. But Carolyne Roehm seemed to be willing to do just about anything to get ahead. She was raised as Janey Smith in Kirksville, Missouri, the daughter of a teacher and school administrator. Though Janey was raised in a modest home by parents with modest ambitions, she determined at an early age—she says it was thirteen—to break out. And the escape route she liked to dream about most was the fashion world. "At a very early age, all I did was play dress-up," she told the *Daily News*.[5] One of her favorite stories of her youth is how she saved up her pennies to buy a costume-jewelry tiara. Once she obtained it, she pranced around the house with it on, all day long. Little did she know that she would one day come to wear an emerald, diamond, and pearl tiara necklace that had once belonged to Aga Khan III.

After graduating from Washington University in St. Louis, Janey made her way to New York where she got a job mastering the art of polyester skirtwear for a company that sold clothes to Sears. It wasn't what Janey had had in mind for herself, however, and after several other false starts, she ended up designing sportswear for Oscar de la Renta. Happily, de la Renta was among the primary members of the Nouvelle Society that emerged with a vengeance in the mid-1980s and was chronicled in *W* and the book *Chic Savages* by John Fairchild. De la Renta took a liking to Carolyne and decided to introduce her into his set. She was equally determined to become a part of it. Smith taught herself to cook, to speak French, and to ride horses—all the accoutrements of life as she hoped to know it. "She was very aware of who the right people are," recalls one of de la Renta's assistant designers.[6]

Apparently, the metamorphosis was total, according to a dress designer who knew her both before and after. "She's a different person now . . . a different voice—everything," Victor Costa told the *Washington Post*.[7]

To the extent that it helped trap Axel Roehm, the strategy worked. Janey moved to Germany, joined the aristocracy, and changed her name to Carolyne, the name that her parents had given her at birth but which she had never used. Today, one thing she cannot abide is to have her name spelled the *common* way. "It drives me crazy," she told a Houston-based reporter. "It's Caroline with the Scottish spelling."[8]

Carolyne didn't last long, however, in cold and isolated Germany. It was not what she wanted, after all. So after only eleven months there, she decided to pack it all in, ask for a divorce, and come back to the sanctity of New York. There, her mentor, Oscar de la Renta, welcomed her with open arms and gave her back her job.

Henry met Carolyne at a cocktail party during the pre-Christmas festivities in 1981. At first, the two were just friends. They dated, of course, but both were still recovering from failed marriages, and neither seemed particularly eager to lock themselves into another permanent relationship. Gradually, however, as each of them became more established in their own fields and more successful, the two grew closer. They helped reinforce each other's rise.

With time, Carolyne became more confident of her design abilities and was eager to emerge from under de la Renta's shadow and design her own collection of evening wear. "I always knew I was attracted to expensive clothes," she once explained.[9] After watching Carolyne spend six months trying to interest a group of backers, Henry decided that she had proven her determination and that she would make a good investment. By this time he was not only smitten with her, he seemed to be taken with the access she had gained through the de la Rentas to New York's upper-crust society: Henry Kissinger, Anne Bass, Blaine Trump. It was a far cry from the cluster of mostly Jewish Upper East Side lawyers and investment bankers that he and Hedi had grown so close to over the years. As Henry spent more and more time with Carolyne, darting from one society ball to the next, he became increasingly removed from those old friends. Although they continued to invite him over for dinner and to their parties, he stopped going and never repaid their invitations with ones of his own. His friends began to feel that they made him uncomfortable, that they reminded him of a previous life he was now concertedly trying to shed.

Carolyne and Henry had their formal debut, as it were, in April of 1985. It was the spring fashion show, and Carolyne had designed a series of evening gowns that would have done Marie Antoinette proud. "I'm not out to dress Middle America," she told the *New York Times*, "just that portion that goes to places where they need dressier clothes and can afford them."[10]

The reception to her first collection was wonderfully gratifying. When she walked out on the platform afterward to receive the applause of her cheering admirers, many of whom were investment bankers hoping to do some more business with KKR, the crowd rose to its feet and gave the young designer a standing ovation. She was overcome with emotion, and the tears tumbled down her face. She blew a kiss to Henry, who was seated in the front row. He was crying, too.

The next month, Henry proposed. Carolyne, who had been complaining to Oscar that Henry was taking too long to make a commitment, was absolutely thrilled. "I need to have a man in my life," she once explained. "I don't need a lot of people, but I do need a man."[11] To seal his love, Henry offered Carolyne an enormous diamond. When one reporter couldn't resist asking its size, Carolyne insisted that she had no idea. "Nice girls just didn't ask such questions," she replied coyly.[12]

With the exception of their glaring height difference, the two were the perfect couple. He seemed to love the association with someone as worldly as Carolyne. She seemed to thrive on his wealth and what it could provide for them. Readers of the society pages were treated to a steady diet of Henry's amorous advances—jewels under her pillow, jewels stuffed in her tennis shoes, lengthy and luscious love letters, houses galore. *Fortune* magazine later bestowed on Roehm the title "trophy wife." But they may have gotten it wrong.

Perhaps it was Henry who was really the trophy. Carolyne liked to refer to him as her "Jewish cowboy."

The two were engaged to be married at the end of November 1985. In anticipation of the great event, Carolyne began redecorating the sixteen-room duplex apartment that Henry had acquired for $5.5 million in a fashionable Park Avenue building. Out went all of Henry's tacky modern furniture and those modern-art prints that he had collected with his brother, George. They were all put away in storage. Carolyne said she couldn't relate to them at all. With the help of an expensive Upper East Side decorator, in came the Louis XV furniture, the Regency dining table, the long silk drapes, the Persian rugs, the Renoirs and Tissots, and the enormous painting by Sargent that filled almost an entire wall of their dining room. By the time she was finished, the apartment resembled the inside of a French château—the perfect backdrop for the marriage ceremony of the decade. In the final hours, Carolyne had six thousand flowers flown in from Europe, the windows and stairs hung with garlands, and gold candelabra entwined with flowers for the center of each table, where the 101 guests would enjoy a splendid sit-down dinner. After the ceremony, which was conducted by the Kravises' rabbi from Tulsa, Carolyne, looking ravishing in her black velvet and white lace gown, her hair strewn with lilies of the valley, presided over the evening with aplomb.

The wedding was only the first of Carolyne's many performances. The apartment served as a splendid stage set for advertisements of her evening gowns, which she insisted on modeling for the photographers herself. Magazine readers were treated to photos of Carolyne in a variety of haughty poses: parading in front of her Sargent, pausing coyly in an anteroom with her long, full gown flowing behind her, or draped Marilyn Monroe style over a settee with her brown hair cascading over a pillow. She was the very embodiment of the classical female fantasy. When the *New York Times* decided to do a special issue on the resurgence of formal entertaining, it put Carolyne Roehm on the cover as the arbiter of good taste. There she was, dressed in her signature ball gown, inspecting her exquisitely laid dining-room table for any flaws. Among her dessert suggestions: small meringue nests filled with homemade pistachio ice cream, flanked by frosted grapes. To get the right effect, she explained, her chef dipped the grape clusters in lightly beaten egg whites and then sprinkled them with granulated sugar before refrigerating them on waxed paper for several hours. One must take care not to prepare the dessert too far in advance of the meal, or the sugar will melt. "Carolyne sees herself, I think, as a princess. And she's fulfilled her dream," said Michael Wilsey, a friend of both George's and Henry's.

With his princess by his side, Henry finally had the life he had been prepared for since he was a child. He was a successful businessman; he had a net worth of several hundred million dollars, and now he had the final piece of the puzzle: an accomplished wife who could convey upon them "star" status. She even had the requisite terrier named Pookie. By now, the pain and humiliation of Hedi's rejection was buried deep. Henry was a happy man.

Having remade herself and their apartment, Carolyne began to train her sights on Henry. The couple was within a hairsbreadth of being accepted in New York's most exclusive social circles, but Henry still had a few rough edges. To be more precise, he lacked culture. One of her first campaigns was to train him to appreciate music. Carolyne had always loved opera: "It speaks most directly to my soul," she once told a *New York Times* reporter.[13] Opera had long been considered the true litmus test of good breeding, and Carolyne set out to educate her new husband in this area quickly. She played arias on their stereo constantly, at full blast. And she insisted that Henry and she go to Salzburg once a year for the world-famous music festival. "I know very little about music," Henry admits. "Carolyne has gotten me into it." For the last eight years, he says, they haven't missed a festival: "I love it. I love going to the concerts."

But music was only the starting place. There was art, too. Henry had dabbled in fine art by collecting sporting paintings. But Carolyne told him she couldn't relate to them at all. Classical painting, the Impressionists, that's what he needed to be schooled in—the art of the upper class. It was something Henry knew little about. Indeed, when he was showing visitors around his new apartment just after they moved in, he had to consult an index card in his breast pocket in order to identify the paintings he had just bought and the names of the artists. "The first time we went to Italy together and spent all of our time in museums and churches, Carolyne knew so much and I knew so little," Henry told a reporter from *W*. "Since then we've called on the experts and used them to help us," he said.[14] Henry would go to galleries during lunchtime, to bone up on his new challenge. As he grew more confident, he started making appearances at Sotheby's and Christie's, buying with the aid of a consultant, Robert Moeller, who had been a curator at Boston's Museum of Fine Arts.

These were heady days for Henry—the art, the music, the people. His new wife was introducing him to a whole new milieu. "Carolyne acquired a lot of the aura of almost European royalty. She learned a lot. That's been good and helpful to Henry. . . . Before that, Henry was just business and his kids," said Wilsey.

Though Henry was a diligent student, the transformation would be incomplete without a proper country house. Even before they were married, when Henry was still trying to resolve things with Hedi, Carolyne found the perfect spot. In the fall of 1982, the couple was traversing the Connecticut countryside in search of a weekend retreat when they came across a handsome pre-Revolutionary stone house called Weatherstone in the small but terribly upstanding town of Sharon. When Roehm saw the house, she knew it was "the place." She started running toward it "like a person in a strange dream."[15]

Henry, of course, had to get it for her. And even though he was in the midst of finalizing his divorce settlement with Hedi, and her advisers were combing the earth in search of any and all of Henry's assets, Henry did not let his princess-to-be down. He arranged to buy the house for $1.2 million through a company called Weatherstone Corporation. He reportedly told the broker that if Hedi ever got wind of the deal, he would call the whole thing off. Hedi did hear from some Connecticut friends that Henry had bought a mansion, but though her financial investigators searched town record halls, they could not find his name on any properties. She asked Henry's lawyer Dick Beattie if the reports were true, and claims he said they were not. (Beattie denies keeping anything from Hedi.)

Once Carolyne and Henry's wedding was behind them and the Park Avenue apartment was complete, Carolyne and her decorator turned to their next project. It was a perfect location—sitting perkily on what the locals referred to as Millionaire Row—and not far from the country homes of de la Renta and the Kissingers.

As land became available, Henry gradually assembled about 270 acres. Guests to Weatherstone, which was built in 1765 and is listed in the National Historic Register, drive through stone pillars, up a gravel driveway to the handsome home built of natural quarry stone. There are usually four or five vehicles parked outside, including Henry's Jeep and his motorcycle. Inside is a dark wood-paneled library, a pool-room flanked with elegant corner banquettes, nine fireplaces, and the requisite oil paintings.[16]

While the house is elegantly understated, it is the grounds of Weatherstone that really excel. Henry and Carolyne's involvement with the Central Park Conservancy made them think of remaking the gardens around Weatherstone in that park's image. Carolyne, ever the connoisseur of fine living, knew just the role model: the eighteenth-century landscape designer Lancelot "Capability" Brown, who designed those enormous formal English estates at Kew Gardens and

Blenheim Palace. With the help of a landscape architect, they filled the grounds with a variety of flowers and trees to replicate those in Central Park: primroses, irises, willow, dogwood, beech, and pine trees.

But that was only the beginning. Behind Weatherstone was a hill that rose rather steeply, up about 120 feet. Henry and Carolyne had something more subtle in mind. Their landscape designers suggested that they make it roll gradually and have a waterfall come cascading down gentle steps that would be etched into the side of the hill. "We made points and peaks and valleys and greatly increased the drama of the landscape," one of the designers told a writer from *Avenue* magazine who was writing an article on the project.[17] Henry also wanted his own trout pond, preferably one where it would be easy for him to fish.

For nearly three years, as many as twelve bulldozers and a team of laborers dredged up the earth to fashion the landscape of Henry and Carolyne's dreams. The property now has three lakes and a series of ponds stocked with enough plants and insects for the fish that Henry likes to catch. Through a spokesman, Henry denies that the work was ever that extensive. Though the *Avenue* article was based on interviews with the landscape designers who did the job, it was "so factually inaccurate that it is not worth commenting on," said the spokesman. When pressed for details, he replied, "You don't have the space."[18]

While the land around Weatherstone was being recast, Carolyne and Henry began concentrating on a new barn. In Carolyne's eyes, it was to be just a "simple" barn, "something just a step nicer than a little tin shed to ride inside."[19] After all, the Connecticut winters could be cold, and by this time, Henry, and particularly Carolyne, had become avid equestrians. If they had an indoor riding ring, they could ride and jump fences all year long.

By the time they were finished with it, the simple barn had turned into a six-building, 42,000-square-foot "farm complex." There were the stables—large enough to house their seven horses, including Napoleon, Henry's favorite. There was the gazebo, a simple, wood-paneled room with the required eighteenth-century portrait and a big fireplace. And the centerpiece of the complex: a 200'-by-80' riding ring with a 40'-high ceiling and no columns supporting it, so that guests in the viewing gallery would have an unobstructed view of the riders. To construct such an enormous building without any vertical support struts, the couple hired the firm that engineered the Sydney Opera House. The estimated cost of their new farm complex: over $7 million.

A reporter once asked whether Carolyne had gotten everything she'd ever dreamed of when she was a middle-class girl in Kirksville, Missouri. "Roehm, with typical earnestness, thinks for a minute, as if in prayer, and then lifts her heart-shaped face. 'Yes,' she says softly. 'Yes.' "[20]

JERRY RETURNS

When Jerry Kohlberg finally returned to work on a full-time basis in 1985, it was a strange and different world that he encountered. In the year of his full and then part-time absence, the firm had been turned completely on its head. Corporate management was no longer considered an ally, but a bunch of free riders on whom Henry and George had declared war. CEOs now regarded KKR's advances with suspicion. The firm's financing partners were no longer stodgy insurance companies but the aggressive Michael Milken and Drexel Burnham Lambert. KKR was making money hand over fist from investment-banking fees, a complete departure from Jerry's original intention. And Henry was no longer under his control, but seemed to represent the social-climbing nouveau riche that Jerry despised.

The work atmosphere had changed drastically, too. Henry and George were more assertive, caught up in the swirl of activity that the takeover era had spawned. They were always running off to meetings that Jerry had not been told of, and they seemed to have little time or inclination to bring him up to speed. "When he first went back, he would kid about it. He would say, 'They're having a hard time accepting me back.' But he thought, 'This is inevitable, natural.' He talked about it as a father who is watching his kids grow up and experiment," says Kohlberg's daughter Karen. "He kept thinking, 'Maybe it's a phase, maybe it's because of my operation.'"

Over time, however, Jerry needed to become a part of things again. Regaining his position and authority was an important way to affirm his full return to health and vitality. For Henry and George, however, ceding control was next to impossible. Having run the firm themselves for over a year, they made it clear they found Kohlberg's return intrusive, especially since it came at a time when KKR was engaged in a high-stakes battle against tough new competitors. It was a tense, difficult time for all three; they were each locked in the grip of their own demons: George fiercely committed to winning, or at least to not losing, in the takeover spree; Henry obsessed with promoting his image as a clever and daring dealmaker; and Jerry struggling to reaffirm his abilities after an encounter with his own mortality.

It is at this point that the stories sharply diverge.

The most commonly accepted version of the dispute that ensued between the three, and of Kohlberg's eventual resignation, is that which appeared in *Barbarians at the Gate,* an account of the acquisition of RJR Nabisco by two *Wall Street Journal* reporters, Bryan Burrough and John Helyar. The Harper & Row book, which used the literary device of reconstructed dialogue to give the reader the feeling that he or she was there, quickly became a best seller and earned widespread praise for its readability. It gained further readership through mention in society maven Liz Smith's column, and because of excerpts that ran prominently in the *Wall Street Journal* and *New York* magazine.

In this account, Henry, George, and the firm's other

partners gave a variety of reasons for Kohlberg's departure. But in the main, they cited his age and poor health, implying that his operation left him unable to work or to carry his fair share of the load. "Jerry was older, and he never wanted to work as hard," Roberts is quoted as saying. Paul Raether, another partner, offered an even more damaging assessment of Jerry's capabilities, one that would easily frighten off any investor: "Jerry wasn't always there. He lost his train of thought easily. Jerry doesn't believe it. If you told him I said that, he'd say I'm full of shit. But it's true. It's just a fact. Sometimes he just wasn't there."

An encounter between Kravis and Kohlberg makes the older partner seem feeble, even pathetic:

> "What should I do?" Kohlberg would ask.
> "What do you mean, 'What should I do?' " Kravis would reply. "I don't have to tell George or the others what to do. Doesn't that tell you maybe it's time for a change?"
> They had the same arguments over and over. You want it the way it was in the old days, Kravis would say, and it can't be. It just can't be. Times have changed.
> "But we were partners when we started," Kohlberg said. "That's true," Kravis said. "But life changes. The business has changed."
> The simple fact was, Kravis and Roberts no longer needed their former mentor.[1]

One of the most interesting things about this particular passage is how misleading it is to the reader. Although the authors quote Kohlberg, they do not reveal anywhere that they never actually interviewed him. Using the technique of reconstructing dialogue, they present their account of the dispute as complete, without giving any indication that they are only telling one side of the story. And a very controversial story at that.

The book goes on to attribute the parting of the ways to Kohlberg's wanting too much money and too much power. The firm's younger partners maintained that Kohlberg wanted too great a stake in the firm given the minimal work load he was carrying, and that he resisted allowing equity in the firm to be more widely distributed to the firm's dozen or so younger executives. Moreover, the book says Kohlberg suddenly began demanding that votes be unanimous, a move that would in essence give him veto power over decisions when he was at odds with his younger partners. By the time a reader is finished with this passage of the book, it is hard not to feel considerable sympathy for the plight of these talented young men who are trying to extricate themselves as delicately as possible from an untenable relationship with a frail and doddering old man who is trying to cling to some shadow of his former past.

"It was painful for the two cousins to tell Kohlberg he wasn't pulling his load," the authors explain. Roberts, they suggest, suffered in particular:

"The decision we made for him to leave was best. But personally, it was very tough on me. Still is," he is quoted as saying.[2]

To Kohlberg, such touching displays of sensitivity are pure, unadulterated bunk. The truth about his departure, he insists, is far different from the sanitized version presented by George and Henry. And although he has always shunned the media, preferring privacy, he has become sufficiently distressed about the distortions to be willing to share his side of the story.

In describing his return to work, Kohlberg makes no bones about the fact that he was sick and weak. What shocks him is that his younger partners were not willing to wait out his illness and be supportive, and that they instead chose to portray him to those outside the firm as permanently debilitated.

His ex-partners, Kohlberg believes, deliberately exaggerated his health problem to people in the business community. They invariably referred to his acoustic neuroma as a brain tumor, which most people interpreted as cancer, even though they knew Jerry's growth was, by definition, benign. "They made much of Jerry's operation," says one financial executive who knows both sides well. " 'Tumor' sounds worse—most people either didn't know or didn't want to take the time to find out."

The impression that Kohlberg's health was permanently impaired certainly helped to mask the extent of George and Henry's disloyalty to a person who had reared them in the business, even to the point of bankrolling them in their early years. At the same time, it was hard not to feel sympathy for the two cousins' plight: who could help but wince at the thought of two bright young men having to tiptoe around the unrealistic musings of an old man so frail he was often "not there."

Kohlberg was not, however, permanently stricken. His headaches did go away and his strength did return, although it took longer than either he or his doctors expected. Today, at sixty-five, he works the same lengthy hours that many on Wall Street do, shuttling between his midtown Manhattan office and one closer to his home, in Westchester. And he travels extensively, albeit in the comfort of his own private plane. Calls to Kohlberg & Company will find him in California one day, Oregon the next, Colorado the day after. He swims laps in his pool and continues to be a demon on the tennis courts, playing fiercely for hours at a time, three or four times a week. Business associates who work with him, as well as some of his new investors, say that Kohlberg is more vigorous than many men twenty years his junior.

It is difficult to prove that there was a sudden decrease in Kohlberg's day-to-day involvement in the firm after he returned, as the account in *Barbarians at the Gate* suggests, because Jerry had been somewhat removed for years—that was how all three men seemed to like it. Henry and George always insisted on doing things themselves, on being left to their own devices. They disliked close supervision. Jerry, in turn, enjoyed playing the role of the proud father and was happy to see his two young protégés showing such initiative. He also felt that after twenty years in the business, it was appropriate for him to pull back and devote more of his time to *pro bono* work. In the early years of the firm, George and Henry praised Jerry for the autonomy he gave them. Later, they cited his lack of hands-on involvement as evidence of his neglect. And Jerry did not see their turnaround coming.

"He was deliberately turning over power, cutting down his own financial portion and turning over decision-making to them—leaving himself veto, and letting them cultivate the contacts," said Kohlberg's daughter Pam. "In a way, the 'Boy Scout' part of him played right into their hands."

As for George and Henry's claim that Kohlberg wanted too much money and power, that he was unwilling to share ownership of the firm with other executives, it simply doesn't square with the facts. Long before he got sick, Kohlberg had already been steadily reducing his share. He claims he has always been a big believer in letting younger people build up their ownership in the firm, a contention that would seem to be supported by the fact that when he founded the firm, he agreed to give George and Henry 30 percent each, despite their minimal capital contribution. Kohlberg then cut his share of the firm's profits further: from the 40-percent level when he founded KKR in 1976, to 30 percent by 1981, to 25.8 percent by 1985. By the time he finally left in 1987, Jerry's stake was 20 percent, or *half* what it had been eleven years earlier. Henry and George's stakes, meanwhile, had been shrinking, too, as they shared ownership with other executives. But the amount by which they reduced their ownership position was not proportionate with Kohlberg's. Their shares went from 30 percent at the time the firm was founded, to about 25 percent at the time that Kohlberg left, a reduction of just 5 percentage points.

Jerry, according to his personal adviser, Arthur Aeder, was prepared to reduce his stake even further. "In the course of the negotiations, one thing that Jerry made clear was that he was prepared to go down, at any time, proportionate with Henry and George, provided that the interests they would give up would go to the newer, younger partners, because he firmly believed in the institutionalization of the firm and developing the next cadre of management," he says. But George and Henry, says Aeder, refused to accept a reduction in their stakes.

Aeder speaks with great precision about the negotiations, and especially, the financial options that were considered. He is a trained accountant and was the senior partner of the accounting firm Oppenheim, Appel & Dixon and Company. In that capacity, Aeder served as the chief accounting adviser to two Wall Street firms: Bear Stearns and Oppenheimer & Co.

Throughout the interminable discussions, Jerry simply couldn't understand Henry and George's obsession with money. After all, by this time the three were each worth several hundred million dollars. How much more did they need? Kohlberg says he told them, "We're so damn lucky, what difference does it make? We've already taken care of ourselves, our children, even our grandchildren's needs." He says he believes it was George who then said he wouldn't stop until he had made a billion dollars. "George knew his net worth daily," says Kohlberg. "When a deal came in, he would update it mentally in his head."

Kohlberg says that at one point he offered to sell his stake and get out of the firm altogether, but George and Henry dismissed the idea out of hand, on the grounds that the sum he wanted was too high. Ironically, had George and Henry accepted Kohlberg's proposal, they would be better off now, because Kohlberg and Aeder had placed conservative estimates on the values embedded in those stakes. At another point, Kohlberg proposed that if he was not going to play a management role in the firm, that he be allowed to have his name taken off the door. They rejected that idea, too. Although they did not think Kohlberg's contributions to the firm had any value, they apparently thought that others might.

About the only part of the account in *Barbarians* that Kohlberg feels gets close to the truth is the passage concerning veto power. Kohlberg readily concedes that he wanted votes in the firm to be unanimous. What he says is misleading in the book is that it was made to look as if this were a sudden (and power-grabbing) demand on his part. He says the firm had always operated on the basis of unanimous voting. In 1982, when the charter was amended to take in a new partner, Robert MacDonnell, who is George's brother-in-law, Kohlberg says a new clause was inserted that made that premise ambiguous. Kohlberg says that he was unaware of that change until years later, when he and his partners were struggling for control of the firm. In any event, Roberts felt that the 1982 agreement gave Henry and him the right to govern using majority rule.

The argument may sound technical. But the issue underlying the dispute was fundamental: in what direction was the firm going? For George and Henry had one vision of the firm, which was quite different from Kohlberg's. They wanted to go after large companies, earn huge fees, and, if need be, resort to hostile tactics in pursuit of their goals.

Kohlberg, however, was appalled by the fees the firm was charging. Even though he could see that they were getting away with it, he thought that it completely violated the firm's founding principle: that they would make money *with* their partners. Of course, George and Henry still had some incentive to invest prudently: their reputations were at stake, not to mention the fact that they would get 20 percent of any profits on their deals. But what bothered Kohlberg was that they *also* got handsomely rewarded even if they made bad investment decisions; they got the upfront fees, but didn't have to share in their investors' losses. And that, he felt, could distort their judgment. If votes were not unanimous, he could not stop his younger partners from taking the firm in a direction he found repugnant. Likewise, if they could not overrule their former mentor, they would be restrained from building the business the way they saw fit.

Previous reports have speculated that it was the hostility KKR displayed toward Beatrice's management that finally pushed Kohlberg over the edge. But Kohlberg says the breaking point had more to do with the fees that KKR was charging, first the $45 million for Beatrice and then the $60-million investment-banking fee they charged for buying Safeway. "I was starting to urge that we take lesser fees as a percent," he says, because he felt that the initial standard of 1 percent of a transaction no longer made sense once KKR's deals grew to the multibillion-dollar level. Looking back on it, "I looked ridiculous. I was the old fogy. I was always the one that said we should charge less. It's a very difficult position to defend when you've got happy investors."

The realization that the partners' differences were irreconcilable did not arise overnight. In fact, it took a full year of emotional pulling and tugging before Kohlberg became convinced that he had no alternative but to leave the firm that he had founded. That was how torn Kohlberg was over admitting that he was no longer compatible with the two men he had adopted as sons. Even after his acceptance of the turn of events, it took another fifteen months before the three were finally able to agree on the terms of his departure.

The negotiations were, by all accounts, excruciating. The sessions were almost always held in Jerry's office, a Spartan room in the midst of KKR's lavish New York quarters. Henry and John McLoughlin, the attorney from Latham & Watkins, would generally sit on Jerry's couch, while Kohlberg, Aeder, and Todd Lang, the attorney from Weil, Gotshal & Manges who was assisting Jerry, would be seated in chairs across from them, on the other side of a long coffee table. George was occasionally present and John Gerson, KKR's chief financial officer, would sometimes drop by for some of the sessions, too.

The atmosphere, says Aeder, was generally civil. "Both parties would bend over backwards to say the right things to each other." The discussions centered on percentages, what involvement, if any, Jerry would have in future deals, his ability to participate, whether he should be paid a lump sum and allowed to close the door on his KKR past, and whether he could take his name off the door within a year of leaving. The process was emotionally draining for everyone involved. "There were an incredible number of negotiating sessions, offers put on the table, taken off. It went on and on, and it was ultimately a wearing-down process," recalls Aeder. "Up until just literally weeks before the final agreement, everything was put back on the table every time we met."

Making everyone's life more difficult were the complicated relationships involved. By this time, Kohlberg had become very judgmental about Henry and Carolyne's lifestyle. Henry's private life was certainly none of Kohlberg's business. But this disciple of Quakerism and the Judge Solomon school of etiquette held such strong views about wealth and the "correct" way to handle it that he could not contain himself. "Very frankly," says Kohlberg, "I was becoming disgusted with Henry's lifestyle."

Many of Kohlberg's friends thought he was being excessively rigid. They urged him to forget it, to ignore Henry, but Kohlberg could not let it go. He would harp on and on about it. "I think Jerry has always been uncomfortable with conspicuous consumption and displays of wealth. Jerry's given a lot of money to institutions, and none of it has his name on it. None is ever announced. He was becoming somewhat uncomfortable with Henry before he got ill, but later on, every time Henry and Carolyne's name would appear in some big splash, it made him very uncomfortable, almost as if it reflected on him. . . . I can call it puritanical, but people who would use that word would use it in a derogatory way, and I don't mean it that way. Some might call it old-fashioned, but maybe he simply didn't accept the eighties," says his friend Aeder.

*   *   *

Kohlberg understood that his differences with Henry were irreconcilable. But he kept looking to George to make things right among the three. Kohlberg simply could not believe that George would sit there passively and let the partnership dissipate. After all, he felt this was *his* firm. It was *his* idea. He had bankrolled the firm through the early years, helped George buy his house, lent him money to invest so that he could build up some net worth, made his home their home. It was inconceivable to him that George would let the whole thing go up in smoke.

But George would not be drawn in. He stayed in San Francisco, working at his desk, safely three thousand miles away. Only twice was Kohlberg able to get George to meet with him privately, and they were extremely painful encounters. Kohlberg reminded him of their history together, the bonds he thought they shared. When he tried to suggest that George might have some obligation to stand up for him now, Kohlberg recalls that "George's answer was, 'I've fulfilled my obligation to you. We're even.' "

It was George's attitude that was ultimately more hurtful to Jerry than his actual separation from the firm. For him this power struggle was about much more than KKR, money, or percentages: his whole philosophy of life was on trial. Since his early years, Kohlberg had made a conscious decision to invest his time and energy in helping to bring along young people. His motives were not entirely altruistic—he enjoyed it. It made him feel good about himself. It was his way of expressing his own ego. In George's case, he had picked the boy up from out of nowhere—a twenty-one-year-old college kid with unfortunate family problems who was in New York on a summer internship—and helped make him into something great. And together, with George's cousin Henry, they had made KKR into something great. KKR had become Kohlberg's identity, his way of showing everyone—his ambitious mother, his critics at Bear Stearns—that he could do things the right way and succeed.

For George to stand there before him and say that none of that mattered was like saying that Jerry's whole life didn't matter, that the people he had handpicked as surrogate sons, and to whom he had passed along all his knowledge and experience over a period of twenty years, had never shared the same regard for him. It was a total refutation of Jerry's judgment and it made him feel naive and foolish.

There are some individuals close to Kohlberg who think that George, more than anyone else, bears the greatest responsibility for the partnership's breakup. Only George, they maintain, was in a position to stand up to Henry and refuse to let the firm splinter. "George was unwilling to take any real responsibility," says one. "One of the things that really disgusted me was that George tried to hide behind the distance and Henry."

Kohlberg took the strife among the three extremely personally. Mary Lou Murray, who was still working at the firm but was no longer Kohlberg's secretary, says that when she would occasionally run into him, he would seem almost ghostlike. "He looked very, very troubled," she said. "Sometimes when he would pass by, he almost looked like he was on the verge of tears."

At the same time that Kohlberg was trying to understand what was happening to his relationship with George, he was perplexed by the behavior of another young man he had befriended: Dick Beattie.

Beattie stayed away from most of the formal negotiations. Perhaps he felt too conflicted. After all, Kohlberg and he were kindred spirits—liberal Democrats in a world dominated by conservative Republicans. Kohlberg had taken a shine to Beattie when he was an associate at Simpson Thacher & Bartlett working on the Bear Stearns account. When Kohlberg left to form KKR, he continued the relationship with Simpson Thacher. And a number of years later, when the lead attorney on the KKR account left to become the general counsel at Paramount Communications, Beattie, who had been doing more and more work for the firm, took over.

Kohlberg was delighted with the change. Like George and Henry, Beattie was young and enthusiastic. But unlike them, Dick shared Kohlberg's broader, political interests. To Kohlberg's way of thinking, far too few lawyers cared about the communities they worked in or donated their time to correct social ills. Beattie, on the other hand, wanted to help those less fortunate than himself. He had campaigned for John Kennedy in the sixties, did *pro bono* work for a legal aid office in Harlem, and in the late seventies, served for several years in the Carter administration, first as a deputy general counsel, and finally as general counsel to Joseph Califano, the secretary of health, education and welfare.

Kohlberg wanted to help Beattie prosper so that he could continue to pursue those other, broader interests. He personally gave the young lawyer $20,000, followed by another $15,000, to invest in KKR deals where he was not acting as counsel. (Kohlberg felt strongly, and he says Beattie agreed, that investing in deals where he was acting as an attorney would embroil him in too many conflicts.) Kohlberg says he wanted Beattie "to become more independently wealthy and therefore do some of the things he might like." If Beattie got asked to go back to Washington again, Kohlberg wanted him to be able to have the financial wherewithal to accept the position. "He said he'd pay me back," Kohlberg continued, "but he never did. In fairness, I intended it as a gift, because I liked Dick." Beattie declined to comment.

Kohlberg's concern was that if KKR continued to prosper and Beattie saw that George and Henry were earning so much more, he might be tempted to stray from his ideals. He noticed that the young lawyer seemed to be easily impressed by people with money and influence, and he feared that the temptations might become harder to resist.

* * *

Now it was Kohlberg who needed support. He turned to his friend Beattie expecting that he would act as a bridge between the aggrieved parties. Jerry would explain his positions on issues to Beattie, give him the full background, explain where he could compromise and where he could not. Beattie always seemed anxious to help and offered to act as a sounding board. Throughout the fifteen months of negotiations, Dick positioned himself as an honest broker, as a mutual friend who was trying to bring the two sides together, so they could come to some acceptable solution.

By the end of the process, however, Kohlberg came to doubt Beattie's impartiality. The turning point was a meeting that Aeder had with Beattie. Kohlberg thought it would be helpful, since the two were each helping to advise him, if they met and exchanged views directly. Aeder went downtown to Simpson Thacher's lower-Manhattan office and met Beattie for a cup of coffee. The two sat on opposite sides of a table in the law firm's cafeteria. Aeder, a short, pudgy man with a balding head, spoke in short, clipped phrases that were direct and wasted no words. Beattie, his thinning blond hair and ice-blue eyes making him look every ounce the Dartmouth man that he is, spoke in his soft, husky, seductive voice. What Aeder came away with was a vivid impression that Beattie was not, as Kohlberg had assumed all these months, a friend and a confidant, but someone who was in fact collaborating with the other side. It wasn't anything specific that Beattie said that triggered Aeder's reaction, just the lawyer's tone and demeanor that conveyed that bias.

When he got back to Kohlberg's office, Aeder told his friend that Beattie was Henry Kravis's messenger and not the peacekeeper or trusted friend that Jerry thought he was.

"I remember it as clear as day. I said 'Jerry, he's totally committed to Henry and George, and regardless of what he says, he represents them and their interests exclusively.' I remember leaving the building and feeling totally negative, because maybe I anticipated meeting someone who because of history and consideration of Jerry's feelings would at least keep Jerry's interest in mind and not hurt or take advantage of him."

It was only then that Kohlberg began to understand that the lines were being drawn.

JERRY QUITS

On March 13, 1987, after nearly two years of emotional wrangling and intense negotiation, Jerry Kohlberg signed an agreement in which he withdrew as a general partner of Kohlberg Kravis Roberts and ceased to have any decision-making role. The agreement, which became effective on May 7, stated that he would continue to hold his shares of companies KKR had already acquired, and that he would have the option of investing in future deals for the next nine years, but that his interest in future deals would steadily decline. Thus, in 1987, Kohlberg would be entitled to a 20.541-percent stake of KKR's interest in any new companies that the firm acquired. The following year that figure would decline to 17.625 percent. By 1990, it would be only 12.625 percent, and it would go down to 7 percent in 1995.

About two weeks later, at KKR's third annual investment conference, Kohlberg announced his withdrawal to the firm's investment partners. Standing at a podium looking out over the 120-some investors who had gathered for the meeting in the luxurious Versailles Room at the Helmsley Palace Hotel, Kohlberg took the opportunity to deliver a rousing defense of business ethics, a speech that some in the room might have interpreted as a veiled critique of his younger partners.

"Twenty-two years ago," he told the group, "I had a small dream—that companies could be bought, and investments made, in undervalued businesses where we, as financiers, would put our money, time, and effort right alongside management. We would do everything in our power to ensure that our investment *and theirs* turned out well. We would *both* risk a great deal—capital and reputation." (Emphasis in the original.)

What held these financial principles together and created KKR's success, he said, were the precepts of integrity and ethics. "I chose to mention this today because all around us there is a breakdown of these values—in business and government. It is not merely the difference between insider trading and legitimate arbitrage. . . . It is not just refusing a suitcase of cash, it is not just the overweening, overpowering greed that pervades our business life. It is the fact that we are not willing to sacrifice for the ethics and values we profess. For an ethic is not an ethic, and a value not a value, without some sacrifice to it. *Something given up, something not taken, something not gained.* [Emphasis added.] We do it in exchange for a greater good, for something worth more than just money and power and position. The great paradox of this philosophy is that in the end it brings one greater gain than any other philosophy.

"We all must insist on a resurgence of these values. Because if we do not, the great luck, hard work, intelligence, and decency that we have all brought to these successful investments will wither and decay. We must all insist on ethical behavior or we will kill the golden goose." With that, Kohlberg said that he was turning over active management of the firm to George and Henry, and he turned and sat down.

It was an emotional moment for everyone. The renunciation of a dream for Jerry, freedom for Henry and George, and a perplexing end to an era from the standpoint of KKR's investors. Henry and George, who had not known what the unpredictable and intransigent Kohlberg would say in his farewell speech, were stunned by his references to greed and a general moral breakdown. But all three tried to put the best face on it. Despite the hurt feelings, none of them had any interest in seeing KKR undone by the breakup.

It wasn't until a month later that the business press got hold of the story. In an interview with the *New York Times,* Kohlberg acknowledged that there had been some philosophical differences, but said, "The time has come for the younger guys to run this place." George told the reporter, James Sterngold, that "Jerry may have felt that the deals were getting too big." Dick Beattie was especially effusive: "Among the special things about Jerry is that he is decent, honorable."[1]

Kohlberg took the opportunity to announce that his departure from KKR did not mean that he was retiring. Although he was sixty-one and had an estimated net worth of over $300 million, Kohlberg announced the formation of a new firm, Kohlberg & Company, with his son James, who had worked with George in KKR's West Coast office since 1984.

Kohlberg wouldn't say much more about the new firm, except that it would be doing leveraged buyouts, and that the deals would probably be smaller scale than those of KKR. "I won't restrict myself to small transactions," he told Sterngold, "but I'll stick with deals where reason still prevails." Those who were familiar with the tensions that had existed inside the firm took his comment as a pointed reference to his ex-partners' behavior.

Henry and George, Kohlberg recalls, were not happy about his decision to form a new leveraged buyout firm and did not want his fund-raising activities to compete with theirs. They were just about to start a new round of visits to investors and were concerned that Kohlberg's departure could unsettle them and draw some away. "They asked us not to try to raise any money until they'd finished," says Kohlberg, a request he more or less met.

While Kohlberg tried to figure out where his office should be, what its focus would be, and how he could best market his idea, Henry and George were fast off the mark. Though they still had $1.3 billion left in their 1986 fund, they launched plans to raise a new one. This time they intended to knock the cover off the ball, to raise more money than anyone could even imagine. Their new fund would establish KKR once and for all as the preeminent leader in the field and leave their nemesis, Forstmann Little, not to mention Jerry Kohlberg, in the dust. George wanted to cross the finish line with somewhere between $3 billion and $5 billion. That would be enough equity to buy several Fortune 500 companies without fear of being outbid by any competitors.

Just weeks after Kohlberg bowed out, Henry and George took off on a fund-raising spree. Within a short time they had called on many of their previous investors—some in person, some simply over the phone, obtaining commitments before their elder ex-partner could barely even get his stationery printed.

Their fund-raising pitch was compelling. In the document they circulated to their investors, they noted a series of "firsts": they had completed the first *large* LBO of a public company, the first *billion-dollar* LBO, the first *large* LBO of a public company by way of a tender offer, and the *largest* LBO in history, Beatrice. (Emphasis added.)

On top of all these firsts, Henry and George said they had achieved an annual compounded rate of return of over 59 percent, on investments of over $2.2 billion. That figure was considered breathtakingly good by members of the investment community, who often had to be satisfied with annual returns in the low-to-mid teens on ordinary stocks. In parentheses, KKR acknowledged that their returns dropped to 49 percent if their own 20-percent cut of the profits was taken out. But they did not indicate that even that 49 percent number was optimistic. For it included an estimated return for Beatrice of 192 percent.

There are a number of ways to massage numbers in the LBO field. Investments, for example, are often valued on the basis of time. The longer that it takes for an investor to enjoy a given dollar return on his or her money, the lower the return will be; likewise, the shorter the time period that an investment is valued at, the higher the return will appear. In the case of Beatrice, KKR placed an estimated value on the company after owning it for just over a year. By placing a high estimate on a company that had only been held a short time, and by assigning that 192 percent number to an $8.2-billion investment—by far the largest commitment in KKR's portfolio—the effect was to skew the numbers, which created a highly inflated picture of the firm's track record.

When KKR finally sold Beatrice three years later, the return was more like 50 percent. That is still an impressive figure, but it's nothing like 192 percent. Had a more realistic estimate for Beatrice been included in its 1987 fund-raising literature, KKR's annual compounded return to investors, after deducting its 20-percent cut, would have been more like 35 percent instead of around 50 percent.

Of course, to most people, a 35-percent annual return would be an extraordinary achievement, one that they would consider themselves lucky to experience even once in their lifetime. However, in the high-powered world of LBOs, KKR's record was not unique. Indeed, at least three other LBO groups, Forstmann Little, and the investment units of Morgan Stanley & Company and Merrill Lynch & Company, were giving their investors annual compounded returns, after deducting their 20-percent cut, that were as good as KKR's if not better.

Every LBO group calculates its returns slightly differently from everyone else, so it is difficult to compare them with the precision one might like. However, it is safe to say that both Morgan and Merrill have generated annual returns of around 40 percent for their investors. Forstmann, in turn, has given its equity investors an 86-percent return on the deals it has completed. Critics of Forstmann like to point out that many of its investors also participate in its debt fund, which has generated returns below that of many junk bond funds. However, even if one blends together its debt and equity returns, investors in Forstmann Little would still have gotten 39 percent on its deals.

By comparison, KKR's overall returns have generally declined from their lofty levels when the firm first started. KKR estimates that the annual return to investors in its 1982 fund is 41.8 percent, after deducting its 20-percent cut. The comparable figure for investors in its 1984 fund is about 30 percent. And the annual return on its 1986 fund is estimated at 29 percent; however, that figure assumes that investors lose none of the $138 million they have invested in one company that filed for bankruptcy protection. KKR did not provide an estimate for its 1987 fund, much of which is tied up in its relatively recent purchase of RJR Nabisco.

Not only have other funds matched or superseded KKR in terms of investment performance, they have also charged less in fees. Neither Merrill Lynch nor Forstmann charges the companies they acquire an annual fee to monitor them —they consider that their job as an LBO sponsor. Nor do either of them charge a fee when they sell a company. And none of the three charges directors' fees for having their executives sit on the boards of the companies they control. Again, they regard that as part of their responsibility.

On Wednesday, June 24, just six days after Kohlberg publicly announced his withdrawal from KKR and the establishment of his new firm, George Roberts flew up to Portland. George had previously called Carol Hewitt, who was then the Council's chairperson, and asked if he could take her and the other Council members out to dinner before making a presentation to the Council the next morning.

Accepting such an invitation, strictly speaking, violates the Council's operating procedures, since their meetings are required by law to be open to the public. But Hewitt and the others accepted. After all, they had known George for years. They were happy to meet with him; they would just consider it an informal get-together.

Early that evening, the Council members and George gathered around a table in a private dining room at the RiverPlace Alexis Hotel, a swanky new hotel built with the help of Council funds on the banks of the Willamette River. While evening strollers sat outside drinking beer, eating ice cream, and enjoying the sunset by the river, George and his friends were inside going over KKR's grand plans. George wanted them to contribute 10 percent of the next fund's total, as they had done several times in the past. The only difference was, this time, because the fund was so large, 10 percent might amount to as much as $600 million, or three times the size of their previous commitment.

It was a breathtaking sum. But Jim George had come up with some numbers ahead of time that showed that even if they lost every dollar of this new commitment, they'd still come out well ahead. Up until that point, KKR had invested $2.2 billion in equity and given its partners back $2.4 billion. Jim George estimated that the investments that hadn't yet been sold were worth about $5.8 billion. Even if they lost every penny of this next commitment, which he regarded as a virtual impossibility, Oregon would still end up with returns on their KKR investment in the mid- to high teens. And if this next investment performed anywhere near as well as previous ones, they'd be heroes.

That was exactly how the members of the Council chose to think about it. They didn't worry about placing that much money with just one investment firm. They didn't think about how KKR was doing relative to other buyout firms: whether its returns were higher or lower than its competitors, or whether KKR's fees were reasonable or not. All they knew was that up until now they had enjoyed large profits, and that if they lost everything going forward, they would still be doing all right.

Since Jim George's numbers had already prepared them, George had little trouble that night persuading his Oregon friends to make another investment. The mood at the table was festive, like partners getting together to celebrate their past successes and toasting the exciting frontier they hoped to conquer next. George, nonetheless, gave an unusually animated pep talk. Normally, when George met with Council members, he was his low-key, placid self. He would explain the firm's impressive results and then temper his presentation with a considerable dose of humility. He would emphasize that the economic climate had been favorable and warn that one could never be sure of sustaining such returns in the future.

This time, however, George "put a little sizzle into it," says Council member Swindells. Almost like a salesman trying to sell a new car model, George reminded them of how good the returns were, how pleased they must be, how, if KKR had even more money, they could *really* turn the world upside down. "This time he was rather expansive, explaining the real leverage of this fund," recalls Swindells. "I remember at one point he looked down the table and said, 'With this much money'—six billion dollars I guess it was—'there's no corporation in America that we can't buy.' And I thought, 'Whoa, this isn't like George.' "

At nine o'clock the next morning, Roberts went through his drill again, this time for public consumption. The values they placed on the companies in their portfolio were "very conservative," George assured the group. He acknowledged that other competitors were crowding the field and that there was a lot of money chasing leveraged buyouts. But he assured them the market would not collapse. What he would like, he said quietly into the microphone, was for the Council to commit $500 million to KKR, with the option of increasing that amount to $600 million depending on the final size of KKR's fund.

"At that time, that was a huge amount of money," recalls Doug Le Bon, Oregon's consultant from Wilshire, who was seated in the audience. While other money managers often try to give a peppy sales pitch, Le Bon was struck by the low-key manner with which George addressed the formal gathering. "He very quietly laid out what he wanted to do, and he wanted to ask for six hundred million dollars. Nobody in the room said anything," said Le Bon.

Several people who were there remember that Chairperson Carol Hewitt actually cut George's speech off, so quick was she to make a motion to give KKR up to $600 million. One of the other members moved to second her motion, and George's request was passed unanimously. A group of five people had just signed off on what is believed to be the largest pension-fund commitment ever given to a single independent investment group. Yet they had voted on it in a matter of minutes, as if they were deciding where to go for lunch. According to several observers, George said thank you very much, closed his briefcase, and left for the airport.

Many in the audience were taken aback by the size of the numbers being bandied about. After all, this was a Council that prided itself on grilling its money managers at monthly meetings about why a particular stock in a portfolio was performing poorly, or what steps were being taken to rent an office building in Washington, D.C. Council members had been known to insist on personal tours of potential real estate investments before they signed off on them.

They could be incredibly difficult and ornery with some money managers, but when it came to KKR, they were almost blasé. Looking back on their $600-million decision, none of the Council members remembers anything striking or even bold about their decision. By then, of course, many of the Council members had known George and his colleagues at KKR for years. They had earned more on their LBO investments than with any other type of investment. They had been to the firm's annual meetings, sat through endless conference calls, and discussed investments over meals together. KKR was well on its way to becoming the largest single employer in the state. Not only did it control Fred Meyer, Safeway, Red Lion Inn, Motel-6, and PacTrust—all of which had big operations in Oregon—but it would soon buy other companies with local operations, including RJR Nabisco.

"There was so much comfort with KKR. KKR was more like family," recalls Swindells. "They set up the concept, yet we helped improve that concept—Roger did, and the Council. And we evolved together."

When Kohlberg finally arrived in Portland three months later on his own fund-raising mission, he met a very different reception. If George and Henry were family, he was a distant relative. It did not help that his meeting with the Oregon Council fell on the day after the stock market had dropped 508 points—a day that became enshrined in the public's mind as Black Monday. (The day before, when the crash actually occurred, Kohlberg had the misfortune of calling on the state of Washington.)

Kohlberg made his pitch. He would only buy companies on a friendly basis and would make that commitment contractually binding. Furthermore, he would not engage in any "toehold" investing because he thought it bordered on hostile and because he felt it was, in effect, no different from gambling on the stock market, which he did not feel qualified to do. He would be unlikely to do deals of more than $1 billion or $2 billion in size because once they got any larger than that, it usually necessitated breaking up the company and selling off the pieces, and he did not believe in that. And after setting aside a $15-million fund to cover expenses of transactions that might never be consummated, he would split any fees he charged for doing a transaction with his investment partners on a fifty-fifty basis. He hoped they would consider giving him $50 million, or about 10 percent of the $500-million target he had in mind. He and his associates would be committing $20 million of their own money to the fund.

Kohlberg's presentation met with a cool response. Everyone seemed predisposed to think he was still in frail health, and that he was only trying to raise money to help set up his son Jim in business. And they had heard that Jim didn't have much experience as an investor. Wasn't he a tennis player? they asked. The goodwill that Kohlberg had expected to find, given the Council's long and happy association with KKR and his own role in bringing about the Fred Meyer transaction, had totally evaporated.

Every Council member seemed to have a different excuse. Carol Hewitt thought Kohlberg's firm was too small and too dependent on Kohlberg. She worried that Jim did not have enough investment experience and that another partner, George Peck, was known more for his management-recruiting skills. However, Kohlberg had addressed that concern in advance by stipulating that if anything happened to him, the firm would cease making any further investments.

Jim George's position was even stranger. He said he was concerned that the Council would be investing with a group that might compete with KKR. Yet Kohlberg was only trying to raise $500 million and clearly wouldn't even be in the same marketplace as a firm that had $5.6 billion.

Though Roger Meier was no longer on the Council, he was still influential with many of the current members. He continued to receive investment reports, attended virtually all the Council's monthly meetings, and was frequently consulted by other Council members and Jim George for his advice. Judging from Meier's remarks about Kohlberg, he was still part of the decision-making process.

Was turning down Kohlberg a hard decision? "It was. We all liked Jerry, he'd done a great job," said Meier. "I said, 'Look, you know, we've got this major commitment to KKR, and I think it should be left there.' And again, Jerry's business was going to be much smaller. I was concerned that it would be smaller. We had our commitment and we should live with that one."

Swindells said the Council had no problem with the concept of Kohlberg's fund. If anything, they liked it better: Kohlberg was putting more of his own money into deals, he was raising concerns about gouging investors with fees, about loading up companies with more debt than they could handle. "He was doing it just right," said Swindells. As for concerns about his age or health, "I think it was more of a cop-out," he conceded. "I think we said, 'We've got this relationship [with KKR] and we're as full up as we need to be. Let's keep it simple." As for Kohlberg, says Swindells, "He was hurt. He should have been."

When Kohlberg tried to raise money with other state funds, he encountered a similar reaction. They all seemed to have formed a prior opinion that his health was poor, that his son was inexperienced, and that even though Jerry had fathered the original concept of an LBO, he had lost his edge.

"Some were glad to see Jerry. Some said, 'Why did you do this coincident with the crash?' And there was some indication that some wells had been poisoned. Some people told us that Jerry was not going to work, that he was creating a haven for Jim. Those comments were unkind, unfair, and inaccurate," says one person familiar with Kohlberg's fundraising efforts. This observer added: "Jerry's sickness was the best propaganda they could have had. In this case, it was easy to say, 'Jerry's older, he's been hurt by the operation.' "

Kohlberg got the distinct impression from his conversations with investors that the consultant Doug Le Bon had done his best to keep potential investors at bay. "He told the pension funds, where he was influential . . . that I was ill and that I was over the hill and that they [George and Henry] had really been responsible for the firm, they had done all the work. You know, I heard it back."

Le Bon denies having said anything like that, and adds that he cannot recall a client ever asking him to review Kohlberg's new fund. Had they asked, he says his view was that Kohlberg & Company, "did not meet our normal criteria of collective investment experience and track record."

Kohlberg made a few calls to other state funds, but their responses were all so similar, as if they were all reading from the same script, that he eventually gave up. Not everyone reacted that way. The charitable trust of Fred Meyer gave Kohlberg & Company $5 million. And GTE's pension fund, which is considered in the financial industry to be a particularly savvy group, invested in Kohlberg's fund, too. In fact, John Carroll, who is in charge of that area for the telecommunications company, says he kind of enjoyed using Kohlberg to make a statement about the LBO movement. GTE's pension fund had invested in KKR's 1984 fund, but Carroll refused to participate in others after that because he objected to the fees they were charging, which he feared could distort their judgment. "Who are they in the game for: their limited partners, or themselves?" he asked. When Kohlberg left KKR, Carroll invested in his LBO fund, a move he said, in a way, ratified his decision not to go with KKR.

Kohlberg ultimately rallied over twenty investors to join him in his new fund, including major banks such as Manufacturers Hanover and large insurance companies. The amounts they were each willing to commit, however, were relatively small, and Kohlberg came away with only about $300 million in total. He was disappointed with the showing, but in the postcrash environment, raising anything was considered an achievement. It gave him enough to get started. And since then, he, Jim, and two other partners, along with a staff of about six members, have bought three companies: the Welbilt Corporation, a foodservice-equipment manufacturer, Colorado Prime, a direct marketer of gourmet foods and food appliances, and B. Manischewitz Co., the country's largest matzoh-producer—for a grand total of $450 million.

It is difficult to assess Kohlberg & Company's record, since none of the companies have made it through their entire buyout cycle and there are no financial statements publicly available on the private companies. There are some in the business community, however, who have had a chance to observe Kohlberg's new team in action and maintain that they are not as aggressive or as sharp-elbowed as their counterparts at KKR. Kohlberg will say little about his investments other than that two of the companies are performing well, while Welbilt's earnings have declined substantially and its debt rating has been downgraded, requiring a recent change in top management. It remains to be seen whether the new management can turn Welbilt around and make it a profitable investment.

OUT OF CONTROL

It's fair to say that anyone, armed with $5.6 billion, has the potential to be a menace. But if it happens to be two people with something to prove, and little restraint on their ambition, the combination can be explosive. In the case of George and Henry, it was.

By 1986, both men were exhibiting signs that too much money and power had gone to their heads. Their appetite for winning seemed insatiable, and they now had the wherewithal to achieve their goals. By this point, moreover, the economic interest of virtually every entity they came into contact with was bound up in the ongoing success of the KKR money machine.

Investment banks would turn cartwheels for the chance to work with KKR. There were the $20-million advisory fees, plus $80 million or more in underwriting fees, if they played their cards right. Since individuals were losing faith in the stock market and brokerage commissions were way down, "deal fees" were where it was happening. An assignment from KKR could make an investment banker's career and sharply boost his or her bonus. By this time, KKR had also figured out that the best way to ensure a loyal following among investment bankers was to spread the goodies around: dole out an assignment to Drexel one month, Goldman Sachs the next. When Eric Gleacher, the merger star of Morgan Stanley, left to start his own firm in early 1990, Henry sighed and said, "Now there's one more mouth to feed."

Commercial banks had become equally tied to the money machine. LBO lending had become a mainstay for the industry: from 1987 to 1989, U.S. banks made about $255 billion in loans to companies that were highly leveraged. With traditional lending activities languishing and many bad loans on the banks' books, the LBO business became the only decent source of profits the industry had.

At the two banks that were almost always KKR's lead or colead banker—Manufacturers Hanover and Bankers Trust—the dependence became very visible. By 1989, LBO activity contributed as much as 10 percent and 20 percent of their net incomes, respectively. Not only did they get fees from making and distributing loans, but KKR would frequently give those it worked most closely with a chance to participate in special investment opportunities. Manufacturers Hanover was allowed to buy an entire issue of preferred stock in Stop & Shop, the East Coast grocery chain that KKR bought in 1988. First Chicago, a longtime investor in KKR's funds, was a part owner of L.B. Foster, one of KKR's first acquisitions. And its venture-capital unit bought Georgia-Marble, a subsidiary of Hillsborough Holdings, from KKR. Getting and then keeping KKR's business was a ticket to the top for a smart banker. Mark Solow, for instance, who spearheaded Manufacturers Hanover's ties to KKR, enjoyed a meteoric rise within his bank. In 1985 he was promoted to executive vice president, in 1986 he was named a senior managing director, in 1990 he became a group executive, and in 1991 his responsibilities were expanded again.

No, it was unlikely that lenders or advisers were going to do anything to curtail KKR and its activities, which by this time had become a fountain of opportunity.

Unlike his cousin Henry, George had up until now remained relatively untouched by the frenzy of dealmaking and the publicity surrounding it. He was a family man at heart, devoted to Leanne and his children. He tried to be home as many evenings as possible—the couple rarely participated in San Francisco's society life—and was often in bed by nine-thirty, according to his mother, Carolyn. The Robertses would occasionally show up for the opening-night festivities of the San Francisco opera, and George made the local papers when he donated $250,000 to the San Francisco Fine Arts Museum. But otherwise, observers from the outside would not have guessed that the headiness of the moment was having any impact.

With George, the telltale sign was the house. Perhaps because he had experienced such a precarious financial existence as a child, George had always been reluctant to take personal financial risks. He was extremely afraid, for instance, of buying a house in the early days of KKR, despite the fact that his growing family cried out for it and prospects at the firm appeared bright. Instead, he and Leanne remained for many years in a small apartment in San Francisco.

Finally, however, George and Leanne bought a house in Atherton, California, a well-to-do suburb about half an hour southwest of San Francisco, just a five-minute drive from the prestigious Stanford University, which had rejected George on three different occasions.

The Robertses' house on Valparaiso Street was a nice enough place that might have belonged to any number of successful upper-middle-class business executives. But there was certainly nothing special about it, nothing to suggest that one of the most successful financial tycoons of the decade lived there.

In 1986, however, George and Leanne hired a well-known local architect, who designed an enormous house for them that is estimated to be over 25,000 square feet. In Atherton, locals refer to it as the "huge" house, and indeed it stands out as a mighty monument even in a community filled with impressive mansions. Behind the six-foot wall that surrounds the property and is interrupted by an imposing electronically controlled gate stands a rust-colored house that soars into the sky. Neighbors can see the home from two blocks away—a fact that has been the source of considerable complaint.

An eclectic blend of hacienda and post-modernism, the house is entered through a series of columns that are at least thirty feet high. The main feature of the living room is a soaring, vaulted ceiling. The house includes a pool and cabana, a tennis pavilion and three courts, each with different surfaces, a wine cellar, and maids' quarters.

After nearly four years of designing and building the house, the Robertses finally moved in in the spring of 1990. "*Fancy*'s probably not the right word, but it is a *huge* house," says George's friend Wilsey. "He's shy about it. If you asked him how big is the house, he'd say he doesn't know." The vastness of the house seems particularly at odds with the diminutive Roberts family. Visitors say they are struck by the contrast between the huge, open rooms and the tiny specks of people sitting inside them.

Wilsey says the house is so enormous that members of the family frequently lose themselves in it. Occasionally, when he would call George on the phone and the maid would answer, "she'd say she'd go and find him. Sometimes it would take five minutes for her to find him because nobody knows where anybody is and they're very quiet," says Wilsey in a mock whisper. Sometimes, if one of George's three kids answers the phone, the problem can get even more acute. "They say they'll go see and then they never come back. What my wife and I do, if we want to talk to them, you have to drive over."

If George was breaking out of his mold, Henry was positively exploding. By now he had shed virtually all of his old friends—the ones who knew him well enough to bring him back down to earth—and substituted for them a new and altogether different crowd.

Working the de la Renta network with the diligence of a scientist on the track of a new vaccine, Carolyne and Henry courted the movers and shakers of the New York society set. They threw parties in their stage set of an apartment that were oohed and aahed over for months to come. At one particularly splendid affair, Henry had arranged to have Midori, the world-renowned sixteen-year-old violinist, give his guests a private virtuoso performance. They sat the young prodigy, dressed in pink taffeta and silver slippers, in their drawing room, where they had set up gold ballroom chairs for their one hundred or so guests. Among those soaking in the evening were American Express chairman Jim Robinson and his wife, Linda, Donald and Ivana Trump, corporate raider Saul Steinberg, cosmetics magnate Ronald Lauder, and Georgette and Robert Mosbacher. The latter was named secretary of commerce shortly thereafter. After a breathtaking performance, they all sat down to eat in Carolyne and Henry's peach-colored dining room, under the watchful eyes of an enormous portrait by Sargent. After pasta with white truffles, the dinner guests were treated to venison and "unborn" vegetables. Dessert was a simple but elegant fruit compote topped with whipped cream. Suzy, the society writer, rated the party a twenty on a scale of one to ten.[1]

There was no question, Carolyne knew what she was doing. First she transported them to the pinnacle of Manhattan's Nouvelle Society. And once that position was secure, she made sure they became part of a transcontinental elite. They wouldn't just throw parties in New York, at Weatherstone, or in Vail, where they had torn down an old ski hut and erected a cross between a Swiss chalet and a French château, called Woodhaven. No, wherever they went, Carolyne would entertain royally. In Salzburg, for instance, they gave a dinner for twenty and arranged to have the flamenco dancers from *Carmen* entertain their guests between courses. In Paris, they managed to get invited onto a special committee formed to help support the Paris Opera, ensuring them a place at black-tie affairs sponsored by France's prime minister and attended by friends such as Henry and Nancy Kissinger. "The money that fuels Nouvelle Society is the same that fuels the creative process," Carolyne explained matter-of-factly to a reporter. "Where would the Renaissance have been without the patrons?"[2] Henry and she certainly were good patrons. They started underwriting entire performances at the opera and the ballet.

In addition to their own private parties, they would throw themselves with abandon onto the charity scene. Carolyne had never worked with charities, but Henry showed her how. He had been on the board of the New York City Ballet since 1984, and now he introduced Carolyne to its inner circle. It was a very political board, but it didn't have the same rigid social criteria of the Met. Carolyne had her "coming out" party there: she was asked to chair the ballet's spring gala in 1986. It wasn't so hard after all, she told a *New York Times* society reporter: Henry got the whole event underwritten by his friends at Drexel Burnham Lambert.[3]

That seemed to be how it worked. Henry bought companies using his investors' money, and then those companies paid him and his investment bankers enormous fees. Out of gratitude, many of those investment bankers then donated some of that money to Henry's favorite charities, often in his name. The nonprofit organizations, in turn, were only too happy to have someone with financial muscle on their boards. It was a perfect system. Everyone won, or almost everyone.

But that was just the beginning. Henry began getting interested in Channel 13, where his friend Dick Beattie was general counsel. And in 1989, after several years of lobbying by Beattie, Henry was named that organization's chairman of the board. He also became a trustee at the Central Park Conservancy and quickly became the chairman of a newly formed Campaign for Central Park Conservancy. By 1989, Henry and his network of wealthy investment bankers had become something of a savior of the organization. Its board chairman, Jim Evans, wrote in the 1989 annual report, "The Park's renaissance would not be possible without the unflagging energy of campaign chairman Henry Kravis and his marvelous team, who have raised $39 million of the Conservancy's $50-million fund-raising goal." By the end of the next year that amount had risen to $42.5 million, with the help of generous contributions from KKR's extended family. While Henry and Carolyne gave their usual gift of more than $250,000, the RJR Nabisco Foundation kicked in over $250,000, Beatrice donated over $50,000, Duracell contributed over $25,000, and Dick Beattie's firm, Simpson Thacher Bartlett, contributed over $10,000.

Henry could deliver—both by making his own donations and by persuading people he knew to do likewise. And in the 1980s, when federal grants to cultural organizations were being reduced at the same time that expenses were growing geometrically, people with money ended up in positions of enormous leverage.

The experience of the venerable Metropolitan Museum of Art is perhaps the best example of these changing fortunes of such organizations. In the old days, a handful of New York's finest families always saw to it that the Met was financially sound. When the curator needed money for a new exhibition or the purchase of a fine painting, he would simply call up one of the Astors or the Morgans and a check would arrive on his desk the next day. It was almost as simple as that. But as those families' wealth was passed down through the generations, it became less concentrated and therefore, less potent. Out of necessity, the Met became increasingly dependent on other sources to help preserve its position as the preeminent fine art museum in the United States.

234

In the 1980s, of course, it was mostly Wall Street men who had money. Financiers had never really been considered the right caliber for the Met. To many of its board members, stockbrokers were nothing more than bookies with fancy titles. They had no intention of allowing such ill-bred figures with little or no taste to penetrate the inner sanctums of their fine institution. Saul Steinberg learned of this bias the hard way, when he tried unsuccessfully to gain access to the Met with a $10-million contribution. With his swaggering ways and corporate-raider reputation, he was regarded as simply "not right" for the Met's lauded board of trustees, although they gladly took his check. "It's how you behave yourself. You have to work at it," explained a Met trustee.

Henry Kravis, however, was another matter. For starters, he had polish. The years of Ray's careful training, boarding school, and Carolyne's good influence had definitely paid off. No one would say Henry Kravis wasn't charming. And though trustees dismissed his claims to be "a collector," he did at least make an effort to appreciate art. But his ace in the hole was William Luers, the museum president, who was responsible for keeping an eye on the business health of the Met and was an ex officio member of the nominating committee for new Met trustees. Like many others in this era, Bill and Wendy Luers were social animals, only they never made it past the periphery. They were popular. But they just didn't quite have what it took. Luers was a tall, gangly former ambassador to Czechoslovakia and a friend of Henry Kissinger's. A mutual courtship began. Luers's friendship was no doubt helpful to Carolyne and Henry in securing the magnificent Temple of Dendur for private parties. Bill and Wendy, in turn, must have been delighted by the enthusiasm that was suddenly turned in their direction.

In December of 1987, Henry decided to take a leap and give the Met $10 million for a new wing that would have his name on it. Larry and Preston Tisch, two highly regarded Manhattan investors, had done the same thing one year earlier and ended up with their photo in the front of the Met's annual report alongside Arthur Sulzberger, the museum's chairman. There were no promises made, but many who know Henry say he hoped that his gift would grant him access to the Met's prestigious board. A picture in the next annual report shows him standing in front of the construction site looking slightly out of place. The caption read, "Henry R. Kravis surveys construction of the wing to bear his name."

"This is history," he told *U.S. News* to explain his generosity. "This has been done for years, whether it's the Mellons or the Carnegies or the Vanderbilts. They accomplished, they made money, and of course money and power is what's attractive to these institutions. You look down the boards, you don't see a lot of unknowns."[4] If the magazine's editors saw any irony in a financial engineer comparing himself to men who had spent their lives pioneering new technologies and building up industrial companies from scratch, they made no comment.

Six months after his gift, when there was still no public mention of Henry's board seat, Henry and Carolyne took Bill and Wendy Luers in their private jet for a tour of the Soviet Union. Luers, having spent many years in Czechoslovakia and considering himself something of an expert on communist countries, no doubt had many interesting observations to make as the two couples toured the country. And Bill and Wendy cannot have been unhappy about traveling through the impoverished country in such fine circumstances. "Henry Kravis cultivated Bill Luers, and Bill Luers cultivated Henry," said one Met trustee. Finally, about a year after Henry's gift, he was invited to become a trustee. Friends say he was elated. And just several months after that, Bill Luers was invited to become a director on one of KKR's companies, a small machine-tools company named IDEX. In exchange for his counsel, Luers takes home $25,000 a year and has been granted stock options in the company—2,000 a year.

Kravis insists that his donations to places such as the Met and Mt. Sinai Hospital, where he also gave $10 million for a new wing, are purely charitable and that he expects nothing in return. "I was taught to give something back," he insisted to a reporter.[5] But the assiduousness with which he has courted the city's cultural institutions and the prestige those board positions, in turn, have conferred on him have unquestionably enhanced his business image.

The pattern of Henry's donations, moreover, is strikingly similar to that which Ray employed in his bid to gain acceptance in hard-bitten Tulsa. Henry says his mother always taught him that life was like a house—it needed a strong foundation. And if you built it one block at a time, the house would never crumble. All Henry was doing was building his house. First he built a business reputation, then he parlayed it into entrance to higher society, ingratiating himself with prominent cultural organizations, one by one. At the same time, he was developing ties to the Republican Party, a platform from which he amassed at least a limited power base in Washington. One block at a time. Just as Bessie said.

Today, Henry sits in his magnificent forty-second-floor office exuding the satisfaction of a man who has conquered. "I've had fun with Central Park," he says, nodding his head toward the window, which affords a splendid view of the city lawn that runs almost to the foot of his building. "Chairmanship of Channel 13," he says, clearly savoring the sound of it. "That's going to be a kick. I can bring my business background to that, my interest in television, my interest in education, and I'm having a lot of fun!" he says, displaying all the enthusiasm of a boy with a new toy.

Armed with $5.6 billion and egos that could fairly be described as robust, Henry and George went on a buying spree the likes of which this country has never seen. From 1987 to 1989, they bought eight companies with a total price tag of $43.9 billion. Among their new wards were Owens-Illinois, the glass container maker, Duracell, which makes batteries, Stop & Shop, the northeastern supermarket chain, and RJR Nabisco, the food and tobacco giant. Not even J. P.

Morgan in his heyday tried to amass an industrial empire on the scale of KKR's. From a close look at the companies they went after, the people they aligned themselves with, and the abandon with which they dispensed other people's money, it is clear that they became quite unhinged from the values and business practices the firm was founded on and to which they continued to pay lip service. "To me, the story is about power and what power does to people," says one investment banker who knows KKR well. "That's what this story is about—the influence of power, and how in this case, three personalities handled it."

The message that KKR began to send out was perfectly straightforward: work with us and you'll be amply rewarded; get in our way and you'll be sorry. Nowadays the deal that KKR is most associated with, and that people regard as most symptomatic of the excesses on Wall Street, is RJR Nabisco. But RJR Nabisco was not a departure; it was the culmination of a process that had gone badly out of control. The only thing different about the RJR Nabisco deal was that it was larger, and therefore more visible, and that it came at a time when critics of leveraged buyouts were looking for a scapegoat. But KKR had committed equally, if not more, egregious acts with other companies long before RJR Nabisco.

Of the six companies that KKR has acquired since 1987 (the year that Kohlberg resigned) one—Jim Walter, also known as Hillsborough—has filed for bankruptcy protection, and two others, Seaman Furniture and RJR Nabisco, have required KKR to shore them up with more equity. As for working with management "partners," they have been ousted in Stop & Shop, Seaman's, and RJR Nabisco. KKR's skills as a money manager may not be too good either. According to a report in the *New York Times*, the firm purchased $810 million worth of stock in the public market, which at the end of September 1990 had a value of only $457 million, a 44-percent decline.[6] Since the market has rebounded somewhat, so, presumably, have KKR's investments.

George Roberts is quoted in *Barbarians at the Gate* as

saying that Jerry simply had to go because he wasn't with it, wasn't reading, wasn't keeping up with the times. While Jerry's presence might not have forestalled any of these disasters, it is at least arguable that George or Henry were not "with it" either. As Kohlberg's friend Aeder sees it, "What they were really saying was, 'These are new times, and they have the beat.' They obviously didn't have the beat."

A close look at some of KKR's deals reveals just how far the firm strayed from its original precepts. Consider Seaman Furniture Company, a family-run outfit that for years has been selling home furniture to the New York area's middle class.

Until Seaman's, the firm had always resisted buying a company that had a limited product line that sold in a narrow geographic market. Given the debt loads the firm was heaping on its acquisitions, that would be suicide. Yet that is precisely what KKR did in the case of Seaman's, which derives 25 percent of its revenues from the relatively small market of Long Island and the rest from stores in nearby New Jersey and Pennsylvania.

Clifton S. Robbins, however, was a hard-charging twenty-nine-year-old KKR dealmaker, and he seems to have been determined to make Seaman's his catch. He had only been with the firm three months before he persuaded the partners to launch a bid for Seaman's. With that, Robbins certainly made a quick mark. In the world of KKR, deals are the currency in which one trades. Robbins convinced KKR that he knew Seaman's financial picture fairly well because he had looked into the company when he was working in Morgan Stanley's mergers department, before he joined KKR. He knew that the family had its wealth tied up in the company, and he thought that they might respond to an invitation to get their money out. KKR gave Cliff the okay to pursue the company, and the firm ended up acquiring about 80 percent of it with $41.5 million of its investors' and its own money, and a $265-million bank loan organized by

Manufacturers Hanover. The Seaman family and other managers retained the rest. For its troubles, KKR pocketed a $5-million investment-banking fee. Salomon earned $2 million for acting as an adviser, and banks, lawyers, accountants, and others were paid another $13 million.

In Seaman's, however, KKR got more than it bargained for. As it turned out, Morton Seaman, the company's wily, white-haired CEO, had sold his company at the peak of the market. From his family's perspective, it was an exquisitely timed transaction. Almost immediately after KKR acquired it, the Long Island economy began to soften, and the company's sales plummeted. Less than two years later, Seaman's was on the verge of bankruptcy. KKR managed to convince the banks to help it restructure the deal rather than let the company go under. *Restructuring* is a euphemism for taking an otherwise bankrupt company and making it look whole again. Inevitably, someone must accept losses, however, and an intense struggle arose over how those losses should be apportioned.

In the end, after months of bitter wrangling and eleventh-hour discussions, the banks wrote off $115 million of their loans. KKR injected another $28 million of its investors' money into the badly weakened company just to keep it alive. And KKR put in $7 million of its own money. That was probably the minimum injection it could get away with without losing face.

KKR executives dismiss criticism of the deal as unfair. They concede that with Seaman's, they took their eye off the ball. But it was a small deal, they say, a mere pimple on an otherwise outstanding record. It may have been small in size, but it was hardly an aberration. About the same time that it acquired Seaman's, KKR did a leveraged buyout of Jim Walter Corporation, a construction-materials and home-building company based in Tampa, Florida. The firm paid $3.3 billion for the company, of which George and Henry and their other partners contributed a grand total of $1.5 million. Their investment-banking fee on the transaction—$35 million.

Jim Walter had been around since 1955 and was one reason that hundreds of thousands of Americans lived in prefab houses. It was also, unfortunately, the manufacturer of products containing asbestos. A year and a half after it was acquired by KKR, the company filed for Chapter 11 bankruptcy protection, after fears of the potential asbestos liability made it impossible for the company to refinance some of its debt before a deadline. Court documents that have emerged since that time show that KKR was aware of the risks that asbestos presented, but was determined to do the deal anyway. In that determination, the safety of their investors' funds seems to have been of secondary concern.

KKR came to acquire Jim Walter because it caught the eye of another of KKR's rising stars. Michael Tokarz had been calling on the company since the 1970s, when he was a loan officer at the Continental Bank in Miami. KKR's young bucks were given free rein to roam—indeed, it was their job to seek out and pursue potential acquisitions. If they found a good opportunity, and Henry or George or the other top partners gave their approval, it could be a real feather in their cap and would likely increase their year-end bonus.

"I thought it would be a good investment opportunity, and I asked Mr. Kravis if I could give him [Jim Walter] a call," Tokarz said in a court hearing in the fall of 1989 having to do with the jurisdiction of a class-action asbestos suit. "What did Mr. Kravis say?" an attorney asked. "He said if I was that up on the company, sure I could give him a call,"[7] Tokarz replied. It was the beginning of a year of fierce efforts to make the deal happen.

Tokarz ran various financial projections through his computer to see what would happen to the company's financial performance if it was loaded up with debt. Having convinced himself that it could stand up to the pressure, Tokarz suggested that he and Kravis fly down to Tampa in late January 1987 to have a "get-acquainted" meeting with management and discuss a potential buyout. In that and a subsequent meeting, Jim Walter, the company's chief executive and founder, told them he was pleased by their interest but that the company faced the prospect of having to pay off thousands of past employees who had worked with asbestos. The liabilities associated with a class action suit, he warned, could be enormous, and any buyer would have to study the issue thoroughly before talks progressed any further. He also said that he had no interest in selling the company if it would have to be split up and sold off in pieces in order to make the deal work.

Tokarz and Kravis promised they would explore both subjects fully and flew back to New York scratching their heads. Walter had presented serious obstacles, but Tokarz was determined to try to overcome them. Over the next few months, he tried to structure the deal so as to meet Walter's criteria and still make a profit. Whenever he could snatch time away from other projects, he would study the issue, turning it over and over in his mind, sometimes with the help of Drexel executives. Kohlberg, who was then on his way out the door, says he warned Kravis and Tokarz that they should not go ahead with the deal unless they could obtain insurance for the asbestos liabilities.

With the help of some creative financing ideas from Drexel and some thoughts about how to restructure the company in order to isolate the asbestos claims, KKR finally made a $50-a-share bid for the company in July. Their action promptly drew other bidders, including Paine Webber and a buyer affiliated with Citibank, into the fray. To stay in the game, KKR raised its bid twice, finally to $60 a share plus a dividend payment. When it came time for Jim Walter's special committee of directors to consider the final bids, Henry, who had been supervising Tokarz on the transaction, was off in Turkey on a yacht he had chartered for a vacation with Carolyne and the children. At the last minute, George was drafted to step in for Henry to make KKR's final presentation.

According to a presentation paper that KKR had prepared, various executives assured the Jim Walter directors that KKR had fully explored the asbestos issue and had received the necessary opinions stating that the company was solvent at the time that it was sold. "KKR has already obtained the necessary opinions with respect to solvency and fraudulent conveyance which serve to protect the incumbent Board as well as to satisfy a closing condition of the lender," the outline stated. "KKR already has *in-hand* [emphasis in original] the necessary legal and accounting opinions required to avoid a fraudulent conveyance problem." (The latter concerns whether it was known that a company was insolvent at the time of its sale.) KKR used its preparedness on these various issues to put other bidders at a competitive disadvantage. "Have other bidders resolved tax issues, asbestos-related issues, and solvency/fraudulent conveyance issues? Have other bidders demonstrated proven track records which assure the Independent Committee that they can complete a $3-billion deal in this most difficult transaction?" the notes asked.

Two years later, in court hearings, a lawyer asked Tokarz about this presentation. "Did you in fact have opinions by this point in time?"

Tokarz replied, "No. I did not have any written. . . . I just had an understanding that they would be forthcoming on the basic financing issues."[8]

Not only did Tokarz not have the necessary opinions, but they would prove extremely difficult to obtain. As KKR, its bankers, and debt underwriters sought to organize the financing for the deal, the asbestos liabilities became a key issue. If there were ever large legal settlements, they could wipe out the company's financial reserves, leaving bank lenders and junk-bond investors with claims on the company that could turn out to be worthless. KKR hired the accounting firm of Deloitte, Haskins & Sells to do an audit of Jim Walter's financial status, and to write a letter affirming the company's solvency. (KKR almost invariably uses Deloitte as its accountant. The LBO firm and the companies in its empire make KKR one of Deloitte's largest clients. In addition, Deloitte's team leader in this case had already expressed an interest in buying a subsidiary of Jim Walter with some friends once the deal went through.)

Deloitte did its financial analysis, but was worried about evaluating the company's solvency without making some judgment about the potential asbestos liabilities. Without a statement from Deloitte affirming the company's solvency, it would be virtually impossible to get money for the deal from either the banks or bond investors. The deal would be dead in the water. "We needed the DH and S letter," Tokarz confirmed to a lawyer during a court hearing.

At the last minute, Deloitte decided it could not give its stamp of approval without first obtaining a legal opinion on how the company's asbestos liabilities might affect the company's solvency. KKR asked the building company to get its lawyers at Latham & Watkins to provide the opinion. The choice was especially curious because the Los Angeles–based Latham & Watkins was one of two firms that KKR usually used, and because it was being asked to analyze Florida state law as it applied to the potential for asbestos-liability claims on a Florida-incorporated company. Yet Latham & Watkins was not licensed to practice law in Florida and therefore could not be considered an expert on the state statutes.

One can't help but wonder where Latham & Watkins's loyalties stood at this point. The would-be buyer, KKR, had hired Latham & Watkins on March 3 of that year to research the asbestos issue. Yet ten days later, Latham & Watkins went to work for the would-be seller, Jim Walter, to advise it on the same matter. (KKR said it had no problem with the law firm's switching sides because at that time it had decided against doing a transaction. Yet through much of that month and into the next, Tokarz continued to pursue the deal.) Now one year later it was being asked to give a letter that would provide assurances to Deloitte.

Long after the Jim Walter board thought the issue was resolved, Latham & Watkins finally delivered a letter stating that it had determined that Jim Walter was legally insulated

244

from any asbestos claims. Two years later, Tokarz admitted that he did not even bother to look at the letter until after the tender offer for Jim Walter's shares had been completed. But with that letter in its files, Deloitte could give its full-steam-ahead opinion. And with that, the lenders and junk-bond underwriters were able to come up with the money.

The end result is just as Jim Walter feared: to meet interest payments, KKR has had to sell off substantial divisions of the company, at least partially dismantling it. In the first nine months after the company's bankruptcy filing, sales declined compared to the previous period and the company suffered a loss of $83 million. In a report to its investors, KKR stated that the bankruptcy had caused some disruption and that "it is too early to determine whether there will be any long-term damage to the various Hillsborough businesses."

The relationship between Latham & Watkins and KKR is quite complex, and raises questions about the law firm's independence. The connection dates back to the early 1970s, when Kohlberg asked Clint Stevenson, then one of the firm's partners, to help Bear Stearns with some legal work that George needed done on the West Coast. Stevenson assigned one of the firm's bright young lawyers, John McLoughlin, to handle Kohlberg's work.

The first major assignment that McLoughlin worked on was George's acquisition of the Cobblers Co., the troubled California shoe company, in 1971. McLoughlin was then a thirty-five-year-old associate, eight years out of law school. Because of the CEO's suicide, it was a deal neither man will ever forget.

Despite the unpleasant circumstances, George and John worked well together. And when it came time to do several more West Coast transactions, Kohlberg gave Latham & Watkins the nod. At the time, it was a small account, prestigious but not especially profitable. Latham & Watkins, meanwhile, was focusing more on Hollywood-related legal work. In those early days it was not apparent that McLoughlin was developing a relationship with a client who would turn out to be one of the firm's most important.

A certain rapport gradually developed between the two men. They were both quiet and unassuming, without the slightest interest in the limelight. Their personalities complemented each other well. George liked to control things, and having been trained as a lawyer, he knew exactly what legal work he wanted performed and how it should be carried out. McLoughlin, by contrast, was highly accommodating, according to those who saw him in work situations. Though good at carrying out directions, he showed no aptitude for trailblazing himself.

McLoughlin appears to hold his client almost in awe: "He is exceptional among the exceptional. . . . I'll bet he charmed the hell out of you!" McLoughlin was particularly impressed with the way that George retains numbers from a host of different transactions and juggles them effortlessly in his head. George's memory, he says, takes his breath away.

No matter how hard McLoughlin tried to come up with ideas that George might not have thought of, he says he was rarely, if ever, successful. "I think I'm pretty good. . . . I've worked with them for a long time, and I think I sort of know the way they think, and yet I'm always amazed. . . . They will think of considerations and aspects down the road that, once they say it, you say, 'Of course, that's exactly what we should be thinking about!' "

McLoughlin's deferential nature and Roberts's determination to be in control were a perfect match. They work well together, but otherwise maintain a fairly formal relationship, unlike Henry and his lawyer Dick, who frequently dine and vacation together. George and Leanne attended a wedding of one of McLoughlin's daughters, and John and his wife were invited to the Robertses' tenth wedding anniversary. But other than formal family events, they maintain their separate, private lives.

As KKR's business grew, so did McLoughlin's status within Latham & Watkins. He went from being a well-respected attorney to one of their rising stars, to one of their senior rainmakers. The fees from KKR's business exploded. In some years they exceeded 5 percent of the firm's total revenue—a level that McLoughlin says made some partners uncomfortable because they feared it signaled an unhealthy dependence on one client. So important was KKR's happiness to its own welfare, the fifty-seven-year-old West Coast firm finally decided in 1985 to open a New York office. Today that office holds eighty-five lawyers, many of whom work on KKR-related business. Of the thirty-eight deals KKR has done since it was founded, Latham & Watkins has been involved with at least twenty. It has also given some of its own flesh and blood to the cause. Mike Michelson and Saul Fox worked for many years at Latham & Watkins before they joined George in KKR's San Francisco office. The two men now make several multiples of their previous salary, and Fox was recently named one of the firm's two new partners, bringing the total to six.

In fact, the tentacles between McLoughlin, his firm, and KKR extend much further than many people realize. Early on, George Roberts would frequently offer McLoughlin seats on boards of companies that KKR was buying. The offers were somewhat unusual, and many lawyers are wary of accepting such positions, because it vastly complicates the attorney-client relationship. Suppose the company on whose board a lawyer is sitting chooses to engage in an activity that the lawyer considers illegal or unethical. Is the lawyer obliged to uphold the law, as any officer of the court is sworn to do, or should he or she assist the client, with whom the lawyer hopes to do much work in the future? To prevent potential conflicts of interest that might arise out of situations like this, many of the country's leading law firms simply prohibit their lawyers from sitting on the boards of their clients' companies.

In the case of Latham & Watkins, McLoughlin was allowed to sit on a KKR company's board, but the firm would not allow him to accept director's fees. They would have to go to the partnership, rather than to him personally. McLoughlin says George was not satisfied with that arrangement. "George wanted me as the director, *me* getting the fees, etc. And he found out that the firm was getting them and on the next deal he said, 'We don't see a lot of sense doing that, we can get all the legal help we need from you anyway, we don't need you on the board.'" Though he was disappointed by George's decision, McLoughlin resigned his seat.

George rewarded McLoughlin another way. He offered him stakes in some of the companies that KKR was acquiring. Again, such a step was highly unusual. Most large law firms get uncomfortable when a relationship between one of their lawyers and a client is anything other than at arm's length. They like clean lines; they don't want there to be any questions about loyalties; and they certainly don't like partners accepting remuneration from clients other than through the partnership. That is, after all, the whole essence of a partnership; what belongs to one belongs to all. When a partner receives money on the side, it leaves open the question of whether the firm as a whole was fully compensated for the legal services it provided. While some small firms allow it, many large law firms such as Davis Polk & Wardwell and Wilkie Farr & Gallagher remove any ambiguities by simply banning special deals like that altogether.

Initially, says McLoughlin, his firm's rules inhibited his ability to accept stakes in clients' deals. However, "we got a little more into the twentieth century in our policies here, and I invested in four or five companies before the eighties." After some of McLoughlin's partners became jealous of the financial rewards that he was reaping because of his special relationship with George, they asked if they could get in on it, too. The arrangement, says McLoughlin, began in earnest at the time of KKR's first formal fund-raising effort in 1982. Initially, it involved about ten partners. Today, he says, about two hundred of Latham & Watkins's partners participate in KKR's deals through a pool.

Among the companies in which it has invested are Storer
Communications, Motel-6, Union Texas Petroleum, Owens-
Illinois, Fred Meyer—and the now-bankrupt Jim Walter,
which was their client at the time it was negotiating its sale
to KKR, and on whose behalf the law firm wrote a letter that
became pivotal to KKR's ability to finance its purchase of the
company.

Henry and George's penchant for bestowing handsome
rewards on those who went the extra mile for them was
exemplified in the case of Macmillan. By the late 1980s, the
old-line publishing house was in a weakened financial state
and in danger of falling prey to a hostile takeover. One investment group, led by the wealthy Texan investor Robert
Bass, had already circled around the company in the fall of
1987 and acquired a substantial stake in it. In May of 1988,
he made a formal offer to acquire the entire company.

By this time, the company's CEO, Edward P. Evans, had
spent considerable time telling his board of directors how
unfortunate it would be if Bass took over the company. Evans
persuaded them to issue the usual array of antitakeover devices: lavish golden parachutes for top management, poison
pills, stock options—all items designed to help entrench management in the company, and which Henry generally regarded with contempt.

On the advice of Lazard Frères, Macmillan's board
spurned Bass's offers and made plans to move ahead with a
management-led buyout sponsored by Evans and a group of
top managers. Lawsuits filed by the Bass group prevailed,
however, and in July of 1988, with Bass looking as though
he had won the company, Ned Evans began holding urgent
talks with KKR.

At this point, a host of other bidders jumped into the
fray, including the eccentric British publisher Robert Maxwell, who was looking for American publishing properties.
While Macmillan's board held talks with other bidders, Evans
spent the next five weeks conferring with KKR, providing

information about the company's financial health, and negotiating how large a stake Evans and his team would have in the company as part of a KKR-sponsored buyout proposal.

KKR agreed that Evans and his group of managers could own up to 20 percent of the company if they won. The offer had the effect of reducing the share that KKR's investors would receive by the same amount, and therefore their share of future profits. KKR also insisted that it should receive a $29.3-million fee if its offer was rejected because someone else made a higher bid.

In late September, shortly after all the bids were submitted, Evans and the company's president, William F. Reilly, asked the company's financial advisers how the bidding was going. Though Evans and Reilly were clearly aligned with one team and therefore should not have received any flow of nonpublic information, the advisers, who had been closely involved with Evans and Reilly from the start, told them the details of the various bids. Evans promptly telephoned a KKR representative and "tipped" them to Robert Maxwell's bid, according to a description by a Delaware judge. "In this call, Evans informed KKR that Maxwell had offered '$89, all cash' for the company, and that the respective bids were considered 'a little close.' After a few minutes of conversation—but not in time to stop Evans from giving them the information they needed—the KKR representative realized the impropriety of the call and abruptly terminated it."[9]

If KKR was disturbed by what had transpired, it kept mum about it for three days—just long enough for it to revise its bid to counter Maxwell's and for the board to meet, consider the bids, and agree to award the company to KKR. Later, when KKR admitted having received the tip, it attempted to "trivialize this extraordinary act of misconduct," according to the Delaware judge.

KKR already had valuable information concerning its main competitor's bid. But Bruce Wasserstein, enfant terrible of the dealmaking world and an adviser to Macmillan's management, subsequently telephoned KKR, according to the

Delaware supreme court, and guided Henry and George as to how to structure their final bid so as to top the others. Although Wasserstein disputes the court's description of his behavior, the judge concluded that he left Maxwell with the mistaken impression that they had already submitted the highest bid. Thinking he would only be bidding against himself, Maxwell chose not to bid again, leaving the way clear for KKR.

In a court decision in the fall of 1989 by the Delaware supreme court, it concluded that "this auction was clandestinely and impermissibly skewed in favor of KKR. The record amply demonstrates that KKR repeatedly received significant material advantages to the exclusion and detriment of Maxwell to stymie, rather than enhance, the bidding process." The lack of an evenhanded bidding process meant that Macmillan's shareholders did not receive the highest price they might have for their shares.

The document continues: "This 'immaterial' tip revealed both the price and form of Maxwell's first-round bid, which constituted the two principal strategic components of their otherwise unconditional offer. With this information, KKR knew every crucial element of Maxwell's initial bid. The unfair, tactical advantage this gave KKR, since no aspect of its own bid could be shopped, becomes manifest in light of the situation created by Maxwell's belief that it had submitted the higher offer."[10]

The Delaware judges said they considered Wasserstein's comments to KKR as "in reality another form of tip." They concluded that "the eventual auction results demonstrate that Wasserstein's tip relayed crucial information to KKR: the methods by which KKR should tailor its bid in order to satisfy Macmillan's financial advisers. It is highly significant that both aspects of the advice conveyed by the tip—to 'focus on price' and to amend the terms of its lockup agreement—were adopted by KKR. They were the very improvements upon which the board subsequently accepted the KKR bid on Wasserstein's recommendations. Nothing could have been more material under the circumstances. It violated every principle of fair dealing, and the exacting role demanded of those entrusted with the conduct of an auction for the sale of corporate control." As a result of the various court skirmishes, KKR's initial victory was overturned and Maxwell ultimately won the company.

Although the behavior of the people that KKR was dealing with in the Macmillan case had been called deceptive and unfair by a state supreme court judge, the firm did nothing to distance itself or its investors from them in the future. Indeed, just a few months later, Evans helped KKR acquire a subsidiary of Macmillan, called K-III Holdings. Although he has no official role in the company, he works on the same floor where the company is located and reportedly acts as an unofficial adviser. Evans's sidekick, William Reilly, in the meantime, has resigned from Macmillan and has become the president of K-III. KKR and Reilly intend to build K-III through acquisitions into a major publishing force.

As for Bruce Wasserstein, just a few months after the Macmillan battle was over, he was retained by KKR to advise it on its bid for RJR Nabisco. Like other advisers on the transaction, all of whom KKR later said played a minimal role, Wasserstein's firm received a $25-million fee.

But the zeal that KKR exhibited in its bids for Seaman's, Jim Walter, and Macmillan was nothing compared to the abandon with which it pursued RJR Nabisco. While the details of that chase have been fully recounted elsewhere, there is one perspective that has not received a lot of attention: that of investors who owned bonds of the company before it was acquired and loaded up with even more debt.

One such investor, the Metropolitan Life Insurance Company, owned $340 million of the RJR Nabisco bonds, some of which were not due to mature until 2016. Up until that point, the insurance company had enjoyed a long relationship with KKR, having invested with the firm since the early days in transactions such as Fred Meyer. So executives at Met Life were particularly surprised when KKR rode roughshod over them in its determination to win RJR Nabisco. The insurance company sued RJR—and by inference, its owner, KKR—claiming that it had breached its contractual commitments to bondholders.

In the fierce battle for RJR, KKR made increasingly higher bids for the company. The only problem was, it would eventually have to come up with the money—$32 billion to be precise. No one was actually sure there were enough lenders in the world to come up with that gargantuan sum—it was more than anyone had ever attempted before. At the time of the bidding, RJR Nabisco had $5 billion on its books of low-interest-rate, high-quality debt. If it did not have to repay that debt, but could leave it in place, that would be $5 billion less that KKR would have to come up with, and thanks to the low 8.2-percent interest rate, less in interest that would have to be paid every year.

To find out if that would be possible, James Greene, a KKR associate and former Bankers Trust lender, asked lawyers at Simpson Thacher to look at the company's forty-one indentures, notes, and other lending documents. In less than a week, the lawyers at Simpson Thacher came back to Greene and said yes.

By his own account, Greene did not ask too many questions: "I had a lot of things on my mind, as you can appreciate in those days, and not the least of which was raising an awful lot of money in a very short period of time. And so when I became aware, and when we became aware, that we could put our financing in place and not be in violation of the pre-LBO debt, I said, 'Thank you very much,' and I moved ahead and I left that behind me. . . . From my vantage point, that's what I wanted to hear. That's what I needed to hear to do what I was doing, which was raising a lot of money."[11]

From the Met's standpoint, it was bad enough that KKR left existing bondholders in place and did not repay them. But what really disturbed the insurance company was the amount of debt that RJR Nabisco finally incurred to finance the leveraged buyout and the tiny amount of shareholder's equity that was left afterward, which could be used as a cushion against insolvency and default on its bonds. At the same time, the Met complained in its suit, RJR Nabisco engaged in some fancy legal footwork that resulted in assets of the company being pledged to the banks as collateral, which meant they were removed from the reach of the company's original bondholders. The Met was concerned that if the company ever faced a financial collapse, the banks would end up whole and the original bondholders would be left with nothing. In questioning KKR's lenders, the Met's lawyers established that the banks had insisted on that collateral as a condition for their loans. KKR had not been in a good position to argue if it wanted its deal to go through.

This might not have been so serious had RJR Nabisco's debt load not been so huge. But in order to finance the buyout, KKR had arranged for RJR to issue a veritable mountain of junk bonds. And since the company acknowledged that its earnings were not sufficient to pay interest on all that debt, KKR and its advisers had the company issue what are known as payment-in-kind bonds, where interest is paid by issuing more junk bonds. (Payment-in-kind bonds were popularized by Michael Milken and became commonplace on Wall Street during the late 1980s.)

At the time the deal was done, KKR executives pointed to these non-cash-paying bonds as evidence of their aversion to risk. "It's as conservative a deal as we've ever done," said Paul E. Raether, a KKR partner.[12] Met Life's lawyers calculated that of the $11.5 billion in junk bonds that RJR issued to finance the buyout, $9.3 billion were not obligated to pay interest in cash until 1994 or after. But because of this pay-in-kind feature, they also estimated that RJR would have to make over $20 billion in principal payments by 1995, long before its bonds would come due.

In January 1991, RJR and the Met settled the suit out of court. It was clear from the terms of the settlement that the Met achieved its objectives. RJR Nabisco agreed to repay the Met and other bondholders the full amount of their bonds, and to do so fifteen years before those bonds were originally scheduled to come due. It thus agreed to move their claim ahead of the company's more recent junk bond holders. RJR also agreed to pay the legal and other expenses of the Met and another plaintiff, which the *New York Times* estimated would come to nearly $15 million. And RJR agreed to let the Met swap certain other bonds for equity in the food and tobacco company, a step that will further dilute the ownership position of KKR's own investors.

Indeed, KKR's investors are in the peculiar position of watching the company's financial underpinnings get stronger but at a stiff cost to their prospect for returns. Under the terms of the original agreement, KKR's investors put up about $1.5 billion in equity in exchange for 55 percent of the company and the same percentage of any future profits.

However, RJR Nabisco's heavy debt load soon proved so unworkable that KKR had to revamp the company's financing by raising several billion dollars of new equity and using that money, plus some bank loans, to pay off $11 billion of high interest-paying bonds. Unfortunately for KKR's original investors, by inviting in so many new equity investors KKR diluted their interest in the company and their claim on its future profits. KKR's investors had to cough up an additional $1.7 billion, but they only have about the same percentage ownership to show for it. Because KKR's investors have had to put up more than twice as much to get almost the same percentage profit, the restructuring has, by definition, lowered the ultimate return on their investment in multiple terms, by half.

KKR's investors hope that RJR's earnings will improve enough to offset at least some of that dilution. And certainly, the company's profit margins have improved under the watchful eyes of KKR-appointed chief executive, Louis V. Gerstner, Jr. But industry analysts caution that it is too early to make intelligent predictions about RJR Nabisco's long-term prospects. They do not know whether the cost savings that were generated in the first year and a half can be continued to the same degree in the future. They cannot foresee what will happen to potentially large overseas markets such as Eastern Europe. And they remain concerned about the risks to the company of tobacco liability. There are enough unknowns, in other words, to reserve judgment on whether RJR will turn out to be a smart investment for KKR and its partners or not.

WASHINGTON

Washington watched this orgy of dealmaking on Wall Street with mounting concern. It wasn't just KKR that seemed to be spinning out of control—although it was certainly among the more visible examples. But it appeared that almost anyone with a half-baked takeover idea and a few million dollars could persuade Drexel or one of its competitors to help them buy an old-line American company and disassemble it. As more and more of the nation's financial resources were funneled into the business of trading companies like so many baseball cards, a backlash began developing in Washington against Wall Street deal mania.

The first rumblings could be heard in 1985, when several congressional committees held hearings on takeovers, their impact on companies and local communities, and the rise of corporate indebtedness. There was much hand-wringing and beating of breasts, but in the end, Congress couldn't make up its mind what to do. Plenty of economists, after all, were saying that the restructuring of corporate America was a healthy development that signaled the dynamism of a capitalist system. At the end of the day, policymakers quietly slunk back to their offices, content that they would at least get credit for having examined the issue.

Kohlberg Kravis Roberts wasn't taking anything for granted, however. By early 1986 it had retained the services of five different lobbying firms in Washington. Although each had a slightly different assignment, their overall purpose was to monitor and if need be, help deflect any potential for legislation that might restrict merger or LBO activity or limit the tax deductibility of deal-related interest payments.

Besides its lobbying efforts, KKR sharply increased its contributions to political candidates. George, who had not shown much interest in supporting national political figures before, became an avid check-writer beginning in 1987. Federal Election Commission records show that in addition to generous contributions to key members of the Senate Finance Committee such as Lloyd Bentsen, the committee's chairman, John Danforth, Bob Dole, and Bill Bradley, George also gave $100,000 in 1988 to Team 100, the Republican National Committee's group of largest contributors.

George's activities, however, paled beside Henry's. In the 1987–88 election season, Henry gave over $80,000 to an assortment of senators, congressmen, Republican PACs, and the GOP's national committee. On top of that, Henry also gave $100,000 in Bush's election year to the party's Team 100, which gained him admission to that elite group.

Once again, Henry had a good teacher in Ray, who had long been one of the Republican's leading contributors. Since the late 1970s, Ray had regularly been giving as much as $40,000 a year to the party's national and senatorial committees. His generosity won him a place on the Committee to Re-elect the President, not to mention an invitation to dinner at the White House. In 1976, for instance, Ray and Bessie attended a dinner there hosted by President and Mrs.

Ford in honor of France's president, Giscard d'Estaing. Bessie's dinner partner that evening was Donald Rumsfeld, the secretary of defense, while Ray sat at a table with none other than Henry Kissinger, who was then secretary of state.[1]

Until the mid- to late 1980s, election records show that Henry and Ray gave to many of the same candidates, sometimes writing checks on the same days for the same amounts. By the time the 1987–88 election season rolled along, however, Henry's interests veered off slightly, as he and George began focusing their efforts on the Senate Finance Committee, which had jurisdiction over tax issues and would therefore be pivotal if any LBO legislation was proposed in the more liberal-leaning House of Representatives. Henry and George gave money to nine of the twenty senators on the committee. Carolyne did her share, too. She gave to five of the same senators, sometimes writing checks for the same amount as Henry on the same day.

The Kohlbergs made contributions, too. In 1988, Jerry gave $90,000 to the Democratic National Committee, and $2,000 to Sen. Donald W. Riegle, Jr., a Democrat from Michigan who sits on the Finance Committee and subsequently became the chairman of the prestigious Banking, Housing and Urban Affairs Committee. Riegle recently came under fire for having been actively courted by Charles Keating, the savings and loan executive. At the time Kohlberg made his contribution, Riegle had been moderately critical of excesses in the takeover movement, even to the point of cosponsoring a bill with Senator Proxmire designed to make abuses of the process more difficult.

Otherwise Jerry and Nancy's other political contributions have generally been in support of liberal candidates—often blacks and/or females—who tend not to have any role in LBO or tax policy-making. Among those who have received money from Jerry are Jim Hunt, for instance, the former governor of North Carolina who fought a spirited battle against Sen. Jesse Helms in 1984, and the Council for a Livable World.

* * *

In September of 1987, as the takeover fever showed no signs of abating, Sen. William Proxmire, a curmudgeonly man in his midseventies who had established his populist credentials by refusing to accept any PAC campaign contributions, decided that he had had enough. On the last day of the month, he submitted a bill aimed at restricting takeovers. Two weeks later, Rep. Dan Rostenkowski, the chairman of the important House Ways and Means Committee, submitted a bill that would limit the tax deductibility of interest on debt used to finance takeovers. Five days after that, on October 19, the stock market experienced the closest thing to a financial earthquake it has ever known. The market fell 508 points in a matter of hours, an event that became known as Black Monday.

Wall Street analysts were quick to draw a connection between the proposed legislation in Washington and the collapse of the stock market. And as that opinion was reinforced on talk shows during the next few days of postmortems, Washington policymakers became increasingly fearful that they were going to be made the scapegoat for the calamity on Wall Street. And since the market's collapse was feared by many to be a precursor to a national depression, that was a charge that few, if any, legislators wanted to be held accountable for.

Not surprisingly, this fear did much to squelch the appetite in Washington for further antitakeover legislation. Though there were those who felt that it was unfair to link Congress to events on Wall Street, their protestations had a defensive ring to them. And since no one was quite sure what had caused the market collapse, it was impossible to prove that the antitakeover proposals had *not* played a role. "Wall Street fed the myth that the Hill had caused it. I heard staffers walking around saying, 'We can't do this because we can't risk causing another crash.' It was an impediment to serious dialogue," says Carolyn Brancato, who was then analyzing LBOs for the Congressional Research Service.

For six months following the crash, there was a deafening silence on Wall Street. Although the collapse left many companies' stock selling at bargain-basement prices, an almost unspoken pact seemed to exist on the part of takeover artists and financiers not to stir things up again. At least, not yet. The crash had, after all, sent the nation reeling. And its aftershocks were felt in the stock markets of Tokyo, Paris, Bonn, and London. But gradually, as nerves grew calmer and the depression everyone had predicted showed no signs of materializing, life began returning to normal. Investment bankers started thinking about the possibilities for mergers, chief executives started eyeing their competitors, and corporate raiders started itching to get back to work again.

The spring of 1988 saw the battle for Macmillan, among others, but it wasn't until fall that all hell broke loose with the bidding war for RJR Nabisco. Polls indicated that the American public felt that corporate takeovers and the Wall Street investment bankers who spawned them were a negative influence on the country and that something should be done to restrict them. Before the year was out, nine different congressional committees had announced their intentions to hold hearings on takeovers, corporate indebtedness, and the negative impact on workers, bondholders, and American competitiveness. And Henry Kravis, who had become something of a household name during the brouhaha surrounding RJR Nabisco, was invited to appear at all of them.

But Henry did not want to be dragged before endless panels of hostile congressmen, where he would be forced to defend not just his business practices but his entire lifestyle. A circuslike atmosphere would almost certainly develop that would be both undignified and extremely unpleasant. "I said that that would turn into a television spectacle; I said no," says Henry. He and George instead decided to launch their own offensive. Dick Beattie, whose political antennae were more attuned than theirs, had convinced them they would have to contend with the publicity surrounding the RJR Nabisco takeover. If overly negative, it could scare off Japanese lenders, whom they were counting on to provide a large portion of RJR's financing. The Japanese are typically wary of antagonizing government officials, and a backlash in Congress could easily send them running for the hills.

To lend support to the case for LBO, KKR commissioned a study from the accounting firm of Deloitte, Haskins & Sells (now Deloitte & Touche) that would document exactly what happens to KKR-controlled companies after they are acquired. As Henry explained in an interview with *Fortune* magazine, "One of the biggest missing ingredients in Congress right now is information and understanding about LBOs. We're prepared to take the necessary time, as are others in the business, to try to increase public understanding of these transactions."[2]

Deloitte's study was intended to provide definitive answers to such nagging questions as, how many jobs are lost after an LBO? Is it true that spending on research and development is sharply cut back? Are companies that undergo LBOs raped and pillaged? Deloitte is the accounting firm that KKR has used for years to audit the financial statements of most of its companies. Deloitte has earned millions of dollars in fees from that business, making KKR one of if not its largest client.

Deloitte's survey found that the seventeen companies that were then under KKR's umbrella flourished after they were taken private in a leveraged buyout. Neatly packaged in a white booklet that ran over thirty pages, the study showed that the total number of employees in those companies grew from 276,000 the year the buyouts were done to 313,000 three years afterward. Spending on new plant and equipment, meanwhile, was 14 percent higher on average than it was before the deals were done. And despite constant worries about a decline in spending on researching and developing new products and ideas, KKR's companies' spending on those items actually rose by 15 percent after the companies became privately held. Not only did the study suggest that KKR's buyouts were good for the companies and the communities that they were located in, but it also implied that LBOs were good for America. Productivity rose, making those companies more competitive with their foreign counterparts. And contrary to popular opinion, Deloitte found that the U.S. Treasury did not lose out because the shareholders of those companies that were taken private had to pay hefty capital gains taxes on their windfalls. And those amounts far outweighed any loss of revenue that the Treasury suffered when companies were able to deduct the interest they paid on their debt.

KKR's study furthered the confusion on the Hill over how to think about LBOs. At hearing after hearing, congressmen and their aides had listened to sharply differing assessments of the LBO movement. The research of some academics showed that companies taken private in leveraged buyouts *did* generate new jobs. But other research showed that those companies generated fewer jobs than others in the same industry. There were eminent professors who said it was terrible to see so many of America's fine companies broken up and sold off in little pieces. And just as many others said those conglomerates should never have been assembled in the first place, and that those units were only being returned to their rightful homes where they could be better managed. There were industry executives who demonstrated that the debt levels of companies that underwent LBOs were no higher than those of their counterparts in Germany or Japan, and it hadn't seemed to have hurt them. And other analysts said it was unrealistic to compare the U.S. to those countries because their cultures and legal systems were so different.

"It gets really esoteric and people don't really want to listen," said Jennifer Hillman, an aide to Sen. Terry Sanford, a Democrat from North Carolina. "In the end, people felt that if they couldn't come to a substantive decision on whether these transactions were good or bad, then they shouldn't act."

On an issue where definitive conclusions seemed impossible, KKR's white paper had the benefit of being concrete. It was about real live companies with real live employees and real live budgets. And the numbers were impressive.

Ever the enterprising salesman, Henry was determined to see that the study was widely read. Rather than testify in any hearings, he decided to meet with legislators one-on-one. He always felt he could be most effective if he could meet someone in person, turn on that Kravis charm, and show them he was just a reasonable guy like anybody else trying to make a living. "Nobody can tell the story as well as we can," Henry said.

He enlisted the support of Tom Downey, a Democratic representative from New York, who identified members of the House Ways and Means Committee who might be receptive.[3] And he used his lobbying team, which included former aides to Senator Dole, Senator Kennedy, and Senator Packwood. "These guys aren't dumb," said one former staff director. "They got together a very good group who did a good job of saying, 'This isn't black-and-white.' And the Hill was on the defensive."

Whether due to his influential lobbyists, his dealmaking reputation, or his role as a major contributor, Henry was granted extraordinary access. Over the next few months, he and his team worked the Washington circuit assiduously, meeting personally with thirty-five of the country's one hundred senators. At every stop, Henry would thrust a copy of his report into the hands of anyone who would take it. "Kravis was here," said Congressman Byron Dorgan, pointing to a big overstuffed leather couch in his Capitol Hill office. "Henry Kravis has open doors. He can get to see anybody."

About the only ones who wouldn't receive him, says Henry, were Senator Dole, who Henry suspects was annoyed with his role as a major Bush contributor, and Treasury Secretary Nicholas Brady. Henry says that he spent time instead with the undersecretary of the Treasury, Robert Glauber.

Despite his charming manner and impressive study,

Henry's appeal did not win much favor with Senator Sanford, who had previously been the state's governor, the president of Duke University, and a board member of the ITT Corporation. Sanford had watched in horror as one company in the region after another—WestPoint Pepperell, RJR Nabisco, Burlington Industries—was taken over and decimated by job reductions and asset sales. "He had a sense that these were marauders from New York," explained his aide Hillman, and that they were getting rich from deals while North Carolinians were losing their jobs. "He came to believe and feel in his bones that transactions in the eighties were done for fees as opposed to for economic sense." It bothered him so much that he started referring to the takeover movement as the "corporate killing fields."

Senator Sanford decided he had to do something to try to stop it. He proposed a series of bills designed to impose restrictions on the deductibility of interest payments used in highly leveraged transactions. One in particular seems to have made Henry see red. Bill S.325 denied deductibility on interest payments of more than $5 million in any transaction where the debt-equity ratio of a company exceeded 3:1 and that ratio was 50 percent greater than it had been before the deal was done.

Henry thought the bill was a terrible idea, so he had one of his lobbyists call Sanford's office and explain that Henry would like to talk to the senator. "Henry called Sanford demanding that we withdraw 325—*demanding*!" says Hillman, still amazed at Henry's gumption. She says he told her and the senator, "You have no idea what you're doing, you don't understand this transaction, the financing." Sanford and Hillman heard him out, then gently tried to explain that there was no process for withdrawing a bill. According to Hillman, "Henry said, 'Oh, there must be!'"

Looking back on the episode, Senator Sanford said he couldn't remember anyone else who ever behaved that way toward him. On the other hand, he said, with a devilish look in his eyes, "I never have put one where it hit someone right between the eyes so well, either." Sanford's bill never garnered enough support to make it to the Senate floor.

Several months later, in May of '89, Sanford's skepticism made him look pretty good. Just as the furor over LBOs was finally beginning to die down, two economists, one of whom was temporarily based at the prestigious Brookings Institution, dropped a bombshell. William F. Long and David J. Ravenscraft released a paper claiming that they had found "methodological problems" that had the effect of distorting the results in KKR's study.[4]

They criticized Deloitte for not disclosing that in seven out of the seventeen companies it analyzed, it had used projections for several years' worth of data, rather than actual performance results. They also noted that if the accounting firm had selected a slightly different time frame for its evidence on research and development spending, it would have shown the opposite result, i.e., that spending on new product research actually went down. In addition, if KKR's results on capital and research spending were adjusted for inflation, the economists said, both would have shown a decline.

"The study looked impressive," said Congressman Dorgan, an LBO critic. "But as it turned out, it was terribly flawed and that injured their credibility." Some members of Congress were so infuriated by what they felt was KKR's deliberately misleading behavior that they actually held hearings on the KKR study. Rep. Edward J. Markey, who chairs the financial subcommittee of the House Energy and Commerce Committee, seemed particularly vexed. He sharply rebuked one of Deloitte's leading tax partners, Emil Sunley, who was sent to defend the report. "I don't think that we should be placing before the subcommittee quantitative data which cannot withstand critical scrutiny," he said caustically. Sunley tried to rebut the critique of his firm's report by saying that Ravenscraft and Long had misunderstood the purpose of the study. He dismissed their criticisms as "mostly nits."[5]

One of Long and Ravenscraft's criticisms that he took particular exception to was their point that in calculating the number of jobs KKR's companies had generated, Deloitte had included acquisitions of the companies in the survey. While that might appear to be a technical issue, the exchange that ensued over the issue revealed two fundamentally different schools of thought about LBOs.

In arguing that it was perfectly reasonable to include acquisitions, Sunley used the example of Motel-6, the low-budget motel chain that KKR owned. "In counting Motel-6 employment, does it make any difference whether Motel-6 buys motels and hires sixty people or instead builds motels and hires sixty more people? In each case, sixty people are employed by Motel-6."

Long disagreed. He said Sunley was thinking like a financier, and not like someone who was building a business. There was a difference, he insisted, between buying a company and building a new one from scratch, one that added new jobs to the economy. If Motel-6 had built a new motel and hired sixty people, that would have been in addition to the sixty people that were already working in the motel that already existed. "The KKR study consistently confuses acquisitions with real economic growth," said Long at the hearings, putting his finger on what many thought was the fundamental issue. Then he offered his own example: "Consider an LBO that lays off four hundred employees and then buys a company with an existing employment of five hundred. The KKR study's logic would lead to the conclusion that the LBO had created one hundred jobs. The real effect is that four hundred people who had been working no longer are working."

Henry may have burned a few bridges in Congress with his ill-fated study. But by this time, he had a much more important ally in Washington: George Bush. Interestingly enough, Henry had known George Bush for some time, thanks to his inimitable father, Ray.

Ray had gotten to know George Bush's father, Prescott Bush, when he was a senior partner at the Wall Street firm Brown Brothers Harriman. Like other Wall Street firms, Brown Brothers used Ray's firm to help it evaluate oil reserves. Ray got to know Prescott so well that when his son George graduated from Yale and was looking for a job, Prescott asked Ray if he would give George a job. Sure, was Ray's response. Only, several days before George was slated to show up in Tulsa, George called Ray and told him that he would respectfully like to decline the job offer because his first preference was to move to Texas. "I know George Bush well," says Ray proudly. "I've known him since he got out of school. His father was a very good friend of mine."

Henry met George Bush several times through his father and saw the president-to-be at various fund-raising events, but it wasn't until the end of 1987 that the two really made a connection. During the early days of Bush's campaign for the primary election, Henry agreed to cochair a Bush fund-raising luncheon at the Vista Hotel in lower Manhattan, to which many Wall Street dealmakers were invited. The reported take that day: $550,000.[6]

But that was just the beginning. Henry kept up his Team 100 contributions: both he and George gave $25,000 to the party in 1989, following on top of their generous $100,000 contribution the year before. (RJR Nabisco also gave $100,000 to Team 100 in '89, the first year in which it was owned by KKR.) After Bush won the '88 election, Henry was given the prestigious task of acting as cochairman of the President's inaugural dinner. And one year later, he became the national chairman of Bush's inaugural anniversary dinner. The gala affair, which was held at the Kennedy Center in Washington, was attended by about one thousand people, most of whom were Republican Eagles, the group that gives at least $15,000 a year to the Grand Old Party. The event planners had decided it would be fun to make it an "oldies night," and they lined up such entertainers as Chubby Checker, Tony Bennett, and B. B. King, who did a rendition of "nobody loves me but my mother, and she could be jivin', too." In his remarks that fun-filled night, Bush took the time to single out Henry as one of "those who did the heavy lifting on this."[7]

Henry was "very helpful to President Bush in fund-raisers," says the President's brother Jonathan, who was the finance chairman of the New York Republican Party. "He admired the President. And also, significantly, on a personal level, his father, Ray, and he [George] were friends from way back. And that meant a lot to Henry. He wanted to be part of that." Jonathan Bush says that Henry has also been a generous contributor to New York's Republican Party. He was even named Man of the Year by that local group, an event that was celebrated with a keynote dinner address by Vice President Quayle.

Henry says it would be wrong to characterize his relationship with the President as close. But, he adds, "he writes me handwritten notes all the time and he calls me and stuff, and we talk." Occasionally, when Bush is mulling over a financial issue, he will seek out Henry's opinion. "We talked on corporate debt—this was going back a few years—and what that meant to the private sector," Henry volunteered.

Since becoming such an important Republican fund-raiser, Henry has found himself increasingly sought after. He says he was given several opportunities to become an ambassador, but turned down the advances. He did decide, however, to accept Bush's offer to become a member of a national trade commission, even though it required him to fill out what he considered irritatingly detailed financial disclosure forms. The Federal Bureau of Investigation conducted its standard background check in December 1990, but as of this writing, no appointment had been made.

Henry insists that he has never asked for anything in return for his fund-raising efforts. "I swear to God, I have absolutely no agenda on this, and nobody understands this," he says. "I want the best person in office, to keep this country competitive and free. I'm very much of a free-market person.

I don't want interference. My life . . . you've listened to my life story, I don't want interference! The best thing to happen to people and this country is a free market system, and I'm very concerned, if we don't keep the right people in office, that we're not going to have this free-market environment. And we should have it!"

FRAUD?

Kohlberg was all in favor of free markets too. But as he watched from the sidelines, he became increasingly convinced that his former partners were consumed by much more than capitalistic fervor.

The first time he began to consider this was the summer of 1988, about a year after he had left KKR and gone out on his own. As a limited partner of KKR, Kohlberg continued to receive quarterly memos and financial statements; only, unlike other investors, he was far better able to interpret them. He noticed that his former partners were offering to buy back stakes in several companies from the firm's own investors at prices he considered surprisingly low. In June of that year, for instance, KKR bought out the position of investors who owned shares in Marley, a heating and cooling equipmentmaker. Kohlberg considered the price to be less than investors would have gotten had the company been sold in the open market, as was usually done. Kohlberg is prevented by his partnership agreement from stating what that purchase price was. However, KKR's sales document from 1987 indicates that Marley was the least successful of all of its transactions, except for two in which its investors actually lost money. The document shows that Marley's investors paid $4.13 a share for the company in 1981 and that in 1987 KKR estimated those shares to be worth only $8 apiece. At that price, KKR's investors would have received an annual return of only 11.7 percent, before deducting KKR's 20-percent cut in profits.

Kohlberg kept abreast of Marley, and not long after KKR bought back the shares from its investors, the company started to register a sharp improvement in its performance. In the first year after the recapitalization, according to a document obtained in early 1989, independent of Kohlberg or anyone at his company, Marley's earnings before interest and tax were 26 percent higher than the projections KKR had distributed to its investors at the time it was offering to buy back their shares. The following year the company's revenues were 30 percent higher than had been projected, and earnings before interest and tax improved by almost as much. To Kohlberg's way of thinking, if KKR's investors had had any idea how well the company would have performed, they would never have agreed to sell their stake for as little as they did. But it was too late; thanks to the recapitalization, KKR's share of Marley's profits had gone from 5 percent to more than 50 percent. Interestingly, among the new investors in the recapitalized Marley were Drexel Burnham employees such as Michael Milken, who were given 7 percent of the equity in the company as part of their compensation for financing the transaction.

Marley was not the end of it, either. In July of 1988, about a month after they launched that transaction, Kohlberg saw them repeat the process with two other companies,

Pacific Realty and M&T Trust, that KKR had merged into one entity called Pacific Trust. Unlike Marley, investors in PacTrust were not given the option of remaining as equity holders in the deal. They had to sell their shares back at a set price to a new partnership made up of KKR and the Oregon and Washington funds. Again, the mandated prices represented a substantial increase over those that the investors had originally paid for the two companies. But again, Kohlberg thought they could have done better in the open market.

Under the terms of the new partnership, KKR and the company's management put in only $2 million of their own money; they bought out the rest of the investors by borrowing against the company's assets. When the transaction was completed, KKR was entitled to 45 percent of any excess cash the company generated over a specified investment target. An independently obtained document shows that KKR estimated that its $2 million would be worth $36 million within five years, or a 1,700-percent increase in value. Kohlberg was convinced that the only way KKR could do so well on its investment was if it had underpaid for the company in the first place, and that would constitute a clear breach of its contractual obligations to act in good faith toward the firm's limited partners, who were, in this instance, the sellers.

He thought back to U.S. Natural Resources, the Oregon company that Roger Meier had been given shares in, and he recalled how quickly the company had improved after KKR bought back half of the company's shares. And he remembered the recapitalization of Houdaille, a machine-tool maker, which occurred in the fall of 1986, while he was still at KKR negotiating his departure. The firm offered to buy back a third of the company's shares from investors at $11 a share. That translated into a 22.3-percent return, before KKR's 20-percent cut, to the investors who had participated in the purchase in 1979. It was a respectable performance, but not great; certainly Houdaille was not one of KKR's more successful deals. Kohlberg realized belatedly that the investors who sold their Houdaille shares to KKR in 1986 made a great mistake. For just a year later, KKR sold the company to a British acquirer for the equivalent of $41.80 a share. Investors who remained in the deal earned almost four times their money. KKR and certain favored investors did even better than that. Three days after selling Houdaille, KKR arranged to buy back several of its divisions with a handful of select investors. They put $1 million of equity into the newly formed company, called IDEX, and financed the rest with debt. Two years later, when they sold a portion of IDEX to the public, that $1 million investment was valued by the market at more than $50 million. It was another extremely astute investment decision by KKR. Again, Drexel executives benefited: through a limited partnership in IDEX, they had a 6.5-percent stake in the company.

In each of these transactions, the message seemed to be the same: seller beware. At first Kohlberg didn't think all that much of it. Placing values on private companies was, after all, not a straightforward business and involved making many assumptions about future prospects. However, as the number of instances grew, and each deal had many of the same earmarks, Kohlberg began to discern what he considered a pattern of suspicious transactions. "With hindsight, KKR always buys things right—just before the earnings go up," says Kohlberg. "After a time, you put it together, and it doesn't seem like coincidence anymore."

Kohlberg was unsure what to do. In general, he believed in working quietly, in keeping to himself. Even if he wanted to, he was in a dreadful position to do anything about his suspicions. For who would believe the criticisms of an ex-partner, someone who had been edged aside? It would just look like sour grapes.

He was also ambivalent because these were his former partners, and despite all the rancor associated with his departure, KKR was still his baby. He hated the idea of doing or saying anything that might jeopardize its future. What pushed him over the edge, however, was a statement he received in the mail several months later, showing that his proportion of KKR's stake in those reconfigured companies had been summarily reduced from the 30-plus percent he had held in the companies as an original investor to 17.6 percent, the amount he was allotted that year for any new deals he invested in.

Now *that* was an issue over which Kohlberg felt he could take a stand. The terms of his separation agreement were black-and-white, he felt, and he could legitimately insist on KKR's observing them. No one could criticize his motives on that score. Before deciding what action to take, however, Kohlberg persuaded George, with whom he still felt he had something in common, to come to his office to discuss the matter. On August 30, 1988, George took his first step through the door of Kohlberg & Company. The two men had not met in the year since Kohlberg had withdrawn. Although Kohlberg & Company was a mere two blocks south of KKR's New York offices, it was a world away in terms of ambiance. Visitors to KKR's Manhattan offices on the forty-second floor of 9 West Fifty-seventh Street cannot even get into the reception area unless they are approved by heavyset security men in blue polyester jackets who ask you your name and then phone it in to the receptionist inside. If you are "expected," a quiet click signals that the wooden doors can now be pulled open. Inside, a gorgeous woman sits primly behind an antique desk, which is floating on a sea of gray and pink marble floors. Behind her, a floor-to-ceiling window offers a breathtaking view of Central Park.

Kohlberg's office is plain by comparison. He insisted that his new abode not be in a building that had a "signature address," and he wanted his new lobby not to have any of that marble or other fancy trimmings that seemed to become de rigueur in Manhattan in the 1980s. Visitors to Kohlberg & Company pass through a dark stone lobby on the ground floor before riding a small elevator to the eighth floor, where the doors open out into a small reception area. In contrast to KKR's polished wood floors, Persian throw rugs, etched-glass partitions, and $10-million worth of furniture and fine art, Kohlberg's office sports blindingly white walls interrupted by prints of birds, gray carpet, and black furniture.

The day that George came to see Jerry, he sat on the gray couch in the firm's small conference room that is tucked just behind the reception area. Jerry stayed over by the conference table, in a black leather chair. Kohlberg recalls that George seemed to be taken aback by how well he looked and that the young man remarked several times during the meeting on Jerry's good health. After George made a few solicitous remarks about how much he regretted the loss of Kohlberg's friendship, Kohlberg remembers his saying that neither he nor Henry was happy with the separation agreement. They felt it was overly generous to Jerry and it was a constant irritant to them. According to Kohlberg, George also said that he resented the fact that Kohlberg had chosen to go out and compete with them. And he had still not forgiven Jerry for the disparaging remarks about greed and a breakdown of ethics that Jerry had made to investors when he announced his departure from the firm. Jerry told George that he and Henry might not like his separation agreement, but that that was no reason for them to ignore it. About the only thing the two could agree on was that they didn't agree on what constituted an old and a new deal.

Kohlberg then told George that he thought KKR was buying back some of its companies at prices that were lower than they could get in the open market. Kohlberg remembers being horrified by George's response. In notes that he took afterward, which I obtained independently, Kohlberg wrote: "He said that he thought Marley could have been sold for a higher purchase price, maybe 25%, grinning the while. I said the same thing holds true for PacTrust/M&T, to which George said that they had obtained several real estate appraisals. My reply to this was that real estate appraisals and investment banking opinions are easily obtainable within a range and that I could demonstrate to him, on the basis of cash flow, that we could have obtained a higher price for the company in the open market. Again, he just grinned."

George has a different recollection of the meeting. He says he reminded Kohlberg that the firm's investors were all sophisticated institutions who had had the opportunity to review each transaction thoroughly. He pointed out that they had been given the option of remaining as investors, and that he had personally advised the two largest ones to reinvest in the reconfigured company.

Kohlberg left the meeting still convinced that KKR was acting with disregard both to him and to the firm's long-standing investors. He agonized about whether he should take legal action.

Several months later, Kohlberg was in Washington and dropped by the offices of Joseph Grundfest, an SEC commissioner. A mutual friend had suggested to Grundfest and Kohlberg that they might enjoy meeting each other, and Kohlberg was following up on that suggestion. Grundfest had recently read a detailed account in the weekly publication, *Barron's*, of the Beatrice warrants and how Drexel executives had retained them instead of distributing them to the company's bond buyers. He made it clear to Kohlberg that he thought the whole situation was curious and noted that Drexel had probably made more money from the Beatrice deal than KKR had or perhaps ever would. Though Grundfest says he does not recall much about the conversation, Kohlberg says the SEC commissioner then asked him whether he or his former partners had ever considered whether they had any responsibility to their limited partners to try to recover the money that Milken and other Drexel executives had made. Since the warrants had not been necessary to attract buyers of the Beatrice securities, the equity interest in the company could conceivably have remained with the LBO firm's investors.

Kohlberg took the meeting as an unofficial regulatory nudge and promised Grundfest he would look into the matter thoroughly. He left the building deeply troubled.

Soon afterward, Kohlberg raised the issue with Henry and Dick Beattie. They assured him that they had investigated the matter fully, and that they were convinced KKR had fulfilled all of its legal obligations to its investors. They promised to send Kohlberg chapter and verse on the matter, explaining in detail how they had reached this conclusion. Over the next five months, Kohlberg repeatedly phoned and wrote Henry and Dick asking for their response. They didn't return his phone calls, and they never sent him the promised material.

With Henry and Dick dragging their feet, Kohlberg began to get extremely worried that his ex-partners had gotten him into something truly nefarious. Concerned that he might have some personal liability to his former investment partners, Kohlberg sought legal advice. He was assured, however, that he had no responsibility. Still, he couldn't understand why KKR didn't do something to try to recover the profits from the warrants, and why they weren't responding to his inquiries.

About the same time that Kohlberg was becoming concerned about the conduct of his ex-partners, he and Nancy had occasion to see Hedi Kravis, Henry's ex-wife. The last time Jerry had seen her was in early 1983, when he was still the senior partner at KKR. She had come to complain that Henry had shut off all contact with her and was refusing to pay the household bills, because she would not agree to his proposed divorce settlement. For several hours she had sat in Kohlberg's office and sobbed, pleading with him to do something. Kohlberg found Hedi's stories distasteful but, frankly, impossible to believe. After listening for several hours, he politely but firmly told her that Henry was his partner and he really couldn't get involved in that kind of personal dispute.

Now, six years later, having grown increasingly distrustful of his ex-partners, and having seen that bullying side of Henry that Hedi had described in such detail, Kohlberg berated himself for having dismissed her cries for help so quickly that day.

Oddly enough, she was in much the same straits as she was in 1983. Her divorce settlement had only called for her to receive maintenance for six years, and that period was about to end. The $60,000 a year that Henry would continue to provide in child support barely covered her rent and utilities bills. And although Henry had given her $4 million in capital, she had had to pay out hefty legal and accounting fees as soon as the divorce settlement was finalized, some was tied up in real estate investments, and the rest she had devoted to maintaining the lifestyle for herself and her children that they had enjoyed prior to the divorce.

Jerry and Nancy were surprised that Hedi wasn't a wealthier woman. They knew how well they had done with the stakes that Jerry had owned in companies that had been purchased before he left the firm. Hedi explained to them that she had accepted a $4-million limit on her interest in the value of those stakes.

It wasn't that she had accepted that figure blindly—she had hired a top financial investigator and accountant to advise her. But they had found it next to impossible to verify independently the value of Henry's assets, since most of them were investments in privately held companies. As part of the negotiation process, Henry had submitted a net worth statement dated December 1982 in which he listed all his assets and liabilities. At that time, he indicated that his total net worth was $9.3 million, the single largest asset of which was his own investments in companies that KKR had acquired, which he estimated to be worth $6.3 million.

But Henry did not include in his net worth statement any estimate for his share of the so-called carried interest, that is, the 20 percent of the profits that KKR would be entitled to when it sold a company. Kohlberg knew that at the time the couple was negotiating their divorce, Henry's share of that 20 percent was worth tens of millions of dollars.

In the court case that eventually ensued over whether

Henry had deceived Hedi about the value of his assets, Henry stated that he did not include any estimate for his share of those stakes because they were not, strictly speaking, assets, but rather a contractual right that KKR had secured from its investment partners. Moreover, he suggested that it was entirely possible that he, and therefore Hedi, would never see a penny from those investments. In an affidavit, he referred to the firm's 20-percent interest as "contingent" and "speculative," while his lawyers painted an even bleaker picture of their potential: "When, as and if a company which it had helped to acquire was sold, if ever, and, after the non-KKR investors recouped their investments—if they did—and KKR recouped its investment—if it did—then 20% of the profit realized by the other investors would be paid over to KKR."[1]

In contrast, when KKR described its compensation to potential investors in its 1982 marketing literature, it seemed to view that 20-percent interest as a much less speculative and much more integral part of its compensation. "In consideration for selecting and supervising the investments for each partnership, KKR will receive 20% of the profits of the investment for each limited partner in each partnership as, and when [note, no ifs], profits are realized by the limited partners." The fact is, the 20-percent carried interest has always been the single largest source of income to the three partners.

In his defense, Henry points out in his court documents that Hedi was well counseled during the divorce and obviously knew about his stakes in the companies, because they negotiated a minimum and a maximum payment for them. However, in reaching a decision on whether a $3-million minimum or a $4-million maximum was fair or relevant, Hedi and her team of advisers had had to rely heavily on estimates of the values of those companies that Henry had provided to them. Had they been public companies, which are required to publish elaborate financial statements and which are closely followed by independent analysts who try to estimate their earnings potential, their task would have been much easier. As it was, Hedi was in the same position as KKR's investors. They all had to rely heavily on the firm's data and estimates and had no way to ascertain independently the value of KKR-controlled companies.

Judging from the descriptions that Henry gave Hedi of the companies that KKR had invested in, it's a wonder the firm was ever able to persuade investors to give them any money. Of the fifteen companies he had stakes in, he identified nine as having losses, while three others were described as having a negative net worth or substantially deteriorating or depressed earnings.

Hedi's investigator, attempting to dig further, asked for feasibility studies that KKR might have assembled prior to making their acquisitions. His written request defined such studies broadly as any "report or analysis that was made by KKR prior to the acquisition of a company with respect to their determination as to whether or not to proceed with that particular acquisition." He was told in a written response from one of Henry's lawyers that "there are no feasibility studies made by KKR prior to the acquisition of a company"[2]—a statement that anyone familiar with the analysis that goes into a leveraged buyout would find quite implausible.

Kohlberg couldn't help but notice certain similarities between the pessimistic assessment of the companies in KKR's portfolio that Henry conveyed to Hedi and the highly conservative projections KKR had made to its investors when it was in the process of buying back shares of companies such as U.S. Natural Resources, Marley, and Houdaille.

He thought Henry would certainly have had some idea of the value of the stakes in the companies KKR owned, since he knew what information had been available to him at that time. He believed that the value of KKR's stake in its companies was worth millions of dollars more than Henry had apparently indicated to Hedi on his net worth statement.

There was, after all, a fund-raising document that KKR had distributed to potential investors in October of 1983, just four months after Hedi's divorce settlement was finalized. In that document, KKR painted a vastly more positive picture of the companies in its portfolio.

The document indicated that many of the companies that Henry had said were doing so poorly had enjoyed an impressive turnaround and were suddenly worth much more. It was not unlike the rebound that seemed to occur with KKR companies after they were recapitalized and KKR had increased its stake in them.

Hedi, at this time, was in the midst of negotiating an increase in Henry's child-support payments. Henry had already agreed to raise the child-support payments nearly tenfold and to pay for a housekeeper since Hedi was now working full-time and their youngest child was still at home. He also agreed to pay her $150,000 a year until she remarried or died. "Please know how much I appreciate your financial response to my request for increased child support," Hedi wrote Henry, according to court records, and went on to thank him for the time and effort he put into understanding her financial needs. When Henry got the letter, he showed it to Dick Beattie, who was then handling the divorce matter for Henry. They agreed that they would send the letter back with a new sentence tacked onto the end that, if Hedi signed it, would amount to a moral commitment by her never to ask Henry for money again. As Henry's lawyers argued later in court papers, "Given Helene's repeated requests for more money over the previous six years, it is understandable that Henry would want some degree of finality with respect to his former marriage."

But given what she was just beginning to understand, Hedi was afraid that if she signed the letter, she would be signing away all her future rights. She returned the letter as she had originally sent it, without the suggested last sentence. At the same time, Hedi hired a new accountant and legal adviser and asked them to investigate Henry's finances one more time. Her new advisers, who were more familiar with the inner workings of leveraged buyouts, told her that Henry had underestimated the value of his interests in the companies in KKR's portfolio by $45 million.[3]

Close friends say that Hedi was stunned when she got the news. She had always suspected Henry of being shrewd, but she had never expected him to go this far. Now she started to think back. There was his purchase of the estate in Connecticut under a corporate name, the omissions in his list of assets, such as the house he had purchased for his driver, Mohammed. And she thought of the bills that Christie's auction house had accidentally sent her for a $14.3-million painting that Henry had purchased—one with and then one without taxes on it, followed by still another with no taxes on it. And his petty attempts to punish her by cutting off her housekeeper's health insurance.

After weeks of hand-wringing, Hedi filed a complaint against Henry in August of 1989 charging him with having submitted a net worth statement to her that was "false and fraudulent." She sought damages of $25 million. One of her central arguments was that it was impossible to explain such a sharp jump in the value of KKR's companies between June of '83, the date of their settlement, and the October '83 document, unless Henry had defrauded her.

In a sharply worded response, Henry accused Hedi of trying to fleece him. He noted that she had waited until five days after getting her final quarterly distribution from him before filing her "newly thought-of claim set forth by her newly hired accountant." He insisted that the valuations he had placed on KKR's companies were as of December 1982 and *not* June 1983 when the divorce agreement was signed. Although he acknowledged that he had personally initialed the net worth statement on June 20, 1983, right next to the day's date, Henry insisted that the juxtaposition was meaningless. In one document, Henry's lawyer argued that the date was written in someone else's handwriting; in another document, Henry said that the initials were not in his handwriting either.

Henry insisted that since the values of the companies were estimated as of December 1982, and not June of '83, it was much easier to explain why their values had increased so much by October of '83, when they circulated their sales literature to investors. In those intervening ten months, he said, the economy enjoyed a sharp rebound, which triggered turnarounds in the companies that had been performing poorly up until that point. Henry's lawyer gave three examples of companies that lost money in 1982 and were back in the black in 1983. As Henry explained in his affidavit, "Assets with fluctuating values fluctuate in value."[4] (In May 1991, the judge accepted Henry's argument that Hedi had waited too long to bring her claim and said she had not proved fraud.)

Back in 1989, however, as Hedi described her legal battles with Henry, one of the things that troubled Jerry and Nancy most was her description of her conversations with Dick Beattie. For when her advisers told her they could not find out much about Henry's net worth, and it came time to decide whether to accept the $4-million maximum payment Henry was proposing, Hedi discussed the issue with Dick.

In notes she made to summarize the conversation, she wrote: "Mr. Beattie told me that the carried and direct interests which Henry had through KKR and its related entities were of questionable value and suggested that a minimum guaranteed payment of $3 million as my share of the business investments which Henry had would be to my advantage since it was unlikely that 30 percent of the value of those investments would equal or exceed that amount."

"In addition," she continued, "Mr. Beattie stated to me specifically that he would make certain that I was treated fairly . . . . Based upon these statements to me, I agreed to the minimum and maximum payment set forth in the separation agreement."

Hedi had figured she could trust Dick Beattie. The two families had often gone on business trips together and spent weekends at the Beatties' country home in Connecticut. She regarded him as a friend, and when he promised her he would not let Henry do anything to hurt her, she believed him. Hedi's experience with Dick was almost a mirror image of the Kohlbergs'.

DICK

Dick Beattie is KKR's secret weapon, the most subtle of the silent partners that KKR cultivated over the years. Outsiders might regard Henry as too egotistical to be trusted, or George as too deviously clever, but no one would ever question the sincerity of Dick Beattie. After all, he recently became the senior partner of the seventh-largest law firm in New York, an officer of the court. And he has displayed a deep commitment to public service, giving his time both in Washington and on New York City commissions. With his relaxed, easygoing manner, his gravelly voice and crystalline blue eyes, it is difficult not to be won over.

Dick is one of those people who makes everyone believe that they're his best friend. Like a politician working a crowd of potential contributors, he works hard at being liked. He is always thinking of ways to be helpful: to make an introduction, to help someone get on a board, to ask after spouses, whose names he always seems to remember. Whether one encounters Dick in person or over the phone, one always comes away with a warm feeling. He's just that kind of guy.

Only as first Jerry and then Hedi found out, Dick Beattie's friendly concern only goes so far. And if being helpful or supportive comes at the expense of Henry Kravis, Dick Beattie is no longer a friend. Only most people don't guess until it is far too late.

"Dick is a great one for playing both ends off the middle," says an investment banker who has worked with him closely. "He wants to be friends with everybody, but he still chooses sides." And if one of the choices is Henry, there is no doubt which side he will end up on.

Jerry and Hedi found out about Dick's allegiances the hard way. So did Peter Cohen. Cohen was the head of Shearson Lehman Hutton, the brokerage firm owned by American Express. A street-smart boy from Brooklyn, he had risen up through the ranks not on the basis of his résumé or his good manners, but because of a willingness to roll up his shirtsleeves when necessary and get his hands dirty. Like other Wall Street firms, Shearson in the late 1980s was trying to move forcefully into the lucrative LBO business. And Cohen's firm decided they would start at the top, by making a bid in conjunction with management for the food and tobacco giant RJR Nabisco.

Now the story of the frantic scramble between Shearson and KKR for RJR Nabisco has been told in numerous places in numerous ways. But what has consistently been downplayed is the nature of the role of Dick Beattie. In *Barbarians at the Gate*, he comes across as almost heroic in his dedication to KKR, and often the only source of reason or wisdom in the bunch. He was always the first to understand the significance of a strategic development, "always," as the authors described, "a voice of reason."[1]

But in accepting the assignment to work for KKR in its

attempted bid for RJR Nabisco, Beattie was turning against a long-standing client. Simpson Thacher & Bartlett had long represented Lehman Brothers. And after Lehman was acquired by Shearson in 1984, Simpson became one of Shearson Lehman's leading law firms. In its bid for RJR Nabisco, Shearson was not advising a client on whether to acquire RJR Nabisco—it was the one actually putting up most of the money. In other words, it was not merely an adviser to KKR's main competitor, it *was* KKR's main competitor.

Beattie says his decision to work with KKR against Shearson was justified, because he was already working on the deal before Shearson announced its bid. Asking Cohen's permission, as was the usual protocol when a lawyer was caught between two clients, would only have tipped Shearson off to KKR's intentions. However, KKR only sprang into action after Shearson made its bid. Up until that point, Simpson's work for KKR on RJR Nabisco had been limited to collecting documents and analyzing tobacco litigation. Beattie could presumably have told KKR he was unable to continue working on that assignment. After all, he was the head of the Shearson account, Simpson's senior-most liaison with the firm. "Any lawyer with client loyalty would have been conflicted," says a dealmaker affiliated with the Shearson side.

Having taken a questionable position on that issue, Beattie proceeded to try to use his relationship with Cohen to influence the bidding process that ensued. Cohen was not stupid; he realized who Beattie was working for and he understood his intentions. But he figured that keeping a channel of communication open between the two camps would be useful, and indeed, at one point the two groups did consider joining forces and making one bid.

But Beattie went one step further. It was just before Thanksgiving and the two sides were locked in a bitter bidding war. Cohen's side was at $100 a share and KKR was at $94. RJR's special committee of directors had just informed both sides there would be another round. Beattie called

Cohen and congratulated him on his winning bid. The conversation was described in detail in *Barbarians at the Gate* and was based on Beattie's account of it:

"That bid was a winner, Peter," Beattie is quoted as saying. "I got to tell you, nice job. Terrific." Beattie proceeded to tell Cohen that KKR's side was depressed, that they might not come back with another offer, that Henry was going away for the holidays. The authors' narrative continues: "After hanging up, Beattie looked at the phone a minute. He hadn't lied. He hadn't intentionally misled Cohen. It was true: Kravis didn't know what he was going to do. On the other hand, he sensed no skepticism from Cohen. *If Cohen got the impression Kravis was out of the bidding, well, so be it.*"[2]

Cohen distrusted Beattie's motives, but the call influenced his next bid nonetheless. According to individuals familiar with the Shearson team, Cohen's adviser, Jack Nussbaum, an attorney at Wilkie, Farr & Gallagher, believed that Beattie was sincere. It wasn't that Nussbaum thought Beattie was obligated to provide Cohen with any *useful* information regarding KKR's plans; it's just that he did not think that Beattie, given his relationship with Shearson and Cohen, would initiate a phone conversation in which he created an impression that was misleading. After all, a lawyer who abused his position of trust with a client with whom he had an ongoing relationship could violate a duty of loyalty.

In the end, Shearson raised its bid just a hair, to $101. KKR, however, raised its bid to $106 and emerged the victor, both in that round and in another. "Our decision not to increase our bid more was based very significantly on Dick Beattie's phone call," says a person close to the deal.

Despite the questionable nature of Beattie's call, the authors of *Barbarians* wrote about it more from the standpoint of whether the ploy had worked than about its underlying propriety. And they weren't alone. Newspaper and magazine articles that recounted the deal's final moments seemed to be taken with KKR's clever fake-out. As one article in the *New York Times* put it, "Perceived as an also-ran, Kohlberg,

Kravis went out of its way to encourage that view with subtle comments that it hoped would filter back to the management group." At one point, the article continued, George R. Roberts, a senior partner in the buyout firm, conceded, " 'We purposely sent out signals that we might not bid.' The idea was to put their competitors off guard, which apparently worked."[3]

Peter Cohen wasn't impressed. As the chief executive of Shearson Lehman, he intended to see to it that Simpson Thacher never billed Shearson for another hour of its time. He sent out an edict to all departments that all work with Simpson Thacher must stop.

At first, Beattie's associates at Simpson Thacher weren't all that worried. They figured that Cohen was just grandstanding. He would relent, they figured, and they would all get back to work. But as the months wore on and the economic pain got worse, Beattie came under increasing pressure at the firm for his actions. Shearson had been an important client to Simpson Thacher, and the absence of its billings was beginning to hurt.

Finally, the firm's senior partner and former secretary of state, Cy Vance, embarked on a peacemaking effort. At a meeting in Cohen's office, according to high-level Shearson sources, Vance told Cohen he understood his anger but thought it unfair to penalize an entire firm for the behavior of one partner. But that one partner was in charge of some of the firm's most important accounts, Cohen is said to have countered. What did the firm intend to do about that? Another leading Simpson attorney, Edgar Masinter, also called on Cohen and tried to persuade him to relent.

Vance says he only remembers discussing broader issues, such as the erosion of relationships that became such a feature of the dealmaking era. Just as Shearson had chosen to work with another law firm, so Simpson Thacher felt it should not be precluded from working with another client, he says he told Cohen.

After several months, Cohen caved in, and the relationship between the two firms was restored. Apparently, that's how forgiving Wall Street can be. But the Shearson account was taken away from Beattie, enabling Cohen to maintain that he had at least won a moral victory. Today Beattie tries to put a good face on the entire episode. In an article in *The American Lawyer* about whether Beattie was likely to become the next senior partner of Simpson Thacher & Bartlett he gave the impression that the change in the senior partner on the Shearson account was his idea.[4] And he told the reporter that any bad feelings with Cohen, who has since resigned from Shearson, have been ironed out—a fact that those who have spoken to Cohen know is entirely untrue. In support of his argument that all is now well, Beattie points out that the firm's 1990 revenues from Shearson were up by about 40 percent over the previous year's. What he neglected to mention was that for several months of that previous year, Simpson Thacher had been virtually banned from Shearson's offices.

Cohen, Kohlberg, and Hedi Kravis all made the same mistake. They assumed that Dick Beattie would not let them down. Cohen and his advisers assumed that Beattie would be bound by some feelings of loyalty to a client. Jerry assumed that Dick would not turn on someone who had gotten him started and who had helped him financially. Hedi assumed that he would not turn on a longtime friend.

They were all wrong because they never fully understood Dick's relationship to Henry and George. Not only did they provide him with prestige and status, which he rode successfully to the top of Simpson Thacher, but his personal finances were intricately interwoven with theirs. For, as I was able to confirm independently, Beattie has been investing in KKR deals on an ongoing basis since the early 1980s.

Hedi first learned about Dick's financial ties to KKR in 1983, when she was trying to decide about the $4-million ceiling for her share of Henry's carried interest. She says Beattie told her that no one had a greater interest in those companies being worth a lot of money than he, because he had stakes in some of them himself. The problem, he said, was that the companies weren't worth much. Hedi should take Henry's offer, he reportedly told her, because her share of Henry's investments would never come to more than $4 million.

She recalled that no sooner had he told her about his stakes than he seemed to regret his actions. He indicated that he never should have confided in her like that. His indiscretion, she remembers him saying, could get him into serious trouble. His own partners at Simpson Thacher didn't know about his stakes in KKR companies, she says he told her, and she must promise never to tell anyone. Still convinced of his friendship, Hedi assured him she never would.

Though Hedi did not understand it at the time, what Beattie had reportedly told her was shocking. Most law firms are formed on the basis of partnerships; they pool their income and an executive committee decides how to divide it up. For a partner to keep individually earned income from a transaction with a client separate from the partnership is highly unusual. Historically, most large law firms have simply prohibited such special arrangements outright; but during the 1980s, when a few select attorneys became closely aligned with takeover artists, exceptions were made. It was that or risk having the partner resign, which could lead to a much greater loss of revenue. In those special cases, however, approval had to be given first by the law firm's executive committee. Beattie seemed to be telling Hedi that he had decided to invest with KKR without first seeking his partners' approval. In an interview, Cyrus Vance, who until recently was the firm's senior partner, said that Beattie was granted permission to invest with KKR, but his recollection was that that had only occurred on a small number of occasions.

As it happened, Simpson Thacher had always had a policy against partners' cutting special deals. "We never believed in that as an institution," says Donald Oresman, who was a

Simpson Thacher partner for many years. And though it considered an arrangement like the one that Latham & Watkins adopted, where the partners invested in KKR's deals as a group, it decided firmly against it.

Simpson Thacher's position was really not all that surprising. Vance was widely regarded as one of the straightest arrows in the legal, or any, profession. The notion that lawyers should not invest in their clients' business interests was the kind of conservative, old-line view that he would be expected to espouse. Although there was obviously nothing illegal about the practice, many lawyers looked askance at it because they felt it created the potential for conflicts of interest.

It was really only when the merger movement started ballooning in the 1970s and 1980s, turning many individuals into multimillionaires, that more intimate financial arrangements between lawyers and their clients were even contemplated. "Lawyers were always conscious that their business clients earned more income than they did. But over the last two decades, those opportunities may have increased," said Stephen Gillers, a professor of law at New York University who specializes in legal ethics and like Kohlberg, was a law clerk for Judge Solomon. To the extent that those growing financial rewards were a factor, he said, "It is not the first time that opportunity for money has influenced judgment."

When asked about his investments in KKR deals, Beattie waffles. At one point he said he had only invested in RJR Nabisco and one earlier transaction. At another point he said it was "a couple" of investments, and in still another, he said he'd "have to go back and check." In all cases, he said he first sought permission from his firm.

Beattie's sense of timing also seems to be confused. When asked whether he had disclosed his KKR investments to a client who was being acquired by KKR in 1988, he said, "I wasn't an investor at that time." Pressed further, he acknowledged that he was in fact an investor then, and that he had fully divulged that to his client. He says his investments were insignificant and not inconsistent with doing his best for his client.

He vigorously denied Hedi's assertion that he had confided to her about her ownership positions in 1983, saying such a conversation could never have taken place because he did not invest in any KKR companies until at least 1986. Among the many deals he seemed to be forgetting was the $20,000 gift, or loan, that Kohlberg had conveyed to him in August of 1985—for the express purpose of investing in a KKR deal.

The burden of Beattie's actions apparently weighed heavily on him. For when Hedi began to make noises in late 1989 about how Henry, with Dick's help, had misrepresented his net worth, Dick called her and asked if they could get together for lunch. On a blustery, cold winter day, the two met at Capriccio's, a fashionable Upper East Side restaurant that specializes in northern-Italian fare. Beattie was his usual, charming self, and, as Hedi remembers it, seemed determined to make peace. She says he told her he didn't know where she had ever gotten the idea that he had betrayed her, but it was simply wrong. After all, he and Hedi were friends, they had confided in each other, shared confidences. Funny, she replied, I remember confiding in you, but I don't remember you confiding in me. Beattie, she recalled, seemed to squirm a little in his banquette and then with a studied casualness said, well, you know, about my stakes—you never told anyone about them, did you? Hedi told Beattie she never had. As a wave of relief passed across his face, Beattie immediately changed the subject.

When Kohlberg was told about Beattie's ownership positions in KKR companies, he was shocked. "Dick Beattie is a decent man," Kohlberg proceeded to muse, more to himself than to anyone in particular. "Frankly, I never thought he would really succumb the way he has."

Despite Simpson Thacher's close affiliation with KKR and Beattie's investments in various KKR deals, in two instances the law firm represented the company that KKR was acquiring: Storer Communications and the grocery store chain Stop & Shop. In at least one of those cases, Stop & Shop, Beattie headed the Simpson team. His firm was retained, however, long before KKR emerged as a "white knight" for the company.

Beattie's close ties to KKR were certainly well known. And if Stop & Shop's executives were willing to continue relying on his advice in spite of that connection, that was certainly their business. On the other hand, if Beattie did not reveal to Stop & Shop executives the full nature of his relationship, it is possible that he could have violated certain duties to his client. Legal experts say this area of conflicts of interest is a very murky one indeed, and the answer would depend on the precise circumstances.

Through a spokeswoman, Stop & Shop's general counsel said that Beattie had fully disclosed his relationship with KKR to the company. But he declined to comment on whether Beattie had mentioned his prior investments in KKR deals. Beattie says he "told them everything. They knew I had invested in one transaction prior to that time."

Why, one cannot help but wonder, would someone with so much going for him take the risk of not fully disclosing his investments. The few acquaintances who claim to know the full extent of Beattie's investments in KKR deals say that they simply cannot understand it. Their best guess is that he has always held a very high opinion of himself, and that it was painful to watch Henry get the credit and the money for what he often felt were his ideas. It was Dick, after all, who paved Henry's way to Channel 13. And it was Dick who was right by Henry's side in deal after deal, providing him with helpful strategic tips and staying calm when the rest were letting their egos dictate their moves. It was Dick, or other lawyers at his firm, who helped extricate Henry from various personal problems: helping with the purchase of Weatherstone, the favorable divorce settlement with Hedi, and George Kravis's plea bargain.

Henry was never the brilliant one; he was the follower. Dick was the real mastermind, or so he may have thought. Although KKR and he discussed his joining the firm as a partner, the talks never came to fruition. Dick says they asked him and he turned it down. Kohlberg remembers that he and George initially resisted the idea, and then Henry ultimately decided Dick would be better suited where he was. If Dick had to remain in the background, where he could not get all the accolades, his acquaintances speculate that maybe he thought he could at least make some money through his stakes and have the last laugh.

The life of Dick Beattie is in many ways the American dream. He was born in the Bronx in 1939, the son of a middle-class Irish family. His father, Richard Sr., never went further than the eighth grade. Instead, he developed a career as a commercial photographer and supported his family by taking pictures for corporate ad campaigns that promoted products such as Coca-Cola, Ford Mustangs, and Camel cigarettes. (In an ironic twist of fate, Camels are now one of KKR's key products, belonging as they do to the RJR Nabisco empire). As Richard Sr.'s financial status improved, he moved his family to better and better suburban communities outside New York. From the Bronx they moved to Yonkers, then to New Rochelle, and finally to the upstanding community of Rye. Most of Dick's boyhood days were spent in a modest cul-de-sac just a stone's throw from the famous Rye Playland and the Long Island Sound. The only feature to mar this otherwise serene picture was the fact that his mother had serious drinking problems, and Dick grew up essentially motherless.

Still, he was the kind of boy whom everyone would be jealous of in high school—he seemed to be good at everything. Thanks to his blond hair, blue eyes, and nice smile, the girls all liked him. (He was voted "best looking" in his senior year.) He was also a real athlete, fulfilling every boy's dream of being the school's star quarterback. Yet he must also have paid attention to his studies, for he was admitted to the National Honor Society. It was in high school, too, that he began to show an interest in political activities. In his senior year, he presided over the Westchester County Association of Student Councils, a forum for local student leaders. As his yearbook described it, "This interchange of ideas proved very constructive and, due in large part to Dick's efforts, the WCASC is becoming more and more active in County affairs."

Although Dick won an ROTC scholarship for Cornell, he decided instead to attend Dartmouth, a college that Dick says his father had never heard of.[5] Just as he had in high school, Beattie quickly established himself as a popular and talented student. He became the star quarterback of the college's all-important football team and was elected treasurer of his fraternity, Beta Theta Pi.

After graduating from Dartmouth in 1961 with a distinction in economics, Beattie joined the Marines. He served for several years as a jet pilot, some of it on a carrier off the coast of Vietnam, and ultimately rose to the rank of Marine Corps captain. After returning home—a moment that was not traumatic since the Vietnam antiwar movement was still nascent—Beattie continued his interest in progressive political causes. Having done a little campaigning for JFK when he was at Dartmouth and having later become enamored with the civil rights movement, Beattie decided the best contribution he could make would be to become a civil rights lawyer. So off he went to the University of Pennsylvania law school, where he spent three grueling years.

After graduation, Dick needed a job. He had married Diana Lewis, one of three sisters renowned in Rye for their striking blond hair and blue eyes, and they planned to have a family, which he would have to support. Dick ended up not as the civil rights lawyer he had envisaged, but as a corporate securities lawyer at the white-shoe law firm of Simpson Thacher & Bartlett.

By day, Beattie tried to find ways to help companies wend their way through all sorts of cumbersome government regulations. By night, he and his wife, Diana, would attend endless benefits that she, as a special events planner, had helped organize for a number of progressive causes: National Public Radio, the NAACP's legal defense fund, the Dance Theatre of Harlem. Whenever he could get the time, he would do *pro bono* work for a community-based legal aid office in Harlem that he helped establish.

Ultimately, Beattie hoped to secure a political career for himself. His smooth, charismatic ways combined with his good looks would certainly help in political circles. But his foray to Washington with the Carter administration came to a halt as soon as Reagan was elected.

In New York, at least, it was still okay to be a Democrat. And it wasn't long before Beattie had developed close ties to the mayor then, Ed Koch, who appointed him to commissions on everything from special education to reorganizing the city's human resources department. Koch liked Beattie's work so much that at one point he asked Beattie to consider becoming a deputy mayor. The lawyer turned it down on the grounds that he couldn't afford to take such a sizable pay cut.[6] He had to put two daughters through college, after all.

At the same time that Beattie was working the political circuit, he was becoming more active in certain nonprofit groups. He has long been Channel 13's general counsel. And as an outgrowth of his interest in learning, Beattie set up the Fund for New York City Public Education. One of his first acts as its chairman was to get Henry to donate $1.5 million to the fund.

Beattie might have been proud of his accomplishments. But he had achieved them in no small part because of his close ties to Henry Kravis. It was his connection to KKR that had catapulted him to the top of Simpson Thacher. It was his stakes in KKR companies that promised to build him a nest egg. And it was his "in" with Henry that made him so desirable to nonprofit groups in need of funds.

It was obviously important to keep that valuable relationship intact. It would not help Beattie to be seen to upstage

Henry, for Henry liked everyone to know that *he* was in charge, pulling all the strings, making the tough decisions.

But in the role that he had created for himself, this bright ex-Marine was always consigned the role of sidekick, the "consiglieri" as he was called in *Barbarians at the Gate*. He was the one who would pave the way for Henry's grand entrance or patch things up if Henry made some thoughtless remark. The smooth-talking, easygoing Dick was always there to pick up the chairs off the floor, smooth the tablecloth, and make things right.

In private conversations, Beattie often makes it clear that he considers himself smarter than Henry, and certainly more politically astute.

Investment bankers who have worked with him on deals say that he will often try to distance himself from Henry and all that he stands for, at the same time that he emphasizes his own, true anti-Establishment nature. He often finds a way to mention that he rides a motorcyle or that he spends his weekends fixing a 1948 Ford pickup truck. And then there are all those liberal causes. . . .

PERCEPTION

As the information about his ex-partners' behavior kept mounting, Kohlberg decided he had to do something. He called his advisers together and told them they should begin to prepare for a lawsuit. His discussions with George and Henry over the way they were recapitalizing their companies and calling them new transactions were going nowhere. He kept giving Dick Beattie deadlines for a response. And Dick kept ignoring them—and him. The tactic was similar to one they had used during his separation discussions. Only now, two years later, Kohlberg was physically and emotionally much stronger and he was determined not to let them get away with it.

Henry and George did not think that Kohlberg would ever go through with a lawsuit. For one thing, they knew how much he cherished his privacy and how distasteful he would find anything that drew him so forcefully into the

301

limelight. And Jerry had amply demonstrated to them during his negotiations over leaving the firm that he found it difficult to make decisions when emotional considerations were involved.

Kohlberg did waver this time, too. A part of him hated to have it come to this. His name was on the door, after all, and he still cared for many of the younger associates at the firm whom he had helped to bring on board and who would no doubt be hurt by his legal action.

But ultimately, Henry and George's confidence that he wouldn't sue made him decide to go through with it. They were so sure he would never pull the plug, and it irritated Kohlberg that they were right. Given his druthers, he wouldn't. But it was their knowledge of his behavior that gave them the freedom to do what they were doing. The only way to stop them, he felt, was to surprise them, to show them that maybe they didn't know him as well as they thought they did. His adviser Aeder agreed: "My position was, he had to sue, that he would get nowhere until he did. Because they simply didn't believe it, they weren't paying any attention to him . . . they simply didn't believe his threats and wouldn't have addressed them unless he sued."

On August 21, 1989, Kohlberg did what Henry, George, and Dick never thought he would do: he filed suit against his ex-partners, accusing them of having breached his contract and having violated their fiduciary duty to him. He wanted to force them to acknowledge that legal agreements were binding. The lawyer in him would not be satisfied until they accepted, as he put it, "the sanctity of agreements."

And he decided he would not be unhappy if his suit also called attention to the way KKR was recapitalizing its companies. In his court papers he stated the following: "Commencing in the mid-1980s, KKR, Kravis and Roberts recognized that the value or potential value of certain of the companies which had been the subject of prior KKR leveraged buyout transactions had increased. . . . However, in and after 1986, KKR, Kravis and Roberts determined not to sell these companies or all their assets to third parties in arm's-length transactions to realize a return on leveraged buyout investments. (Typically, such arm's-length transactions, and in particular the solicitation of competing bids, generate the most favorable price for companies or their assets.) Instead, they decided that it would serve their purposes to retain control of these companies, to substantially maintain or enlarge their own interests, and to transfer interests to certain KKR personnel or other persons or entities which they chose."[1]

There, he had done it. Though it might seem like the ultimate act of betrayal against the investment firm he had created, he had raised a red flag to all his former investors about the behavior of his ex-partners.

Both the *New York Times* and the *Wall Street Journal* featured Kohlberg's lawsuit prominently and regional papers and business magazines across the country followed up the rest of that week. The fact that Kohlberg—a man of considerable standing who had made such a point of shunning publicity his entire life—would sue his former partners in such a public fashion spoke volumes to knowledgeable Wall Street investment bankers. It meant that something must be seriously awry at KKR.

Henry and George were furious. In conversations with them it was clear they had never expected Kohlberg to pull the plug. Compounding their unhappiness was the fact that his suit came at a time when Seaman Furniture and Hillsborough Holdings were in financial difficulty. There was a danger that the story could develop its own momentum, and they seemed to be deeply worried that their magic aura might suddenly evaporate.

As it turned out, they needn't have worried. For starters, KKR handled the media masterfully. With a few carefully turned phrases, they managed to transform a suit about fraud and misconduct into a sad case of an embittered old man trying to throw stones at his former, and now vastly more successful, partners.

The notion that KKR might be doing something detrimental to its investors was simply "rhetoric," said one person close to KKR. In all but one of the recapitalized companies, the investors were given a chance to invest in them in their reconfigured form. That was true, but since KKR seems to have so understated those companies' prospects, the investors were hardly able to make an informed decision.

What the suit was really all about, KKR's public relations team insisted, was the greed of a resentful ex-partner. He was simply trying to wring more money out of the firm. And the terrible irony, they said, was that if Kohlberg was successful, the people he would end up taking money away from were not George and Henry, but those who needed it most —the firm's bright young associates.

Now *that* argument stopped most journalists in their tracks. It certainly made Kohlberg seem unreasonable and seriously undermined the moral high ground he had been able to stake out until that point.

It is true that when Kohlberg left the firm and reduced his ownership stake, some of that was apportioned to other, junior executives in the firm. Therefore, if the deal was not a "new" deal but still an "old" deal, Kohlberg's stake would be raised and that of KKR associates would conceivably be reduced.

However, the dispute over the size of the stakes totally masked the larger issue. Before these companies were reconfigured, KKR's stake in them was tiny—typically less than 5 percent. By persuading its investors to sell their shares, KKR's claim on profits in these companies rose to 50 percent or so. The fact that George and Henry's share of KKR's interest in the "new" Marley was just 26 percent instead of the 28 percent they had previously held was beside the point. For they now had 26 percent of a 55-percent piece, instead of 28 percent of a 5-percent piece. It's obvious which position is preferable.

Unfortunately, details such as this cloud the issue. The dispute seemed so technical, there were so many numbers. KKR's position sounded so reasonable, and many reporters who were covering the story closely knew Dick and Henry well. They had always found them to be decent, even charming, fellows, and they had no reason to distrust them now. On the other hand, they didn't know Kohlberg. Most reporters had never even met the man. He sounded eccentric—he wouldn't talk to them. When it came down to accepting KKR's version or pursuing it further, many reporters dropped it.

Kohlberg, meanwhile, having said his piece, withdrew to the privacy of his office. He was satisfied with having blown the whistle, but he did not feel it was his job to carry the torch for the rest of the world. Kohlberg was no crusader here. Indeed, his own behavior during this period continued to be deeply conflicted. On the one hand, he was openly attacking the practices of the organization he had founded. On the other hand, he continued to benefit financially from the firm, even to the point of investing in KKR's recent deals because the alternative would signify that he was being deprived of his rights. He could assuage his conscience, he said, by giving the money to charities.

Since Kohlberg didn't intend to take any further action, he hoped that journalists would take up the cause. But if they did not, he figured that KKR's investors, at least, would have to investigate. And once they got up in arms, reporters would eventually hear about it and follow up. Or so he thought.

He was right about one thing. Journalists are generally transmitters—not creators—of news. They tend not to go out on a limb and make bold statements themselves. Editors get uncomfortable when reporters appear to be reaching their own conclusions; the idea is that other people should gripe and then reporters should quote them. For all the power accorded to the press, when the game is played according to the rules, reporters are more often than not a medium—passive rather than active participants.

For the story to be taken the next step, KKR's investors would have to do something. Only that was not going to happen. Kohlberg badly overestimated their interest in exploring the charges. At the same time, KKR's damage control in this arena was also very effective. Henry and George made solicitous calls on the firm's largest investors and talked to them personally about the issues raised in Kohlberg's suit. They offered to send them copies of the filings and to have anyone who was concerned speak to Dick Beattie to assuage their concerns.

KKR's investors gave Henry and George the benefit of the doubt. These were, after all, people they had known a long time. Over the years they had become friends, partners, rather than people who had their money and needed to be watched like hawks. They all thought of Henry and George as extremely serious, upstanding people. They could not imagine for a moment that Kohlberg's allegations could be true. Few of them knew Kohlberg well. The insurance companies, after all, were long gone. The firm's current investors were mostly state fund managers and bank lenders whose main contact with the firm had been either George or Henry. And they understood that Kohlberg had "not been well." The explanation that this was a case of sour grapes, a petty squabble over money, seemed totally plausible.

In Oregon, home of the aggressive Investment Council, the reaction was, accordingly, subdued. Carol Hewitt, then the chairwoman, said she was less troubled by the specific details of Kohlberg's suit than the more general, underlying issue of KKR's integrity. George Roberts immediately sent her a copy of the Kohlberg complaint and went over it with her on the phone. Hewitt says George told her that Kohlberg had filed the suit largely to take advantage of negative publicity the firm had been receiving because of the RJR Nabisco takeover and several recently soured deals. She accepted George's explanation and concluded that it was much ado about nothing.

"You can have businesspeople have different views about what an agreement means, or who should pay what percent," she said. "In a worst-case scenario that's the way I read it, the way it came out. I didn't think it would have a big enough dollar impact on them, or reflect badly enough on their character that it mattered," she said.

Hewitt's intentions were good. She asked George if they could talk to KKR's lawyers, which he said they could. And she asked Jim George, the Council's staff person, to look into the matter. But he never got back to her. And Hewitt, who had earned a reputation as a tiger for her decision to defend Dalkon against suits brought by women injured by its IUDs, never even bothered to call Kohlberg or his lawyers to seek further details. "I felt comfortable after listening to George that this would not have any impact on us," said Hewitt. "I can't say I gave it an evenhanded investigation."

Other fund managers were similarly relaxed. John Canning, a banker at First Chicago, said after hearing about the suit, "On all four of those [deals], I reviewed them and I was not unhappy with the prices I received on any of them. I was probably the biggest investor in some of those deals."[2] On the other hand, Canning's career had soared with his company's investments in KKR deals. His venture capital unit at First Chicago had acquired several spin-offs of KKR companies, investments that he presumably thought would be profitable. And he and his colleagues at the bank invested personally in KKR's funds, through an entity the bank had allowed them to form called Madison Dearborn Partners.[3]

Although Canning had a special relationship with KKR, his reaction was, nonetheless, fairly typical. The industry bible, *Pension & Investment Age*, conducted a survey of KKR's investors about a week after news of Kohlberg's suit hit the papers. Its conclusion was evident from the headline: "KKR

Suit Draws Yawns." "Most KKR investors, including officials of several large state and private pension funds, insurance companies and university endowments, said they do not believe KKR boosted the ownership stake of the firm or its associates in any of the five deals at their expense, or that they were shortchanged. They said they are satisfied with the hefty returns they have had on their KKR investments in companies they consider well-managed, growing and strong performers," the article said.[4]

"We've made a lot of money from KKR investments. I haven't had any problem with them. A lot of the publicity on KKR over the last year has been overblown," said Howard Bicker, the head of Minnesota's state fund.[5] Ned Regan, the head of New York's retirement fund, said, "Our investments are in growing, strong, medium-sized companies. The investments are secure. Our net-of-fees returns have been extremely good."[6]

Consultant Doug Le Bon said several of his clients called and asked him to have Wilshire analyze the transactions to see if they were done fairly. He said he was satisfied that they were. But with his career largely built on his recommendation of KKR he may not have been in the best position to provide an independent appraisal.

In the end, not one of KKR's investors ever called Kohlberg or his lawyers, a lack of interest that Kohlberg finds astounding. By contrast, investors in Morgan Stanley's LBO fund, which are mostly insurance companies and corporate pension funds, have proven to be highly critical of stock buybacks that the firm arranged without the benefit of open auctions. After Morgan's LBO group bought back shares of the Silgan Corporation and the Container Corporation at prices some considered unfairly low, as many as a dozen investors filed four separate lawsuits against the firm, all of which were still pending in the spring of 1991.[7]

Kohlberg's complaints, though similar, had no such effect. KKR asked for several postponements and never filed an answer rebutting his charges. The suit was finally settled out of court five months later. One of Henry and George's preconditions was that none of the parties could discuss the terms of the settlement—privately for three months and publicly forever. All Kohlberg will say about it is that "my original agreement was vindicated and confirmed. And that's an understatement."

If the press response to Kohlberg's allegations was muted, it was virtually nonexistent where Hedi Kravis was concerned. Technically, her divorce papers were sealed, as they are in all New York divorce cases. However, several reporters did manage to get hold of them.

The only place the information surfaced in any detail, however, was in a small article in the *Wall Street Journal*. Hedi later heard from another *Journal* reporter that Randall Smith, the author of the article, had used the material as an opportunity to write a longer piece about first wives who were shortchanged by their ex-husbands. The story had all the right ingredients—it scored high on the greed and gossip quotient. Smith told at least one person that he thought an article in which Henry Kravis, the custodian of millions of retirees' funds, was accused of defrauding his ex-wife in a divorce settlement would certainly make the paper's front page without delay. However, many days passed before the story finally ran, and when it did, there was no mention of the word *fraud*. The article was just a few paragraphs long, buried in the middle of the paper's second section. Readers who didn't know it was there would have had a hard time finding it.[8]

When *Seven Days*, a weekly feature magazine about New York, mentioned Hedi's divorce suit in passing, Dick Beattie was quoted as saying that all but one of the allegations were so "convoluted," he simply couldn't understand them.[9]

How is it that Henry and George have been able to dodge so many bullets? They have become expert at working the press. "Getting good press" is a business just like any other.

On the periphery are a handful of public relations firms that specialize in cultivating "relationships" with top financial journalists at such major publications as the *Wall Street Journal*, the *New York Times*, *Business Week*, *Forbes*, and *Fortune*.

These firms seek to exploit the fact that there is intense competition between journalists for the best and timeliest story. To give some idea of the severity of the competition, the *Wall Street Journal* sends someone to the lobby of the *New York Times* building around nine-thirty or ten o'clock at night to buy the first edition of the paper and rush it back to the *Journal*'s headquarters in lower Manhattan. There, the night editor scans it, along with other national papers it has rounded up, for any major stories the *Journal* might have missed. If necessary, an editor will call reporters at home and ask them to start reporting and writing stories that will enable the paper at least to match the competition.

Since the *New York Times* comes out several hours earlier than the *Wall Street Journal*, it does not have the same luxury. Instead, every morning, an editor in the business section reviews the *Journal*, plus several others, to see how the paper's reporters fared against the competition. A tally sheet is then composed, detailing the stories that were missed or a particularly pertinent piece of information that was somehow left out of a story that ran. The list is then circulated to top editors of the paper every day, who may or may not demand a full accounting of a journalist's shortcomings.

The most active public relations, or PR, people spend their days working the phones, or having lunch or drinks with reporters. Part of the object is to keep abreast of stories, so that a PR person can make sure that their clients are mentioned in favorable ones and kept out of the ones that are not. PR consultants may "pitch" an article about one of their clients or try to put a spin on a particular story that deflects criticism from their client and directs it to a competitor.

As mergers came to dominate the front pages of newspapers and the cover stories of magazines, certain PR people who represented dealmakers evolved into positions of great power. Like many other financial journalists, I did my share of mingling.

A good PR person can make a difference. Naturally journalists want to have an exclusive interview with a dealmaker who has just put together a $4-billion transaction and is keen to talk about it. Especially if they also know that their competitors will not be getting a similar call because they foolishly did not develop the same "close relationship" with the right PR person.

Picture it. A young journalist, barely out of college, who earns somewhere between $50,000 and $70,000, has just started watching "L.A. Law." The phone rings, and the person on the end of the line is asking whether he or she would like to "do an exclusive" with the celebrity dealmaker who just helped sell a $10-billion company to a hostile acquiror. The story ends up on the front page. The journalist looks like a hero in the newsroom the next day for his or her "scoop." And the critical role of the PR person is a secret shared between the journalist and the PR person—a bond to be tested another day.

As journalists who covered mergers found themselves increasingly the object of attention, they began to up their demands. They didn't want to talk with some "flak," they wanted to go straight to the source. And gradually, that is what they did. By the mid- to late 1980s, any merger reporter worth his or her salt had the numbers of the home phone, the country home, and the car phone of every top dealmaker in the country. And they would think nothing of dialing them whenever they had to. The dealmakers, in turn, were only too happy to ingratiate themselves with the mainstream journalists. Press coverage was becoming increasingly important and could even influence the outcome of a deal, by altering public opinion or increasing the pressure on boards of directors. Part of a dealmaker's job was to cultivate a special relationship with one or two key journalists who could be counted on to get his point of view, his "spin" on a deal, into the public's eye.

In this game of mutual seduction, KKR proved to be particularly effective. In the early years of the firm, there simply were no press relations as a matter of choice. But gradually, as the takeover business demanded greater visibility, they negotiated the transition well. "To Henry and George and KKR, the press ultimately became part of the overall strategy. It was important for them to look good, to look responsible. Their business relied on CEOs walking through the door saying, 'we'd like to do a transaction,' " said Dick Beattie.

In the beginning, Henry and George played on KKR's historic reluctance to be interviewed. Interviews were granted sparsely, which only helped to further KKR's allure. From a journalist's standpoint, it was far more exciting to obtain an interview with someone who held the rest of the world at bay than with someone who was always readily accessible.

KKR played this to the hilt. Even at the most prestigious publications, KKR would generally deal with only one reporter. That left the rest feeling intimidated and somehow deficient, yet at the same time, admiring and envious of the person whose calls were returned. In my own case, I had the frustrating experience of being turned down several times while I was at *Business Week*, on the grounds that they just didn't do interviews, even though I knew that they did.

In general, Henry "dealt with" the press. George wanted nothing to do with it. He thought it was a total waste of time and was apparently unable to abide the stupid questions. Henry, however, dealt with a select group. After I joined the *Times* and gradually gained acceptance, I was invited several times to have lunch with him in his private dining room for an off-the-record chat. It felt akin to being summoned for an audience with the pope, and other reporters would nod approvingly when they heard where you were going for lunch. Henry would occasionally return reporters' phone calls, just often enough to make it worth trying, but just inconsistently enough that you still felt pleased when you actually succeeded in reaching him. Gradually, many reporters at the *Times* and elsewhere came to think of Henry as a genuinely nice guy. He was almost always smooth and charming, but he had a nice sense of humor that put people at ease. "Henry gets treated well because you're human and you respond to the same things that other humans do. He's nice, he's charming, and most people give people who are successful a certain respect and deference" was how Dick Beattie explained it.

As Beattie clearly appreciated, most reporters are, at bottom, just like everyone else. They respond to kindness and attention, and they tend to develop more of an affinity for the subjects whose company they enjoy. If a source they like also happens to be a source they need, the relationship between the reporter and the subject can become quite subjective. All reporters—whether they cover Wall Street or Washington or the police department—face the issue of getting too close to their sources. Reporters wrestle with the problem constantly, and there are no straightforward answers. Every day, judgment calls have to be made, whether it's to keep a source on background because the information they give is valuable, or to quote them saying something you know they wouldn't want to be quoted on, even though the discussion was on the record.

As media coverage became increasingly important to the success or failure of a merger, and reporters became an integral part of the dealmaking world, the contact between the press and Henry intensified. And the more that reporters got to know him as a person, the harder it was not to be sympathetic, perhaps even a little protective. KKR was one of the most active dealmakers in the world. Even if KKR wasn't directly involved in a deal, Henry might still be knowledgeable because the firm analyzed many companies without ever making a bid. Henry's charm and importance made him a source not to be trifled with. The coverage of KKR, in turn, became increasingly deferential.

Henry's ties to a few select journalists were buttressed by the good works of Dick Beattie. By the late 1980s, the savviest Wall Street journalists knew that Beattie was the source of choice, even more so than Henry. For starters, he was quick to return your phone calls and was almost always willing to talk "for background," that is, as long as it couldn't be traced to him. For reporters working on tight deadlines, his accessibility and cooperation made Beattie invaluable.

But more important than access was the type of information that Beattie passed along. He understood more than almost anyone else in the dealmaking world the kind of information that a journalist needed. And he would often volunteer it freely, even to the point of calling a journalist to make sure they had a certain tidbit, as he did with me, to alert me to an investment decision by the state of Washington's public fund.

It was a wonderful way to help "build a relationship," and many a journalist became indebted. It usually wasn't vital information. But he had an eye for the kind of detail that would lend a story credibility and make it eminently readable. He was always the one who remembered how late in the wee hours a meeting broke up, or who won the poker game that ensued while a board of directors huddled, or whether it was pizza or Chinese takeout that provided the evening's sustenance. And in the "*People* magazine" era of the 1980s, it was tidbits like these that were deemed to make or break a story. The morning after, in the newsroom, fellow journalists would gather by the coffee machine and note with envy such "deft" touches. Editors would send their young journalists notes praising them for their "insight." It was the beginning of "you were there" journalism. And Beattie was adept at facilitating it.

Author Bryan Burrough has been open in media circles about how helpful Beattie was in providing anecdotes for *Barbarians at the Gate*. Some reporters who cover Wall Street were not surprised, then, to see how well KKR came across in the book, and how poorly certain men who have crossed KKR, like Kohlberg, Peter Cohen, and Jeff Beck, fared in the narrative account.

Forstmann, who insisted throughout the deal that KKR was overpaying for RJR Nabisco and warned that that would burden the company excessively with debt, was mocked throughout *Barbarians* for his constant efforts at self-promotion, his almost childish rivalry with Kravis, and his preachings about the dangers of junk bonds, which were labeled in the book as "The Spiel" and dismissed as "diatribe." (As it turned out, Forstmann's forecast proved to be accurate: just eighteen months later, KKR had to redress the company's high debt profile with an infusion of several billion dollars of equity.)

As for Jeff Beck, a dealmaker with Drexel Burnham Lambert, he was described in the book as a suspected leaker of vital information, and Peter Cohen of Shearson Lehman was depicted as little better than a thug in a business suit.

The description of the book proved to be devastating. Forstmann, once tagged, could never shake The Spiel moniker. He became the butt of many jokes on Wall Street, even though his dire predictions about junk bonds proved to be accurate and his sense of the business cycle seemed to be more on target than George's or Henry's. Forstmann wrote a thoughtful reply to an excerpt from *Barbarians* about him that ran in *New York* magazine, which is owned by the same company as the book's publisher. In it, Forstmann complained that journalists had become mesmerized with mergers as a modern-day battle scene and focused all their attention on tactics, "armor," and personalities, rather than the underlying issues that gave rise to the confrontation. Unfortunately, Forstmann wrote, "Acquisitions of companies are far more serious matters. They are economic events that affect the lives and fortunes of investors, employees, suppliers, and customers." His comments were never published.

Jeff Beck was later the subject of another article by Burrough—only this time he was exposed as an irrepressible liar. Cohen ended up resigning from Shearson Lehman, in part because his image had been so damaged by *Barbarians*. Although his boss, Jim Robinson, then a friend of Kravis's, had condoned if not encouraged many of Cohen's steps during the RJR Nabisco transaction, the authors never made that point in their book, and Robinson emerged from the matter with his reputation intact.

The book's success is viewed by many in the media as having enhanced the *Journal*'s reputation for its dramatic and well-written coverage of Wall Street, since, although the paper had nothing to do with its actual publishing, the authors were both then reporters for the paper. The *Journal* ran an unusually lengthy excerpt of the book. And the paper's managing editor, Norman Pearlstine, sponsored a book party for the young authors, inviting all the chief characters in *Barbarians* to a sit-down dinner at one of Manhattan's elegant night spots. Although none of the three KKR founders attended, Beattie was one of the few subjects of the book who showed up.

Beattie has told people that he considers himself a good friend of Pearlstine's, a relationship that could conceivably be awkward, since Beattie is also the one who Henry usually turns to when he wants to convey to a publication his unhappiness with a particular story.

In the case of the *Wall Street Journal*, however, since so many of the stories about the LBO firm have been favorable, it is hard to imagine that many confrontations have arisen. In general, the reporter who covers KKR for the paper is a man named George Anders. (Burrough is off writing another book, having received an astonishing $1 million advance, largely on the basis of his performance in *Barbarians*.) Anders returned to the *Journal* in the summer of 1990 after a year-long leave of absence during which he worked on a book on the history of KKR. In writing the book, he received Henry and George's cooperation, a factor that was undoubtedly helpful in securing a reported $275,000 advance, a sum large enough to earn a mention in a media newsletter. Anders told people that he was finding book-writing difficult and that he returned to the *Journal* with the idea of working on it in his free time while he pondered how to complete the project. Soon after, when RJR Nabisco's bonds were plummeting because of a technical provision that meant the company was in danger of defaulting on its debt, Anders consistently beat other business publications with details of KKR's intended rescue plan.

In general, Anders's articles depicted the financial rescue of RJR Nabisco as a great success story. They emphasized the extent to which the company would be on a sounder financial footing as a result of the equity infusion and the retirement of debt. Although many leading financial executives on Wall Street regarded the restructuring as humiliating for KKR, because it had previously been so dismissive of those who had predicted RJR's precarious financial structure would eventually topple, that viewpoint was not expressed in Anders's articles.

And though Anders wrote that part of the money that KKR was using to bolster RJR Nabisco had been "raised" from a buyout fund that KKR controlled, he did not note that under normal circumstances, KKR would not have been able to impose such a unilateral decision on its investors and that many of them were howling about it. In the past, KKR had always assured investors that their investments would be diversified. It even included in its partnership agreements a clause stating it would not invest more than 25 percent of a fund in any one company.

KKR removed that clause in its last fund, however, a change that few of its investors' lawyers seemed to catch when they were reviewing the contractual agreement. Some investors were startled when KKR informed them that it was increasing their $1.5 billion investment in RJR by another $1.7 billion, resulting in over half the fund being invested in one company. "Suddenly everyone went to their book to look up the clause," said Robert Zobel, who oversees LBO investing for the state of Wisconsin's fund. But the fine print they'd remembered from previous fund documents was no longer there. "If we'd had our druthers, I'd have said, 'Don't do it,' " said Zobel. "We had to swallow real hard on that one."

The RJR Nabisco restructuring illustrates the important role that interpretation can play in press coverage. The facts of the restructuring could have been presented in a far different light. For instance: "In a stunning setback to the nation's leading leveraged buyout firm, KKR announced yesterday that it would have to restructure a deal it arranged only eighteen months ago, by injecting $1.7 billion of its investors' money into the company."

When KKR later negotiated new bank loans for the RJR restructuring, Anders again gave the subject a favorable cast. "Bankers said they have deluged RJR Nabisco Inc. with $7 billion of loan commitments for its debt refinancing plan, more than triple what the tobacco and food company needs" was how he began his story on July 9, 1990. It wasn't until midway through the article that Anders noted that bankers had been attracted to the loan proposal by the fees. Another way to write the story would have been to start out by saying that as an indication of how difficult it was to secure new bank financing for RJR Nabisco's restructuring, KKR had to offer fees that were as much as two times higher than those for typical transactions.

A number of people in the LBO industry have commented on Anders's apparent bias in favor of KKR. "I deal with the financial press a lot, but this guy always seems to be using information in ways that go beyond fair financial reporting," says Bob F. Johnston, president of Beacon Hill Financial, which specializes in helping LBO firms raise money. Johnston has worked for former Treasury Secretary

William Simon, Equitable Capital, and Forstmann Little, among others. "He always seems to have another agenda. He makes me feel that he works for them," says Johnston.

The *Wall Street Journal*'s coverage of the RJR financing was critical to how KKR's plan was received by the rest of the world. The paper is, after all, regarded as the bible by the financial community. It was therefore fortunate for KKR that Anders wrote such favorable pieces about the firm. His exclusive stories concerning RJR Nabisco's restructuring set the pace for the rest of the business press. And thanks to that ever-present herd mentality that seems to plague the journalistic profession, reporters at most other publications were unwilling to strike out in a different direction when they followed with their own stories the next day.

The favorable press coverage received by KKR over the refinancing of RJR, which was widely regarded as one of its most difficult challenges to date, unleashed a host of other favorable publicity. Having successfully wriggled out of that financing bind, KKR's luster was suddenly restored. Feature stories followed in such magazines as *U.S. News* and *Business Week* that provided glowing accounts of KKR's resurgence. "KKR is rolling with the punches," said *U.S. News*.[10] "They are America's reigning champs of leverage." *Business Week* declared the firm not only open for business, but prospering.[11]

At the same time that Henry was cultivating good relations with the press, he was actively pursuing the role of senior statesman, transcending his narrow Wall Street focus. His image was clearly enhanced by being on the board of prestigious institutions like the Metropolitan Museum, Channel 13, the New York City Ballet. And with Carolyne in attendance, the endless photographs of him in his tuxedo, carrying on some half-serious conversation, helped further his aura as "a player."

In his speeches, Henry spoke of such issues as "leadership" and "ethics." Another of his favorite themes was the erosion of values. "What has happened to us? What has happened to the moral base of our society?" he asked with mounting outrage before a group gathered in 1989 for a Harvard Business School annual dinner. "There are so many of us today who are on the fast track, living for the moment, unable to defer our gratification, and worst of all, contending with all of this without a moral compass."

If Henry knew that he was attacking mores that were often ascribed to him by the business community and some members of the press, his speeches did not convey any sense of that irony. The night he endowed a chair in "leadership" at his alma mater, Claremont College, he told the audience, "The first great imperative of leadership is that those who impose risk must be seen to share it . . . those who shy away from risk may well preside over the collapse of the very institutions they have been entrusted with."

So spoke a man who would buy a company using a mountain of debt and only $2.5 million of his and his partners' money, receive an immediate $23 million back in fees, and then pronounce that he shares risk right along with his investors. Here was a man who would freely criticize managers of corporate America for being "renters of corporate assets" while KKR—and indeed the entire LBO industry—was doing essentially the same thing: "renting" the assets of pension funds in order to own companies just long enough to empty their coffers of excess cash.

Henry apparently thought nothing of moaning to congressmen about how terrible it was that RJR's previous management owned eleven jets and belonged to twenty-one country clubs. He seemed to see no parallels in the fact that it was the enormous fees his firm was paid by companies he controlled that enabled him to buy his personal jet and helicopter, four opulent homes, a $7-million riding ring, a $14-million painting, and who knows how many country club memberships. "Greed really turns me off," he told *Fortune* magazine without a hint of irony.[12]

* * *

Having wrapped themselves in the mantle of the Establishment, and having forged crucial relations with the press, Henry and George became insulated from most criticism. After all, who would ever imagine that Henry Kravis and George Roberts and all those famous people associated with them could be wrong? For the most part, those who had any doubts simply kept them to themselves or suspended judgment.

When a few people did try to question them or their motives, Henry and George came down on them with all their might. The journalists who tried to raise questions about KKR's behavior toward its investors were met with a combination of intimidation, personal attack, and disinformation.

In my own case, after I wrote two stories in the *New York Times* in August of 1989 about KKR's troubled deals and Kohlberg's lawsuit, Henry called the newspaper's publisher, Arthur Sulzberger, to complain. Henry knows Sulzberger, another Loomis Chaffee alumnus, through the Metropolitan Museum, where Sulzberger is chairman. The Met, of course, is where Henry donated $10 million for the Kravis wing.

On Friday, September 15, Henry, Dick Beattie, and another KKR partner, Paul Raether, had lunch with Sulzberger, Max Frankel, the editor of the paper, the managing editor, and an assistant managing editor who oversees the business section. I never heard afterward from any of the editors who attended the meeting. It was reported in *New York* magazine and *Seven Days* because it was viewed as a sign of just how influential Henry Kravis had become.

Henry has also, on occasion, called Pearlstine at the *Journal* to complain about its coverage. And there is, of course, that infamous altercation between him and Billy Norwich, a society writer, during which Henry complained about his coverage of him and reportedly threatened to "break both your kneecaps." Though several people attending the affair said they overheard him saying it, Henry later denied having made such a remark.[13]

Hope Lampert, a free-lance writer, encountered the "mean streak" in Henry's personality when she was doing an article about him for *Seven Days*, a feature magazine about Manhattan that had a brief but critically acclaimed life. When Henry heard that she had been given the assignment, he was said to be furious. She'd criticized him in articles in the past, and he wasn't about to endure another round with her without a good fight.

Lampert was told by editors at the publication that Henry placed a call to the publisher, Leonard Stern, and asked that the story be killed. When that proved ineffective, he called her up and demanded that she come to his office immediately. She obliged and was treated to about an hour of berating. At one point in the meeting, says Lampert, Henry told her that he knew where she had been and who she was seeing. "Whatever he meant, he was clearly being threatening," she says. Henry also got Beattie to fire off a letter to Leonard Stern, in which he raised questions about the accuracy of Lampert's reporting. Yet during a private meeting with her, Dick conveyed his embarrassment to her about Henry's behavior. "On the one hand, he seemed to be separating himself," she said, "on the other hand, he wrote the letter Henry told him to."

Despite Henry's and Dick's efforts, Lampert prevailed. The story ran intact and was biting in its tone.

When intimidation does not work, Henry and George simply counter with "their" own story. After my article criticizing some of their business practices ran in the *New York Times*, for instance, George wrote a letter to KKR's investors rebutting its central thesis. In it, he stated that "KKR has only one business, investing with our partners in companies. . . . KKR has no other source of income such as merger and acquisition advisory fees."[14] Yet in 1988, KKR received about $200 million in fees, of which more than $150 million came from doing deals; in 1989, the total came to around

$120 million, $75 million of which came from investment-banking fees on RJR Nabisco, and $10 million of which came from an unusually high fee for monitoring the food and tobacco company. Henry and George like to explain that all those fees are necessary because KKR has to pay legal, accounting, and other expenses associated with deals that do not go through. But other LBO executives said those fees would run no higher than $5 million or $10 million a year, or else the firm was not managing itself well. That still leaves plenty for Henry, George, and their top associates.

The bottom line is that in the last few years, despite their protestations about being at risk and making money with their partners, Henry and George have each received $20 million to $40 million in annual pretax fees—*independent* of any appreciation in the companies they acquired for their investors.

So, too, KKR states baldly in its most recent marketing pamphlet that "we are extremely conservative buyers." But then how does it reconcile that with its high-risk purchase of Jim Walter and its potential asbestos liabilities, or its piling of debt on Seaman Furniture, which has one product line in a small market, or its acquisition of RJR Nabisco in a bidding frenzy that ultimately forced it to put almost 60 percent of its 1987 investors' money into one deal in order to shore up the company's shaky finances?

Perhaps the most chilling example of all concerns George Roberts's testimony in the $3-billion lawsuit brought against the Jim Walter Corporation, KKR, and Drexel Burnham by asbestos victims. During his deposition to the plaintiff's lawyers, he seemed to develop an acute case of amnesia.[15] When asked whether he owned any property in Texas other than his mother's and a friend's condominiums, George said no. His answer bolstered KKR's position that the case should not be heard in Beaumont, Texas, where many of the asbestos victims reside, but in another jurisdiction where they might get a more hospitable jury. At the time, the lawyer representing the asbestos victims, Stephen D. Susman, took

George's answer at face value. The two had known each other when they were both growing up in Houston, and George seemed relaxed and cooperative that day. The following weekend, however, when Susman was at a cocktail party, he learned from an acquaintance that George had teamed up with one of his best friends from childhood and the two had $1.7 million invested in a number of land development projects in Houston. Susman, one of Texas's scrappiest and best-known litigators, confronted George with that fact several days later. On the witness stand in a crowded Beaumont, Texas, courtroom, George turned stone faced and began to list the projects in some detail: a restaurant, a paint shop.[16] "George didn't like that at all," says Susman, adding that he thought George's earlier omission "was highly pertinent."

That was not to be the end, however, of George's apparent memory loss. When Susman asked him during his deposition whether he had ever been sued personally, he said no. Yet his lawsuit with Kohlberg was at that very moment winding its way through the New York court system. When asked why Kohlberg's name remained part of the firm's, George said there was no particular reason and mentioned that, with the stationery already printed and the name on the door, it would have been expensive to change things. When George was asked to explain how KKR's voting procedures amongst its partners worked, he pleaded ignorance. He said that the procedures were "really pretty vague." And when he was further asked whether there was anything in writing to determine whether votes had to be unanimous or not, this trained lawyer who had just spent two full years wrangling with his ex-partner over that exact same issue, this man who remembers obscure numbers from fifteen years ago and never has to take a note, said, "I don't really know."

No, it's difficult to reach any conclusion other than that George and Henry have a loose definition of truth. To them, it seems, truth is adaptable. One recalls Mike Wilsey's comments about his friend George's betting habits. When he loses, he simply alters the terms of the bet so that they somehow end up in his favor.

Henry, in turn, was defining truth in his own way even when he was a little boy. One afternoon when he was about eight or nine he asked his parents if he could spend the night at a friend's house. Ray was a little suspicious, having heard from a neighbor that the boy in question had been seen using slingshots against birds. "Henry," Ray asked, "what will you be doing when you go over there?"

"Just playing," was Ray's recollection of the little boy's determined response. "You sure, Henry?" Ray pressed. "You sure you're not going over there to shoot slingshots?" Oh, no, Henry assured him, whereupon Ray grabbed the overnight bag that Henry was carrying and began looking through it.

"What do you think I found but a slingshot," Ray exclaimed. So he promptly sent Henry upstairs to his room and told him he wasn't allowed to go anywhere for the night. A little while later, Henry was still upstairs crying, and Ray began to feel bad. He wondered if perhaps he'd been too harsh with the boy. He went upstairs to Henry's room and began talking to the boy, who seemed to have learned his lesson. Ray relented and decided to let Henry go after all, but he warned the boy, "No slingshots." A few minutes later, Henry came scurrying down the big winding staircase, ready once again to go out. "Henry," said Ray, "no slingshot, right?" "Oh, no, sir," said the boy, standing on one of the steps. Ray says Henry then held his sack open and volunteered, "You can even check my bag."

"I'm going to do more than check your bag," said the stern-sounding Ray, who promptly began frisking the boy. "Where do you think I found it? He had the slingshot in his underpants!" said Ray, roaring with laughter. It was obvious that he found his youngest son's ingenuity thoroughly charming.

His other son, George, however, was so honest it could be irritating. The day he got his driver's license, George asked if he could borrow Bessie's car. She had an Imperial with a beige roof that all the boys admired. George came home that night around eleven and hung around downstairs in the family playroom seeming disconcerted. Ray asked if anything was wrong and George said no, but he wanted to know when his father would be around the house the next day. George was up early the next morning, hanging around disconsolately as Ray was getting ready to go play golf. Ray still couldn't bring his shy son to tell him what was on his mind. Finally, when Ray returned from his golf game in the afternoon, George pulled him aside and confessed that when he'd turned a corner the night before in his mother's car, he had hit a patch of gravel and was afraid he might have scratched the car. George was so upset that he made Ray bend down and look under the car. "I couldn't see the scratch anywhere," said Ray. "If I looked really hard, I thought I could see a tiny scratch, but no one would ever know it was there." George, said Ray, shaking his head with obvious frustration, was honest "almost to a fault."

CONCLUSION

In the closing days of 1912, the illustrious banker J. Pierpont Morgan was called before a congressional committee that was investigating how a handful of bankers, through a web of interlocking directorships, had come to exercise so much control over the nation's wealth. Morgan was then in his mid-seventies, but his age did not diminish his resolve. Despite aggressive questioning from the committee's counsel, Samuel Untermyer, Morgan insisted that the concentration of ownership did not signify anything ominous. And he denied that it conferred any power upon him whatsoever. Power, he said, could not be derived from money; its only origin was character.

Frederick Lewis Allen, who wrote a biography of Morgan, believed the banker was not being coy when he said that, but was voicing a deeply felt conviction. To buttress his view,

Allen cited the following exchange between Morgan and the lawyer Untermyer:

"Is not commercial credit based primarily upon money or property?" asked Untermyer.

"No, sir," said Morgan; "the first thing is character."

"Before money or property?"

"Before money or anything else. Money cannot buy it. . . . Because a man I do not trust could not get money from me on all the bonds in Christendom."[1]

Morgan's philosophy had no place in the 1980s. Power in that decade *was* derived from money, and character, by contrast, was in extremely short supply.

The history of KKR vividly affirms this. With returns in the 30- to 40-percent range, George and Henry made themselves and their investors very wealthy. In the process, they showered rewards on those outside their immediate orbit, and almost no one chose to spurn their advances. Many of the recipients of KKR's largess then went out of their way to help the firm flourish, displaying a fierce loyalty that was not extended to others and raising the question of whether those individuals' actions were, in fact, compromised.

The form of the reward varied:

• With commercial banks and Wall Street firms, it was unprecedented fees, warrants, and other favored forms of equity.

• With lawyers, it was a chance to become multimillionaires via stakes in KKR's deals.

• With pension-fund overseers, it was a chance to improve their job prospects in the private sector and flirt, no matter how briefly, with members of the jet set, while in a few select cases there was a hope of personal enrichment following the completion of public service.

• With chief executives it was the chance to become multi-millionaires through owning equity in KKR companies.

• With journalists it was the chance to build their reputations through scoops and access.

• With politicians it was a chance to fill their campaign coffers and hobnob with a Wall Street celebrity.

• With cultural organizations, it was the chance to expand their budgets and build new wings; the individual who provided entree to that cultural organization could, in turn, become a director and earn a little pocket money on the side.

By the time Henry and George were through, they had amassed a power base of enormous proportions. They were revered in the investment community, feared by their competitors, and treated with deference in the press.

Some people might say, so what? George and Henry were merely behaving like good businessmen, trying to ingratiate themselves with various constituents. Lots of people make political donations and give breaks to their best customers to engender loyalty. If anyone did anything wrong, it was probably the people who accepted KKR's offerings, and not KKR itself.

And anyway, did anyone actually violate any laws? My own view is that it would be difficult to prove in court. I do think, however, that the relationship between KKR and Roger Meier, the mechanism by which Drexel executives obtained Beatrice, Storer, and Safeway warrants, and the pattern of KKR's stock repurchases from its investors all merit further exploration.

But even if there were no legal violations, the larger and perhaps more important issue is whether the bonds that KKR forged influenced people's judgment or compromised their ability to carry out their professional duties. To the extent that they did, the question is whether that will further aggravate the crisis of confidence that the public has begun to exhibit toward the business community, the financial markets, public officials, and society at large.

It might not have been illegal, but was it good public policy for Roger Meier to be able to commit several hundred million dollars of other people's money to KKR and then several months later move into a position where he was personally enriched by the firm? And even if it was perfectly legal at the time, did it make good sense for KKR to be the largest source of financial support to state treasurers or comptrollers who, after their election, were in a position to assign to KKR state employees' money? And was it good business practice for a Latham & Watkins lawyer or an attorney at Simpson Thacher & Bartlett to invest in KKR deals on an ongoing basis and accept assignments from other clients that placed them on the other side of the table from KKR?

KKR did not simply create conflicts for other people; it created them for itself in its dealings with its own investors. Could it honestly build a business with a view to the long-term when it was receiving enormous upfront fees and bearing little of the pain if there were losses on its investments? And did it serve its investors well by buying back stock from them without the benefit of an auction, raising the question of whether it met its obligation to its partners to act "honestly, loyally, without self-dealing, and in good faith," as Kohlberg stated in his suit?

In the dealmaking frenzy of the eighties, KKR consistently put short-term profit considerations ahead of long-term business interests. In doing so, it was right in synch with the times. Savings and loan executives plundered their institutions and then ran for the hills. Senators and congressmen gratefully accepted their political contributions without any thought to the public's perception. Defense contractors squandered billions of dollars of taxpayers' money and came back empty-handed. Takeover advisers encouraged their clients to participate in bidding wars in which they were the only ones left standing. CEOs got friendly directors to raise their pay into the stratosphere and to award them $15 million "golden parachutes" on top of that. The business press aggravated matters by glorifying those who invented junior senior subordinated zero coupon pay-in-kind debentures, or some such gobbledegook, and minimizing the coverage of individuals who were toiling to create something lasting.

Today the prevailing view is that everyone is in it for themselves. And as a result, a profound cynicism is setting in. It is little wonder that individuals are pulling back from the stock market, questioning the motives of lawyers and brokers, distrusting the health of their banks, and staying away from the voting booth.

KKR had an opportunity few others get, to blaze a trail through virgin territory. But when it turned its back on its conservative origins and started buying companies with a recklessness that suggested its primary considerations were ego and immediate enrichment rather than the prudent long-term investment of other people's money, as was its mandate, it set a tone that others quickly followed. Before long, what had started as a relatively innocent financial tool had spawned a $200-billion industry dedicated to sucking the financial surplus out of one company and moving on to the next.

In good part because of the LBO movement, many of America's tried-and-true companies have found themselves in a recession saddled with debt levels they would normally accrue only in hard times. Already, there has been a rash of bankruptcies involving companies unrelated to KKR. The roster includes such long-established names as Southland, Revco, Interco, Best Products, and Cuisinart. Others, such as Macy's, Harcourt Brace Jovanovich, and Supermarkets General, are, at the time of this writing, teetering on the edge or seeking new infusions of equity.

Some see nothing wrong with this. They say it is just a healthy flushing out of old, tired companies and their replacement with new, more dynamic overseers. If anything, they maintain, the huge increase in heavily indebted companies will make this whole process more efficient, by speeding up the time it takes for a company to undergo a collapse and rebirth.

But few, if any, of the advocates of LBOs are in a position to feel any direct consequence of a company's changing hands, flipping back and forth between private and public ownership, solvency and bankruptcy, as if doing so were nothing more than changing one's wardrobe. It is hard to believe that somewhere, further down the line, there will be no cost to all this disruption and discontinuity.

Defenders of KKR like to point out how rich investors have become from their LBO investments, and how petty it is to suggest, therefore, that anyone was really hurt. Oregon State Treasurer Tony Meeker has estimated that KKR-controlled companies in Oregon have spent more than $350 million on expansion programs, added thousands of new jobs, and made $15 million in charitable contributions within the state.[2] And the state can still point to returns in the 35-percent range on its retirees' money.

But Oregon was lucky enough to invest in KKR in the early years, when reason was still being applied to deals. A more unfortunate victim is the state of Iowa, advised by consultant Doug Le Bon. Iowa did not begin to invest with KKR until 1986. In explaining why it finally decided to do so, Charles Bruner, the board's chairman and a state senator, stated that "two of the specific reasons for investing in KKR as opposed to the other LBO firms were that KKR does not engage in hostile takeovers and does not make substantial use of high-yield debt financing (junk bonds) in its acquisitions."[3] Today, however, Iowa is in precisely the place that Buner said he did not want to be. The state's pension fund has invested $375 million with KKR and some of that money has been used to buy companies in less-than-friendly circumstances that required large amounts of junk bonds. Iowa is also more exposed than others because that $375 million represents almost 10 percent of its total $4-billion fund. Most other state funds, by contrast, have limited their LBO investments to less than 5 percent of their total. And because about half of Iowa's commitment to KKR has been invested in just one company—RJR Nabisco—the state is far less diversified, and therefore less protected against risk, than others.

All of KKR's investors, even Oregon, might have profited even more from their affiliation with KKR if the LBO firm had acted differently. Had Drexel executives not garnered at least $525 million in profits from the warrants of KKR companies, for instance, some of that money might reside in the coffers of public pension funds today. The same could be said for the profits that KKR enjoyed from companies it bought back from its investors at prices that may well have been unfairly low.

All together, KKR's investors may have missed out on as much as $750 million, a not insignificant sum. Since Oregon and Washington each account for about 10 percent of KKR pools, those two states' pension plans might be $75 million richer today if KKR had acted differently. In states like New York, Michigan, and Wisconsin, the amounts would be more like $30 million to $40 million. At a time when many states are facing fiscal shortfalls and having to choose between maintaining adequate police forces, hiring more schoolteachers, and rebuilding roadways and bridges, this missed opportunity is unfortunate.

Unlike many other Wall Street dealmakers who were stopped dead in their tracks by government investigations, the collapse of the junk bond market, or a general disdain for their tactics, George and Henry are still rolling right along. As this book was being completed, they were attempting to raise $1 billion to $2 billion in new funds. There are some nascent signs of resistance, with a few state funds asking questions about the warrants, demanding assurances on diversification of their investments, and trying to force KKR to reduce its fees. Nevertheless, while other LBO funds have spent months trying to raise $200 million or $300 million, George secured $1.1 billion in commitments from Oregon,

Washington, and a few other states by doing little more than picking up the phone.

When George Anders of the *Wall Street Journal* learned of the Oregon fund's commitment, he wrote a generally laudatory article in which he alluded to Oregon's decision as a "kickoff" event. A table accompanying the article put KKR's results in the best possible light. Among other things, it listed KKR's returns without deducting the 20 percent that the firm takes out in profits, a choice that was surprising if his object was to illustrate the return to investors.

Oregon's decision to invest again with KKR was especially curious since just a few months earlier, Treasurer Tony Meeker had stated in an interview that Oregon would have no further interest in leveraged buyout funds. "We're interested in sunrises, not sunsets," he said then. So how does he explain Oregon's recent decision to contribute $350 million to KKR? "That was what they asked us for," he said simply.

One positive development that could come out of the KKR experience is a heightened sensitivity to the activities of public pension funds. With the largest and fastest-growing source of capital in the United States at their disposal, the people who run these funds and the decisions they make clearly deserve more attention. Yet up until fairly recently, they have largely been ignored by their own beneficiaries, state legislators, and local newspapers, who rarely send reporters to cover the funds' public meetings.

States like Oregon have tried to fashion laws and guidelines that will prevent abuse of their employees' money. Rather than trying to anticipate every possible threat, emphasis has been placed on disclosing financial ties and holdings, the idea being that as long as everyone is required to do things in the open, that in itself will be a deterrent.

But other broader issues need to be considered as well. In many states, the pension fund trustees are all appointed by the governor, and as a result, the selections are often based on political rather than investment criteria. Since most trustees are fully employed in other capacities, more attention needs to be focused on the staff members who do the bulk of the work. Public funds should be granted the resources to hire skilled people in sufficient numbers. The notion that a $10-billion fund can be prudently managed by a team of three or four people who earn no more than $50,000 or $60,000 is wishful thinking. The better ones will continue to be lured away to higher-paying jobs in the private sector. If the public pension funds become populated with sophisticated staff officers and vigilant board members, they will be more likely to spot money managers who aren't acting as prudent investors.

Beyond that, J. P. Morgan was probably right to place so much emphasis on character. Unfortunately, that is not a quality that can be legislated or summoned up. As Kohlberg warned his investors when he left KKR in 1987, the trick is to resist taking every last penny, to stay a few feet away from the edge, to turn away and leave something on the table. What Kohlberg was advocating, of course, is a discipline that runs counter to human nature. Henry and George, in their haste to succeed, had difficulty developing this trait. And, as the current unwinding of the eighties makes only too clear, they were not alone in this shortcoming.

EPILOGUE

When this book was published in its hardcover edition in May 1991, the power structure that had grown up around KKR was briefly rocked by the revelations contained within it. But the wagons quickly circled and the unflattering descriptions of KKR and its cohorts were generally overlooked. It was evidently more important to maintain business relationships than to pursue awkward issues of business ethics.

Immediately after the book was published, for instance, newspapers in Portland, Oregon, were filled with details about Roger Meier's investments in KKR funds and his purchase of stock in U.S. Natural Resources at a price that might have been advantaged.

In the hullabaloo that ensued, the state attorney general decided to conduct an investigation into the stock purchase. His staff's inquiry, however, was hardly exhaustive. They found a stock-valuation expert who stated that the price Meier had paid for his USNR stock was, if anything, generous. That opinion was apparently considered enough to invalidate statements by two other stock analysts who had told *The Oregonian* that the stock was worth considerably more than Meier had paid for it.

The attorney general's staff also faxed Kohlberg a list of questions regarding Meier's activities. Thirty-six hours later, before Kohlberg had even had a chance to respond, the attorney general issued his report. The conclusion: There was "no credible evidence providing a reasonable basis to conclude that a criminal offense has occurred."[1]

"Another old-fashioned whitewash," was how one *Oregonian* columnist described the episode. Meanwhile, the state ethics commission, after considering opening its own investigation, declined to do so.

Dick Beattie went through a similarly tense period, only to emerge victorious. The day after an excerpt of the book appeared in the Sunday *New York Times* Magazine, the executive committee of Simpson Thacher issued a memo to all of its partners saying that it had looked into the allegations concerning Beattie in the book and concluded that "most of the information in the book relating to Dick is inaccurate," and that "any implication in the book that (Beattie) acted improperly is incorrect."[2]

However, at least one partner at the firm, Edgar Masinter, was unwilling to let the matter rest. Masinter, who had responsibility for the firm's relationship with its largest client, Manufacturers Hanover, was considered one of the firm's most valued partners. But when Cyrus Vance, the firm's senior partner, got ready to retire, Masinter lost out to Beattie in the battle over who would become the next head of the firm. There was so little love lost between the two contenders that when Masinter lost, he resigned his seat on the executive committee in protest.

The contents of *The Money Machine* apparently stirred him to action. On May 16, he sent a memo to the firm's executive committee, with copies to all partners, a copy of which was obtained by the *American Lawyer* and is quoted as follows:

As a result of disclosures in Sarah Bartlett's book about KKR, Dick Beattie spoke about his investments in KKR transactions at last Monday's partners' lunch. I have been advised that the executive committee plans no further action on this matter and has not even asked for a list of Dick's investments.

I was intimately involved in the development and adoption of the policies which apply to investments in client transactions. Based on what Dick has told us, I believe that there is a serious question as to whether he has complied with those policies. I am sure that this view is shared by other partners. At a minimum, the partners of the firm are entitled to have a complete and independent inquiry and report concerning the details of Dick's investments. I can't believe that anyone would want to make a judgment without knowing the facts.

Since the Executive Committee has decided that it does not want to conduct that inquiry, I think that a committee of representative partners should be appointed by the Executive Committee to conduct the inquiry and report back to the firm. Only after the facts are known can a responsible decision be made as to how to deal with this matter.

In my judgment, the reputation, integrity and character of Simpson Thacher & Bartlett and each of its partners is on the line. I believe that it is the obligation of the partners...to find the facts and address the issues relating to Dick's investments in KKR transactions directly and promptly. To do otherwise risks real damage to the firm and all that it represents.

Accordingly, I formally request that the Executive Committee immediately appoint a committee or representative partners and instruct that committee to find and report to the firm the facts concerning Dick's investments in KKR transactions.[3]

The executive committee, over which Beattie presides,

was apparently not moved by Masinter's request. The next day, the committee responded with the following:

> The executive committee has considered the suggestion in Edgar Masinter's memorandum of May 16 and has unanimously determined that it is satisfied with the scope of the inquiry which it has made and is satisfied it has obtained all relevant information. It is our judgment that no firm interest would be served by pursuing the matter further.[4]

While Dick and Roger were busy fending off criticisms of their behavior, Henry was on the offensive. KKR had no official comment on the book when reporters called seeking a response. But it was clear from conversations that Henry had with friends and colleagues that it had made him see red. Nothing seemed to gall him more than the material concerning his divorce settlement with Hedi.

So it must have seemed like a gift from heaven when, the day after the Sunday *Times* magazine excerpt appeared, the judge presiding over Hedi's lawsuit dismissed the case on the grounds that she had not filed the suit in a timely fashion and had not been able to prove that Henry had committed fraud against her.

Henry clearly saw this as a major public-relations opportunity. His lawyer paid a visit to the legal counsel for Warner Books, which published *The Money Machine*. Henry's lawyer wanted Warner Books to put an insert detailing the outcome of the court case into every book that was still in the warehouse and to have the insert sent to all book reviewers and bookstores. He also wanted the insert included in any promotional material or advertising that mentioned Hedi's complaints against Henry, and he wanted to be apprised of my public appearances.

Other than the decision I had already made to include the dismissal of the lawsuit in future editions, Warner rejected their proposals. The judge's decision, however, had little impact on the substantive points of the book. The description of the lawsuit had included large portions of Henry's depositions and arguments as well as Hedi's, and in many ways, his explanations were the more troubling. The fact that Hedi had not been able to prove fraud before the court did not mean that the facts she presented in her case were untrue, or that Henry's response was not revealing. Indeed, since the judge had refused to allow Hedi to subpoena Kohlberg to testify on her behalf, and since she believed he had crucial corroborating evidence, the fact that the court found that she had not successfully proven fraud was hardly surprising.

Still, the judge's decision quickly made its way into the press. It was front-page news in the *New York Law Journal* and the decision was the headline of a gossip column in the *New York Post*: "No 2nd helping for Kravis ex."

Hedi promptly hired a new lawyer, Stanley Arkin, and began preparing an appeal of the judge's decision. But tragedy intervened. In August 1991, Henry and Hedi's eldest son, Harrison, was killed in a car crash. The sudden and terrible loss was a shock to everyone and seemed to erase, at least for a time, the animosity that had come between them. Hedi decided she could not put her remaining two children through another emotionally draining legal battle and dropped her suit.

While Harrison's death seemed to propel both Hedi and Henry back into their most private lives, it had the opposite effect on Carolyne Roehm. When she decided to close her clothing design business, she took every opportunity to explain to the press that it had nothing to do with the demise of eighties ostentation, but was triggered solely by Harrison's death. The tragedy, she said, had fundamentally changed her priorities.

Carolyne Roehm's career may have plateaued in the summer of 1991, but the same could not be said of KKR. True, in the wake of the book, the firm didn't raise quite as much money in its latest fund-raising round as it had hoped. And in December of that year, Seaman Furniture went bankrupt.

But in the meantime, KKR had acquired a 16-percent stake of Fleet/Norstar Financial Group, giving it access to the fourteenth largest bank in the country. And it continued its buying spree of media properties, including, among other things, *New York* magazine.

The only developments that threatened to mar this relatively calm picture were two lawsuits that grew out of the material in this book. In August, a representative of the state of Minnesota filed suit against the LBO firm in conjunction with a beneficiary of the state's pension fund. The suit claimed that KKR was in fact an investment adviser and should have been registered as such with the Securities Exchange Commission. Under the rules governing investment advisers, the plaintiffs contended, KKR would not have been allowed to charge the high fees it has traditionally levied. The suit called for the state's share of those fees to be returned.

KKR dismissed the suit as "meritless and frivolous" and added that if the firm lost in court it would simply refuse to manage Minnesota's money. The message to other funds was certainly clear: no fees, no high returns that make pension fund managers look good. In the end, it needn't have worried. The case was dismissed on the grounds that the statute of limitations had expired. At the time of this writing, that decision was being appealed.

In October 1991, another lawsuit was filed against KKR. Several beneficiaries of the Oregon and Washington pension funds hired a feisty Seattle-based law firm to represent their claim that they had been defrauded, particularly of the profits contained in the warrants that were given to Milken and his favored circle of investors.

The law firm, Betts, Patterson & Mines, filed a $1 billion lawsuit against KKR and Milken in which it also named the Oregon and Washington funds as nominal defendants for having sat by and allowed the alleged fraud to occur. Besides the arguments about the warrants, the suit invoked the arguments used in the Minnesota lawsuit concerning KKR's role as an investment adviser. As a result of a recent $1.3 billion settlement between Milken and those who have filed civil suits against him, the Seattle law firm's action may well enable Oregon and Washington beneficiaries to recover at least some of Milken's profits from the warrants.

As it did with the Minnesota-based suit, KKR dismissed this second complaint as "baseless and frivolous." The two sides were still sparring in court when this edition went to press.

In the end, *The Money Machine* seems to have made some people a bit wiser about KKR and Dick Beattie's business practices. But few were prepared to act on their newly gained knowledge, and those who did were handily defeated. The power structure that KKR had striven so hard to erect remained intact.

ACKNOWLEDGMENTS

This book would never have been written were it not for the extraordinary help of a few individuals who devoted endless amounts of time and energy to seeing it through. Unfortunately, some of those who deserve the greatest thanks are also those whose names I cannot mention, since public knowledge of their cooperation with this project could harm their professional careers. To those special nameless few, I can never thank you enough.

Happily, there are some individuals and organizations whose help I am able to acknowledge publicly. The staff at the Oregon Historical Society were always cheerful as they guided me through their rich collection of books, photographs, and newspaper clippings. IDD Information Services was generous in helping me to compile statistics. And Rebecca Daugherty at the Freedom of Information Service Center in Washington was a constant source of insight and tactical ad-

344

vice during my ten-month effort to obtain documents from the Securities and Exchange Commission.

The rewarding experiences I had with these organizations, whose staff were so obviously committed to the furtherance of original research, reawakened in me a deep sense of privilege at being a journalist. These feelings were amplified by the support I received from many friends in the journalistic community, who proved that not all reporters are egotistical ingrates and that we can, in fact, be collegial. While they share none of the blame for the shortcomings of this book, individuals such as Karen Pennar and Tony Bianco of *Business Week*, Strat Sherman and Roy Rowan at *Fortune*, Carla Robbins at *U.S. News & World Report*, and Jeff Gerth at the *New York Times* provided just the right blend of emotional encouragement and professional caution. My thanks also goes to Dulcie Leimbach for her help in fact-checking and to Kathy Daly for her assistance in lining up photographs.

Like many writers, I heard the horror stories about literary agents who desert you after the contract is signed and editors who somehow never get around to editing. My experience with John Hawkins, my agent, and with Nansey Neiman, my editor at Warner, could not have been more satisfying. I also heard how difficult employers could be toward reporters foolhardy enough to try their hand at books. Again, my experience ran contrary. The editors at the *Times* were kind enough not to throw me out on my ear when I asked them for a leave of absence. They asked few questions about my project and bear none of the blame for its results.

The task of keeping me sane and well fed fell to a select group of friends and relatives whose patience with my frequent disappearing acts and endless bouts of panic proved unlimited. My husband occasionally fell short in the shopping and dinner-preparation category, but more than made up for it with his attentive reading of early drafts and his editing suggestions, which improved the book immeasurably. To my best critic and most vital source of emotional sustenance, my heartfelt thanks.

NOTES

RAY

1. Courtney Ann and Glen Vaughn-Roberson, *City in the Osage Hills* (Boulder: Pruett Publishing Co., 1984).
2. "Raymond Kravis Constructing Ultra-Modern 10-Room Home," *Tulsa Tribune* (April 17,1950).

THE BOYS

1. Cathy Milam, "They Laughed at Him Once, But Kravis Got the Last Laugh," *Tulsa World* (November 19, 1982).

HENRY

1. "Greed Really Turns Me Off," *Fortune* (January 29, 1989).
2. Ellis Widner, "Guilty Pleasures—Don't Touch What Dial?" *Tulsa Tribune* (March 21, 1990).
3. Affidavit for Search Warrant filed in the Tulsa District Court, May 31, 1990; Criminal Information filed in the Tulsa District Court, June 5, 1990; Chris Schein,

"Kravis Faces Drug, Pornography Charges—Lewd-Solicitation Count Also Expected to Be Filed Against Station Owner," *Tulsa World* (June 15, 1990).

4. Dan Parker, "Station Owner Pleads Guilty to Sex Charges," *Tulsa Tribune* (February 9, 1991).

EARLY DAYS

1. Nick Galluccio, "Do You Sincerely Want to Be Rich?" *Forbes* (July 24, 1978).

2. Steven Kaplan, "A Summary of Sources of Value in Management Buyouts," paper presented at the Salomon Brothers Center, New York University Conference on Management Buyouts, May 20, 1989.

3. Deposition of George Roberts, September 5, 1989, Case No. B-133554: *Joe Larned, Jr., et al.*, v. *Kohlberg Kravis Roberts & Co. et al.* (Jefferson County, Texas).

4. "Buy Outs: The Art and Science of KKR's Henry R. Kravis," interview conducted by Elisabetta di Cagno, *Hermes—Columbia Business School Magazine* (Fall 1983).

5. Ibid.

6. Charles Humble, "Kohlberg Sidesteps Query on More Northwest Buyouts," *The Oregon Journal* (September 13, 1979).

7. Elisabetta di Cagno, op. cit.

8. Ibid.

9. *New York Post* (June 26, 1990), p. 6.

ROGER

1. Leon Harris, *Merchant Princes* (New York: Harper & Row, 1979); and Steven Lowenstein, *The Jews of Oregon* (Portland: Jewish Historical Society of Oregon, 1987).

THE CIRCLE WIDENS

1. Charles Humble, "NY Buy-out Firm Taps State Fund," *The Oregonian* (July 26, 1985).

2. Roger S. Meier, "System Builds Our Economy," *Statesman-Journal* (Salem, Oregon, January 18, 1989).

REWARDS

1. Letter to Bill Rutherford, Oregon State Treasurer, from Robert W. Muir, Assistant Attorney General, March 11, 1985.

2. Russell Sadler, "Rutherford Eyes Private-sector Job," *The Oregonian* (June 4, 1987).

3. Ibid.

4. Alan K. Ota, "Consultant Advises Firing of Oregon Fund Manager," *The Oregonian* (June 6, 1987).

5. Bill MacKenzie, "Oregon Cuts Investment Firm Employing Ex-treasurer," *The Oregonian* (February 19, 1988).

6. Ibid.

7. Charles Humble, "Stronger Role for Oregon Treasurer Urged in Investment Council Report," *The Oregonian* (August 15, 1985).

8. Foster Church, "Rutherford's Role in Campaign Hit," *The Oregonian* (October 25, 1986).

FRENZY

1. Louis Lowenstein, "The Takeover Boom: Lessons for Wall Street from Main Street," Columbia University, paper presented April 12, 1989.

2. Lloyd Watson, "Helping Companies to Go Private," *San Francisco Chronicle* (August 31, 1979).

3. Stephen Maita, "Kohlberg Kravis Roberts Lets Its Deals Do the Talking," *San Francisco Chronicle* (November 25, 1985).

4. Michael C. Jensen, "Eclipse of the Public Corporation," *Harvard Business Review* (September-October 1989).

5. Government's sentencing memo in its case against Michael Milken, pp. 29–30 (September 13, 1990).

6. Ibid., pp. 78–82.

7. Deposition of Henry Kravis, September 14, 1989, Case No. B-133554: *Joe Larned, Jr., et al.* v. *Kohlberg Kravis Roberts & Co. et al.* (Jefferson County, Texas). Transcript, p. 525.

8. Michael Milken indictment, March 29, 1989, p. 34.

9. Theodore Ammon, testimony in Michael Milken sentencing hearing (October 19, 1990), Transcript, pp. 816–817.

10. Aubrey Hayes, testimony in Michael Milken sentencing hearing (October 19, 1990), Transcript, pp. 663–678.

11. James B. Stewart and Daniel Hertzberg, "Expanding Inquiry: Drexel and Milken Are Focus of Federal Probe That Is Growing Wider," *Wall Street Journal* (September 11, 1987).

12. Ibid.

13. Ibid.

14. Testimony of George Roberts, July 30, 1987, and October 12, 1987, SEC Investigation of Drexel Burnham Lambert, Case No. HO-1907.

HEDI AND CAROLYNE

1. Letter from Arthur J. Mahon to William D. Zabel (August 17, 1981).

2. Letter from Angelo T. Cometa to Norman Sheresky (October 8, 1982).

3. Henry R. Kravis, Reply Affidavit in support of motion to dismiss, February 7, 1989, Case Index No. 61458/89, p. 5.

4. Sharon Churcher, "The Very Visible Carolyne Roehm Kravis, Not in Oscar's Shadow Any More," *Avenue* (September 1986).

5. Karen Heller, "You *Can* Have It All," *Daily News* (December 27, 1988).

6. Jesse Kornbluth, "The Working Rich," *New York* (November 24, 1986).

7. Martha Sherrill, "Carolyne Roehm: Rich, Thin & a Slave to Fashion," *Washington Post* (February 21, 1989).

8. Judy Lunn, "The Grandeur That Is . . . Roehm," *The Houston Post* (May 21, 1990).

9. Sharon Churcher, op. cit.

10. Anne-Marie Schiro, "A New Name in Fashion," *New York Times* (August 27, 1985).

11. Susan Alai, "Carolyne & Henry," *W* (June 16–23, 1986).

12. Ibid.

13. Charlotte Curtis, "New Stars on the Circuit," *New York Times* (May 20, 1986).

14. Susan Alai, op. cit.

15. Alice Gordon, "As Rare as a Day in June," *HG* (June 1987).

16. Ibid.; and Richard J. Grula, "The Lowdown on Connecticut's Toniest County," *On the Avenue* (October 7, 1989).

17. Robin Pogrebin, "Barbarians at the Barn Door," *Avenue* (June-July 1990).

18. "LBO King Builds Fantasy Landscape," *New York Post* (June 7, 1990).

19. Bridget Foley, "Roehm on the Range," *W* (January 7–14, 1991).

20. Karen Heller, op. cit.

JERRY RETURNS

1. Bryan Burrough and John Helyar, *Barbarians at the Gate—The Fall of RJR Nabisco* (New York: Harper & Row, 1990), p. 143.

2. Ibid., pp. 144–145.

JERRY QUITS

1. James Sterngold, "Buyout Pioneer Quitting Fray," *New York Times* (June 19, 1987).

OUT OF CONTROL

1. Suzy, "This Party Rates a '20,' " *New York Post* (November 19, 1987).

2. *W* (December 16, 1988–January 2, 1989), p. 27.

3. Charlotte Curtis, "New Stars on the Circuit," *New York Times* (May 20, 1986).

4. "The Powers That Be in Business," *U.S. News & World Report* (February 8, 1988).

5. Teresa McUsic, "Kravis Brothers Inherited Sense of Giving Back to the Community," *Tulsa World* (August 20,1989).

6. Floyd Norris, "KKR Losses: $353 million and Counting," *New York Times* (December 9, 1990).

7. Michael Tokarz, testimony given September 14, 1989, Case No. B-133554: *Joe Larned, Jr., et al.* v. *Kohlberg Kravis Roberts, et al.* (Jefferson County, Texas).

8. Ibid.

9. Written opinion in *Mills Acquisition Co.* v. *Macmillan*, C.A. No. 10168, Court of Chancery of the State of Delaware (May 3, 1989).

10. Ibid.

11. *Metropolitan Life Insurance Company and Jefferson-Pilot Insurance Company* v. *RJR Nabisco, Inc., and F. Ross Johnson*, Docket No. 818, U.S. District Court, Southern District (August 24, 1990).

12. James Sterngold, "The Nabisco Battle's Key Moment," *New York Times* (December 2, 1988).

WASHINGTON

1. *Tulsa Tribune* (May 19, 1976).

2. "Greed Really Turns Me Off," interview with Henry Kravis, *Fortune* (January 2, 1989).

3. Max Holland and Viveca Novak, "King Henry," *Mother Jones* (June 1990).

4. William F. Long and David J. Ravenscraft, "The Record of LBO Performance," paper presented at the Salomon Brothers Center Conference, New York University (May 1989).

5. "Management and Leveraged Buyouts," hearings before the Subcommittee on Telecommunications and Finance of the Committee on Energy and Commerce, House of Representatives, Serial No. 101-49 (February 22 and May 25, 1989).

6. Max Holland and Viveca Novak, op. cit.

7. "Eagle Wing Dining," *W* (March 5–12, 1990).

FRAUD?

1. Reply Affidavit of Robert S. Cohen in support of motion to dismiss, *Helene D.S. Kravis* v. *Henry R. Kravis*, Case Index No. 61458/89, Supreme Court of the State of New York, p. 15.

2. Letter from Patricia Ferrari to Norman Sheresky, August 13, 1982.

3. Affidavit of Frank J. Convertini, in *Kravis* v. *Kravis*, Case Index No. 61458/89.

4. Reply Affidavit of Henry R. Kravis in support of motion to dismiss, *Kravis* v. *Kravis*, Case Index No. 61458/89, p. 3.

DICK

1. Bryan Burrough and John Helyar, *Barbarians at the Gate* (New York: Harper & Row, 1990), p. 486.

2. Ibid., pp. 426–427.

3. James Sterngold, "The Nabisco Battle's Key Moment," *New York Times* (December 2, 1988).

4. Susan Beck, "Old Star, New Star," *American Lawyer* (November 1990).

5. Hope Lampert, "Attorney Beattie: Kravis's Cohort Is a Man in a Hurry, But to Where?", *The New York Observer* (June 18, 1990).

6. Ibid.

PERCEPTION

1. Summons, *Jerome Kohlberg, Jr.,* v. *Kohlberg Kravis Roberts & Co.*, Supreme Court of New York.

2. Sarah Bartlett, "Kohlberg in Dispute Over Firm," *New York Times* (August 30, 1989).

3. Christopher R. O'Dea, "Surprising LBO Player: Stellar First Chicago," *Crain's Chicago Business* (May 22, 1989); and Anice C. Wallace, "Several Giant Pension Funds Investing in Offer for Nabisco," *New York Times* (October 31, 1988).

4. "KKR Suit Draws Yawns," *Pension and Investment Age* (September 4, 1989).

5. Ibid.

6. Ibid.

7. Margaret A. Elliott, "Paltry Paydays?" *Corporate Finance* (December 1989); and George Anders, "Morgan Stanley Faces More Suits Over Buy-Outs," *Wall Street Journal* (January 31, 1991).

8. *Wall Street Journal*, second section, Law Department (January 26, 1990).

9. Hope Lampert, "Has Henry Kravis Lost His Leverage?" *Seven Days* (January 10, 1990).

10. Thomas Moore, "KKR Is Rolling with the Punches," *U.S. News & World Report* (May 7, 1990).

11. Leah J. Nathans, "KKR Is Doing Just Fine—Without LBOs," *Business Week* (July 30, 1990).

12. "Greed Really Turns Me Off," interview with Henry R. Kravis in *Fortune* (January 29, 1989).

13. "Henry the Lionhearted," *Women's Wear Daily* (November 14, 1988).

14. Letter from George R. Roberts to 1987 Fund Participants (August 22, 1988).

15. Deposition of George R. Roberts in San Francisco, September 5, 1989, Case No. B-133554: *Joe Larned, Jr., et al.* v. *Kohlberg Kravis Roberts & Co. et al.* (Jefferson County District Court, Texas).

16. Testimony of George R. Roberts, September 14, 1989, Case No. B-133554: *Joe Larned, Jr., et al.* v. *Kohlberg Kravis Roberts & Co.* (Jefferson County District Court, Texas).

CONCLUSION

1. Frederick Lewis Allen, *The Great Pierpont Morgan* (New York: Harper & Row, 1948).

2. Jeff Wallach and Robert L. Hill, "The Oregon LBO Scoreboard," *The Oregonian* (June 1, 1989).

3. Charles Bruner, "Another Side to the IPERS Investment Story," Letter to the Editor, *Des Moines Register* (December 8, 1988).

EPILOGUE

1. James Long, "State Won't Investigate Meier Stock," *The Oregonian* (June 8, 1991).

2. Susan Beck, "Bar Talk," *American Lawyer* (July–August, 1991).

3. Ibid.

4. Ibid.

APPENDIX

INFORMATION BY FUND

Date	Fund size	KKR contribution	KKR contribution as % of fund	Annual rate of return (%) to KKR's investors	Some companies acquired
1978	$32m	$3.0m	10.6	30.5	Houdaille, Sargent
1980	$75m	$3.1m	4.1	32.2	Marley, Fred Meyer, Lily-Tulip
1982	$316m	$5.0m	1.5	41.8	Dillingham, Wometco
1984	$1.0bn	$7.5m	0.8	28.0	Cole National, Union Texas Petroleum
1986	$1.8bn	$20m	1.1	29.6	Beatrice, Safeway, Owens-Illinois
1987	$5.6bn	$140m*	2.5	N.A.	Jim Walter, RJR Nabisco

N.A. Not available

*Includes additional $80 million that KKR invested in RJR Nabisco

SOURCE: *New York Times* and KKR reports

EXAMPLES OF KKR FEES

Company	Deal size	Investment banking fee	Monitoring fee	Returns*
RJR Nabisco	$32bn	$75m	$10m	N.A.
Owens-Illinois	$4.4bn	$60m	$600,000	15.9%
Safeway	$5.2bn	$60m	$500,000	62.1%
Beatrice	$8.2bn	$45m	$1.1m	50%
Jim Walter	$3.3bn	$35m	$500,000	N.A.**
Stop & Shop	$1.5bn	$28m	$375,000	22.4%
Storer	$2.4bn	$23m	$350,000	60.6%
Duracell	$1.8bn	$24m	$500,000	6.6%
Union Texas Petroleum	$2.0bn	$14m	$400,000	22.1%
Malone & Hyde	$707m	$6.7m	$600,000	22.0%
Amstar	$465m	$5m	$350,000	84.8%
Cole National	$450m	$4m	$300,000	44.2%
IDEX	$192m	$2m	$268,000	N.A.
PT Components	$150m	$2m	$200,000	50.9%
L.B. Foster	$106m	$900,000	$150,000	16.8%

*Estimated or actual, before KKR's 20 percent profit participation
**Filed for Chaper 11 bankruptcy protection
SOURCE: KKR Reports and company reports